ATMOSPHERIC NOISE

ELEMENTS   *A series edited*
by Stacy Alaimo and Nicole Starosielski

ATMOSPHERIC NOISE

THE INDEFINITE URBANISM
OF LOS ANGELES

MARINA PETERSON

DUKE UNIVERSITY PRESS   Durham and London   2021

© 2021 Duke University Press

All rights reserved

Printed in the United States of America on acid-free paper ∞

Text design by Amy Ruth Buchanan

Cover design by Drew Sisk

Typeset in Chaparral Pro and Knockout by Copperline Book Services

Library of Congress Cataloging-in-Publication Data

Names: Peterson, Marina, author.

Title: Atmospheric noise : the indefinite urbanism of Los Angeles /
Marina Peterson.

Other titles: Elements (Duke University Press)

Description: Durham : Duke University Press, 2021. | Series:
Elements | Includes bibliographical references and index.

Identifiers: LCCN 2020035285 (print) | LCCN 2020035286 (ebook) |
ISBN 9781478010708 (hardcover) | ISBN 9781478011828 (paperback) |
ISBN 9781478013174 (ebook)

Subjects: LCSH: City noise—California—Los Angeles. | City sounds—
California—Los Angeles. | Noise pollution—California—Los Angeles. |
Sound—Environmental aspects—California—Los Angeles.

Classification: LCC TD893.3.C2 P48 2021 (print) |
LCC TD893.3.C2 (ebook) | DDC 363.7409794/94—dc23

LC record available at https://lccn.loc.gov/2020035285

LC ebook record available at https://lccn.loc.gov/2020035286

for Cassius

A mosquito buzzes around me as I sit at my desk doing a final round of edits, coming into audibility before flying away. It is small and fast, and I lose sight of it as soon as I clap in its direction. While its sound is distracting, I'm more annoyed by the thought of being stung by an insect swarming in the outside swamp of a Texas fall—hotter and wetter this year than ever before. The mosquito, in its lines of flight, brings into being an atmospheric assemblage of sound, air, and sense that I trace in this book—which, even in its uncertainty, affords new modes of attunement. The origins of this project were serendipitous. Working at the Huntington Library on a fellowship for another project, I came across files on airport noise in county supervisor Kenneth Hahn's collection. Reading residents' complaints and Hahn's attempts to address the problem of noise, I was drawn in by the work noise was doing in amplifying gaps in airspace jurisdiction. Caught up in noise and its atmospheric entanglements, I moved away from the seeming immobility of concrete and water—the matter of the littoral infrastructures with which I had been engaged—and followed noise toward national legislative histories and acoustical engineering, toward the neighborhoods around LAX, toward the airport itself.

The book draws on material found in L.A. area archives that range from those of the Huntington Library and the City of Los Angeles to LAX's Flight Path Museum, the El Segundo Public Library, the Los Angeles Public Library, and the Centinela Historical Society in Inglewood, along with special collections at area universities (UCLA, USC, Cal State Northridge, and Loyola University). National archives consulted include those of the EPA's Office of Noise Abatement and Control and the National Noise Abatement Council. Many people were generous with time and resources. Hillel Schwartz invited me to peruse the material he collected for his omnibus *Making Noise: From Babel to the Big Bang and Beyond.* LAWA's Environmental Services staff was exceedingly helpful in giving me access to various aspects of their work related to noise. Acoustical engineers with Veneklasen and Associates and the Western Electro-Acoustic Laboratory shared their experiences and expertise. After narrowly missing the ferry, Les Blomberg came by canoe to paddle us to the island on which he was staying, where he shared his thoughts on noise, developed over decades as the founding director of the National Noise Abatement Clearinghouse.

Many of the archives were themselves spaces of ethnographic encounters. This was especially true of LAX's Flight Path Museum and Learning Center, staffed by retired airport workers, including a former director of public relations and an aircraft mechanic. They had a wealth of knowledge not only about what was housed in the museum's library and file cabinets, but also about aircraft noise as experienced and politicized. While the Flight Path Museum held an abundance of material, elsewhere there was a palpable absence of archives on airport noise; Inglewood's Centinela Adobe highlighted its nineteenth-century history, and at the city's public library, an archivist was aggressive about throwing things away. Items I read about in congressional hearing transcripts had been saved by people involved in early work around airport noise. I am grateful for their generosity in sharing their memories and materials. Yvette Kovary, whom I found in the phone book after searching for some of the main organizers against airport noise, had a file of papers and photos related to her struggles to keep the airport from taking her home and that of her neighbors. Rudi Mattoni, with whom I talked on the phone but did not meet in person, told me about a box he had of material related to his El Segundo blue butterfly conservation work. Veneklasen and Associates had original copies of their reports from noise measurement surveys in Inglewood, while the mobile units developed for early environmental sound measurement were stored at their acoustic testing laboratory.

Research for the book began while on a faculty fellowship from Ohio University, and the manuscript was completed on a College Research Fellowship from the University of Texas at Austin. Huntington Library fellowships provided additional support, along with a place to work that affords the necessary focus to write, interspersed with walks in their gardens and rich interdisciplinary conversations. Other spaces for thinking with others came through opportunities to present portions of the book, even in nascent stages, when my thought had run ahead of the material. The book has benefited from conversations at the University of California, Irvine's Center for Ethnography in the Department of Anthropology; the Music and Sound Working Group and Department of Comparative Studies at The Ohio

State University; New York University's Music Department Colloquium, the University of Texas at Austin's Department of Anthropology; UCLA's Culture, Power, and Social Change series in the Department of Anthropology; the Digital Writing and Research Group's Digital Field Methods Institute at the University of Texas at Austin; Rice University's Ethnographic Studio Salon; the Modern Studies Group at the University of Texas at Austin; and the Materialities, Texts, and Images Program Brown Bag series at CalTech. Conference presentations allowed me to play with material that solidified into chapters and offered interdisciplinary engagements; especially generative were the Cultures of Energy symposium at the Center for Energy and Environmental Humanities at Rice University; &Now 2015—Blast Radius: Writing and the Other Arts at CalArts; the Music, Property and Law symposium at the University of Texas at Austin; and the annual meetings of the International Association for the Study of Popular Music, the Society for Cultural Anthropology, and the American Anthropological Association. My wind noise recordings were presented as an audio installation in the Society of Ethnomusicology (SEM) Sounding Board exhibit.

Much of my conceptualization of noise came out of thinking about sound and/as energy with graduate students at Ohio University, both in seminars and through the collaborative Energy Soundscapes project. Friendships that are also ongoing intellectual conversations make every book a pause in a process, a web of thought woven from encounters and exchange too rich to disentangle. Colleagues and graduate students who contributed to this book at various stages through their conviviality and generosity of ideas are, especially, Gretchen Bakke, Casey Boyle, Vicki Brennan, Craig Campbell, Jason Cons, Nina Eidsheim, Ofer Eliaz, Veit Erlmann, Cassie Fennell, Andrea Frohne, Nikita Gale, Megan Gette, Michael Gillespie, Brian Harnetty, Keith Murphy, Josh Ottum, Alessandra Raengo, Dario Robleto, Erin Schlumpf, Louis-Georges Schwartz, Jena Seiler, Barry Shank, Jesse Shipley, Stefanie Sobelle, Nicole Starosielski, Katie Stewart, David Suisman, Adel Jing Wang, and Elana Zilberg. Chepo Peña made my life easier by preparing the images.

I am delighted to be working with Ken Wissoker, whose support has anchored the work of writing an idea into being and whose vision of the project has allowed it to bloom. The comments of two anonymous reviewers were instrumental in helping me clarify the stakes of the project. Earlier versions in different forms appeared in *Social Text*, *Postmodern Culture*, and *Between Matter and Method*. Generous readings by anonymous reviewers for *Social Text* and *Postmodern Culture* helped develop and sharpen the ideas guiding the book. A workshop at Banff with contributors to the co-edited (with Gretchen Bakke) volume *Between Matter and Method* provided a space to imagine with others possibilities for play with form.

Enormous thanks to everyone who provided child care while I went to archives, conferences, and airport meetings, especially my parents, John Peterson and Joanna Vaughn; brother and sister-in-law, Jesse Peterson and Mia Doi Todd; Kendra Field and Khary Jones; and Michiyo Suda and Umar Rashid Foster. And of course Hamza, for infusing joy into a child's everyday life, for life together (and apart), and for giving me all the art books on air. This book is for Cassius, who lived the project from the time he can remember and is eager to write a book together—though you may not have written the words of this one, you have infused breath and noise into them.

LAX NAZ—*Los Angeles International Airport Noise Abatement Zone*. The houses had been acquired through eminent domain but had not yet been demolished or removed. John Divola's 1970s photos of homes in the flight path slated for demolition visualize the atmospheric quality of this process (figure I.1).[1] The images captivate in their stillness, their muteness, their silence. The airport mowed the lawns during the week, and teens broke in on the weekends. Divola photographed traces of the latter: the angularity of broken glass and screens gaping in their frames (figures I.2 and I.3). Interior walls spray painted. A garage door a conversation in dueling fonts: KLAN THIS HOUSE SOLD PIG VANDAL GARD DOG WUS HERE REWARD $100. Tire tracks of bulldozers. Unwittingly ethnographic, the images' formality is at once performative, exploratory, and reflexive—a way of moving through the city's margins. Divola's interest lies in atmospheric light, the rendering or imprint of space, the photo as a remnant, as physical evidence of time, place, and action. The images convey the material qualities of a built environment composed by noise, where sound from the sky shapes neighborhoods and lives. Not representational, they are embedded in and emergent from this place, a place in process, where shattered remains of windowpanes register sky, palm tree, or an absent human presence. What the house sees, hears, feels. "The houses are silent witnesses," I offer. "I don't anthropomorphize," he says. The houses are mute—(not-blank) canvases on which are inscribed traces of human activity. A zone of stillness, following the presence of inhabitants, both long term and temporary, preceding the presence of bulldozers.

Each house is singular, connected to another through its own skin. Shadows of tree branches appear as veins emerging on the surface of a stucco wall. Plywood is nailed into window frames, bowing from moisture or patched together like an incipient Louise Nevelson sculpture. These are portraits rather than a totalizing aerial view, which would cast air's potential as one of command and control. The process of removal is registered in re-

FIGURE I.1 LAX NAZ, exterior view W, John Divola, 1975.

lation to individual houses, portrayed in close-up. Though it is evident the houses were once populated, the photos do not suggest a sentimentality of loss or absence, of past pleasures or activities, lives lived and lost to eminent domain. They are not records of urban transformation, of invisible infrastructures, or of a "history of forgetting" (Klein 1997). There is no sense of a desire for recuperation or reclamation of these spaces. They simply exist in their present form, suspended for a moment. There is an immediacy in their presentness, a presence, of photographer and building, of wind, of the singularity of the vandal: ostensibly male, ostensibly teenaged, in another boy's bedroom (figure I.4).

In conversation with Divola, I suggest that many things are indexed beyond the activity of humans; we can see the presence or effects of temporal and ephemeral forces—wind (palm trees moving), time of day (shadows),

FIGURES I.2–I.3 LAX NAZ FE, site 23, exterior views B and A, John Divola, 1975.

climate (vegetation). "Indexes of noise," I say. "Sure, in a broad abstract way. If you take the title at face value," he responds. "But I have no way to deal with it literally, to deal with noise literally, as content." What work does the title do? "Noise abatement zone" grounds the airport in the city, in neighborhoods of people annoyed by the noise of aircraft. Though Divola's photographs are not about noise or noise abatement, there is an ambivalence in his rejection of the title as having any meaning in relation to the images; the series includes photographs of airplanes departing (figure I.5). The sound of airplanes is silent, silenced. Yet the presence of noise pervades. It is agent. "Noise abatement zone" suggests that noise has made these houses what they are, one after the other, one next to another. The airport (LAX) lurks as the source of a process in which the houses are caught up—the specter of infrastructure and its effects on urban landscapes.

Not lenses through which one may glean demographic or historical "information," the photos ask to be taken seriously in and of themselves, for what they offer in their materiality, their palpability. Nonrepresentational, they do not scale out or shift to categorical thought but instead are a cul-de-sac of sorts, a space in which to dwell, where something happened and is happening. Or an eddy that catches up some things—leaves, pollen, plastic—that then move on, drifting downstream or downwind as another force arrives, a stronger current or just a different one that disperses the

FIGURE I.4 LAX NAZ, site 76, interior view I, John Divola, 1975.

temporary vortex. The photos perform the subject of the book—with airport noise responsible for the transformation of this neighborhood and its homes, noise itself withdraws. The invisibility of noise structures perception and casts a quality of impermanence onto sound that is echoed in the muteness, and impermanence, of the houses.

Noise is atmospheric. Palpable in its sensation, noise is nonetheless ephemeral and indefinite; falling away as both sound and category, it proliferates into an array of atmospheric forms. Attuning toward noise is thus also an attuning toward the atmospheric. This is amplified in the case of airport noise. As people listen to sound from the sky, the aerial is drawn into perceptibility, figuring the permeability of bodies and matter. The dif-

FIGURE I.5 LAX NAZ, exterior view Z, John Divola, 1975.

fuse and dispersed quality of noise makes people accustomed to experiencing and conceiving of that which is indeterminate, to dwell, that is, in uncertainty. The atmospheric emerges as a quality coalescing across multiple
registers: that of the aerial and the ephemeral, dynamic relationships between forms of matter, and the indeterminacy of forms and concepts. Thus,
what we learn from noise is a rich and dynamic way of attuning toward and
understanding the atmospheric. And while noise is not the only thing that
does this, the particular ways in which it does make it central for learning
to think and feel the atmospheric. Building on a robust discussion of forces
and attunements that bring the atmospheric into focus, I insist on the significance of sound and listening, and, by extension, a broader atmospheric
sensorium.[2] The atmospheric is audible as well as visible, heard as much as
breathed. Substantiated in sound, it emerges in moments in which noise

matters. Around LAX, these include airspace law and urban land use; the palpable yet unstable nature of "annoyance" and its metricization; environmental imaginaries and the permeable, resonant skin of bodies and homes; and the precarious presence of a neighborhood now home to an endangered species of butterfly.

While the issue of airport noise is not unique to Los Angeles, there is a specificity to the story—and atmosphere—of the city.[3] Renowned for the quality of its light, Los Angeles, it has been said, "glows" (Weschler 1998). The light can pull you into a daze, all spaced out, watching the streets pass by as you traverse the city via its freeways; it can throw "you into such a trance you fail to realize how time is passing" (Peter Bogdanovich, quoted in Weschler 1998, 95). The climate is pleasant, the temperature in a range that casts skin as coterminous with air. A city definitive of sprawl, its verticality goes largely unnoticed—freeways built on embankments such that drivers look down on rooftops of single-story homes, stack interchanges that seem to make cars fly over and under one another, two downtowns of high-rise office towers whose height is limited by the imminent possibility of fault lines rupturing. It is also a relatively quiet city, the sound of freeway traffic blurring into a background white noise punctuated, perhaps, by sirens or a circling helicopter (Manaugh 2017). Airplanes, when they pass overhead with their roar and whine, shatter a stillness in which human speech is the measure of acoustic amplitude.

Airport noise is a condensation of forces and processes already in play, amplifying existing dynamics even as it yields its own effects, tendrils unfolding into newly fabulated fields, or domains encountered anew through sound. In the 1960s and 1970s noise emerges as a pressing concern, bringing into relief broader attenuations and tendencies of the era that foreground atmospheric figurations and logics. These include *The Blue Marble* (the first image of Earth from space); nuclear threat; environmentalism; smog; the Light and Space artists of Southern California, who used aerospace materials to play with perception; Yves Klein's *Air Architecture*; inflatables; Charlotte Moorman playing cello while being lifted into the air by helium balloons; *Atmosphères*, Ligeti's score for the film *2001: A Space Odyssey*; the dematerialization of the art object; the notion of liminality as an indefinite state of ambiguity, a moment of suspension outside what otherwise seems structured; the use of electricity to create amplified sound and electronic music; postmodernism; indeterminacy as a concern of composers and artists; systems thinking then anchored in cybernetics or "ecology," efflorescing as "climate" or "the cloud." This was an atmospheric moment that continues into the present, a sense of indeterminacy lingering as a condition of our time.[4]

NOISE, AN OPENING

Insofar as noise is made, whether as sound or in its designation, it is emergent, approachable principally as an ethnographic concern.[5] Hence I take an "acoustemological" approach to noise, Steven Feld's term for understanding "local conditions of acoustic sensation, knowledge, and imagination," which in this case include sensation, discourse, technology, law, and urban infrastructure (1996, 91). This is a sonic ethnography of how people (and sometimes technologies) listen. Rather than describing sounds I hear, I listen with others, attending to how they listen. I listen to the experiences of residents in the flight path and memories of homes removed as a result of noise. I listen with acoustical engineers measuring and metricizing noise, along with legislators grappling with how to solve the problem of noise. I listen as airport environmental services staff listen to sounds heard by noise measurement microphones and inscribed in noise contour maps. I listen as a microphone listens to a room, testing its eligibility for soundproofing. I listen to the determination in the voice of a man whose career has been spent lobbying for antinoise legislation, as well as to the stilled thrill of another who has long loved butterflies. The noise they encounter is sensed and made sense of; perceived, it is figured as disrupting communication and concentration. It reveals the permeability of buildings and recruits sympathetic publics concerned with hearing, productivity, and sensory experience. It is recorded and measured, construed as something that might be managed even as it seems to escape control.

Always coming into being, noise is necessarily immanent; intrinsic, or inherent, to its instantiations in assemblages of machine, air, body, or building, it provides a way of exploring sound as such. Hence a theory of sound emerges in which sound is not instrumentalizable, containable, or objectifiable.[6] As such, I do not offer a general definition of noise, whether unwanted, ontological, metaphysical, or even relational.[7] Nor do I ascribe a particular value to noise or the experience thereof. Noise, instead, is "an opening"—"anarchic, clamoring, mottled, striped, streaked, variegated, mixed, crossed, piebald multiplicity," it "is possibility itself. It is a set of possible things, it can be the set of possible things" (Serres 1997, 56). There is something curious about how this "thing" of noise that everyone comes together around is not "there"—and how something ephemeral is made to matter through scaffolding that includes metrics, publics, law, and discourse. A material-discursive "monster," a "quasi object," an "unformed object" or "hybrid," noise emerges in and through things: ear, window, air, microphone diaphragm, the creation and circulation of standards, sound transmission graphs and their interpretation, perception and affect, law, regulations, technology, civic mobilizations, and sensation (Haraway 1992; Latour 1993; Murphy 2013).

Proliferating into a multiplicity of atmospheric forms, noise shapes, grounds, and resonates across concrete formations, which include airspace territory, the inscription of metrics, environmental legislation, residential architecture, and infrastructural edge spaces. Not a thing in and of itself, noise is a "compositional node" from which "lines of contact radiate out" and "energies distribute" (K. Stewart 2013). Thus tracing noise as it is heard and made meaningful entails paying attention to emergent forms and concepts; to interconnections and entanglements that are material, sensory, imagined, and social; to movement and shape-shifting forms; and to a proliferation of effects. It means attending not only to how and in what terms *noise* is produced as such but also what is externalized and how they also matter; these are the excesses, the logics and illogics of categories as they are taken up in various contexts. It means attending to how that which is blocked, excluded, and occluded nonetheless percolates, escapes, seeps out the edges, explodes, implodes, expands into and out of gaps that take the form of doubt, noise complaints, love of home, weather, wind, fog, vibration, touch. The management and regulation of noise depends on and draws partially from a modern physics of acoustics, which both curtails and affords wider potentials for the sonic. Hence, while necessarily engaging, and often relying on, a modern physics of sound, I also read against the grain of its role in designating truth value, drawing out both its assumptions and weirdnesses (and in this way, departing from much work in sound studies). And while I aim to avoid reducing its multiplicity to a singularity, I, like others, find noise seductive in its malleability, its ability to be at once material and metaphor, matter and method.

SENSING ATMOSPHERIC MATTERS

Good to think (or sense) with, the atmospheric is difficult to pin down, to make conform to any one thing, to harden into existing categories. At the same time, like noise, the atmospheric is not "out there," either physically or conceptually; rather, it is present, pervasive, and immanent; it imbues, becomes, and permeates; it is perceived, sensed, and heard. In its emphasis on a physicality of the ephemeral, the book is an explicit engagement with and intervention into an expansive literature that falls broadly under new materialisms (Bennett 2010; Coole and Frost 2010; Latour 2007; T. Morton 2013). Informed by the spirit of this work, I write through *things*—noise, atmosphere, annoyance—as a means of attending to materiality in motion. There is something of a lacuna in this literature on the particular qualities of diverse forms of matter and their entanglements. In particular, gaseous or energetic forms of matter tend to be treated in similar terms as those that are more durable and concrete. A now burgeoning literature on air and atmosphere, however, engages explicitly with questions of materiality. Hence, while Luce Irigaray (1999) famously accused Heidegger of "forgetting of air," a recent turn toward the atmospheric by scholars across disciplines has begun to remedy this tendency.[8] As Derek McCormack notes, "atmosphere has become one of the most theoretically and empirically alluring of concepts" (2018, 6). In drawing out qualities of matter and their entanglements, I incorporate approaches that destabilize not only the human subject but the solidity of all kinds of matter. This is what Karen Barad describes as "intra-action," or "*the mutual constitution of entangled agencies*." Relationships, rather than ontological qualities of things, give form to "boundaries and properties" of "components of phenomena" (2007, 33, 139). For Barad, quantum physics provides a means of conceptualizing matter as fundamentally destabilized, consisting not of boundaries between things but the constant movement of electrons. Noise facilitates this openness: animated electrons, it amplifies the indeterminacy of boundaries between forms of matter.[9]

A phenomenal approach to the atmospheric emphasizes sensation and immaterial forms of energy, materializations over materiality—motion, emergence, immanence, in and of air and sense. Attending to listening affords engagement with these processes. As an energetic entanglement across forms of matter, listening is affective, a mode of bringing into being an "intensity of relations," a concrete poetics of encounter that amplifies the sensory as relational and affect as embodied.[10] Listening is an event in which something is happening or stirring, shifting orientations and relationships: "Sound affects: we feel it and it creates feeling" (Kapchan 2015, 40; see also Brennan 2004). At the same time, listening is indeterminate; as Brian Harnetty writes, "Listening is an act of uncertainty. When we listen closely" we are "unsure of what sounds or words we might encounter" (n.d.). Listening offers the possibility of attuning toward one another, or the refusal thereof.

Listening anchors a theory of deobjectified sound, which otherwise remains burdened by a distinction drawn by modern physics between sound and hearing. Such objectification becomes codified in modes of inscription, whether musical composition or recorded sound. To shift from this dichotomy, it is productive to conceive of listening as akin to senses of touch, proprioception, and thermoception—senses that do not distinguish between sense and that which is sensed.[11] Instead, sensory perception figures a body as being part of a world of atmospheric qualities rather than separable from it. Michel Serres, in theorizing the senses as "mingled bodies," locates mingling, or mixture, between body and world in the skin: "The skin is a variety of contingency: in it, through it, with it, the world and my body touch each other, the feeling and the felt, it defines their common edge. . . . I mix with the world which mixes with me. Skin intervenes between several things in the world and makes them mingle" (2009, 80; Connor 2003, 27–29). Or, as Erin Manning writes, "When the skin becomes not a container but a multi-dimensioned topological surface that folds in, through and across spacetimes of experience, what emerges is not a self but the dynamic form of a worlding that refuses categorization. Beyond the human, beyond the sense of touch or vision, beyond the object, what emerges is relation" (2009, 42). Elaborated more fully in chapters 1, 3, and 4, skin figured thus is crucial for the ways in which the atmospheric comes into being through the perception of noise. Approaching listening in this way affords a similar reading of other senses, whether vision or touch, while at the same time shifting from a focus on human senses. In what follows, many things are sensed: images, wind, heat, vibration, and noise. There are also many sensors, including walls, windows, chickens, microphones, and people.

Listening is compositional. Taking place in and through diverse modes of sensing, listening draws together emergent assemblages of matter. This is taken up explicitly in many of the chapters. For instance, in chapter 1 we see how bodily experience is wielded as evidence for the significance of aircraft noise even as its unreliability destabilizes noise as a concern. In chapter 2, noise as annoying is metricized and images become sites of engagement, casting a continuity of sense across hearing, vision, and thermoception. Through a discussion of the emergence of the category of noise pollution, chapter 3 thematizes sound as immanent, figured as airborne even as it is not a substance of air; here noise—pervasive yet diffuse—provides a cipher for environmental imaginaries. Chapter 4 attends to the physicality of sonic encounters that are largely excluded from the case itself, from sound as touch to the effect of fog on noise and the phenomenality of microphone listening.

Chapter 5 emphasizes the sensory capacity of buildings, walls, windows, and microphones, the resonance of which crafts a climate of listening. And in the last chapter, as humans attune toward butterflies, encountering soil and plants in a place where homes once stood, a sense of loss pervades. Lurking in these haptic encounters are shifts in frame offered by discussions of plant sense and multispecies entanglements, of what has been described as "vegetal being," "animacies," and "zoontologies."[12] Of this, work on plant sensing has been especially significant for turning my attention toward the nonhuman in a way that affords an investigation of noise as drawing together diverse forms of matter and ways of being—for attending to how other species, or forms of matter, might be sensing, or at minimum resonating.

Though many emphasize the pleasurable commingling of multispecies entanglements, noise draws attention to displeasurable and unwanted entanglements of body and atmosphere. Noise figures a body as permeable, ear and skin less a protective shield that might make a body "immersed" or "suspended" in sound than vibrating with sound, resonant to its very core (Choy and Zee 2015; Ingold 2011). This is a body threatened by that which is external to it, a body affected by noise, by the vibration of sound.[13] Hence noise has more in common with *exposure*, used to conceptualize a body under threat from a toxic atmosphere that permeates the skin.[14] As this literature demonstrates, a permeable body is not always desirable—we do not always want to be "enwinded" (Ingold 2011) or even vibrate with others. Vibration, at times used for healing, for the experience of trance, or as a mantra of togetherness, can also be an unwanted entanglement, a limit point of shared physicality with others, whether human or not. This becomes evident in the category of *environmental noise*, which draws together industrial sound, pollution, a standards definition of "unwanted sound," and regimes of measurement and control. Its contours, assumptions, and effects secure the significance of noise for the atmospheric. In the mid-twentieth century, infrastructures and technologies of mobility that initiated newfound aspirations for movement and flight also brought new sounds and sensations—the rubber of trucks on freeways and the unmuffled roar of engines, airports, and aircraft noise. These are the sounds of anthropogenic climate change: the combustion engine, fossil fuels, electricity. Their noise affords a sensory investigation of the contemporary condition, in which atmospheric entanglements are increasingly troubled.

GLITCHING, A METHODOLOGY

Writing through noise is improvisational, musical practice providing a metaphor for tracing noise in its movement across atmospheric registers and for sticking with it in its ephemerality and indeterminacy. My writing stays close to things—materials, concepts, noise—in ways similar to how I play cello, one sound becoming another through a physicality of touch and instrument, an indefinite, rhizomatic form. I write with an ear to the sound and rhythm of words and to the ways in which they can convey scenes or moods or ideas. In free improvisation, a sound (that is always a multitude) moves into another; sometimes there is a folding in while at other times a pause or a rupture, a startling switch from one thing to another (Grubbs 2018). Repeating a sound, dwelling in it, the hand slips and something else yields, is opened, explored, drawn out and on until time shifts or another player prompts a change in tone or mood or tempo or volume. We play with and against one another, melding into a drone or an alternating, irregular rhythm; it gets loud and I pause or find a way to break through the bass with the highest pitch possible, sustained, softly. An experiment with materials and their textures, improvisation risks failure, whether falling off the edge of legibility or playing a string with such pressure the spiral paper clip used to prepare it pops off, clattering onto the floor somewhere in the darkness.

Improvisation entails experimentation with the sonic potentialities of an instrument—what the materiality of the cello yields as I draw the bow vertically, a scratchiness or click click click as string yields to and then resists the pressure of horsehair. There are tones to be found on metal parts meant to be still, used as tuners and otherwise unnoticed; whispers and wshswhshwhshses of wood, or paper placed under the bridge. These are glitches—sounds made beyond and against a particular history of the instrument, but nonetheless existing as potential. A glitch is a "noise" interrupting or erupting within an intended sound, a buzz or a squeal that betrays the inner workings or recursive potentials of audio technologies—dirty connections, crossed wires, microphones with too high a signal or held in front of an amplifier, a scratch that cuts across the grooves of a record. A sign of infrastructural failure or the materiality of digital technology, glitches are unintended sounds that are always potentially audible, with as much work required to keep them concealed as to make the intended sound heard.[15] Airport noise is itself a glitch, an unintended effect of infrastructure that makes it possible for humans to move from ground to air. And while most engagements with airport noise aim to control or minimize it,

I hone in on the noise itself, finding in it a means of tracing atmospheric matters.

Glitching as a method of investigation, analysis, and writing, I read documents and ethnographic encounters for textures and qualities of events. Hence images and audio recordings are engaged not only for their content but as objects in and of themselves. And while I attend to something of the specificity of a historical moment, I am not aiming for a totalizing account but instead present discrete, distilled concerns that nonetheless seep out and into one another, in ways that are often unstable and indeterminate. I treat archival material ethnographically, listening to its dynamics rather than situating it as an event in the past. Writing in present tense provides a way of animating ethnographic encounters and historical hearings, excavating the archive for its liveliness, or noise. Moreover, it engages hearings as active processes in which key terms were negotiated. A close reading rather than a comprehensive study, the writing performs analysis by attending to noise and its encounters, which might, in turn, fold into another kind of matter, noise itself receding. Neither the construction of a grand narrative nor an application of theory, the discussion stays close to noise itself, sorting out how it emerges and the matterings attendant to it. In this regard, it finds company in "thin description," what John Jackson describes as a "flat" ethnographic methodology, "where you slice into the world from different perspectives, scales, registers, and angles—all distinctively useful, valid, and worthy of consideration" (2013, 17), and what Heather Love offers as "forms of analysis that do not traffic in speculation about interiority or depth" but provide "exhaustive, fine-grained attention to phenomenon" (2013, 404). I read glitches, and read them as glitch, drawing out indeterminacies that are in or across the message, that are meaningful in their exclusion. A glitch methodology affords an amplification of im/materialities of sound and atmosphere even when that may not be the explicit concern of those with and to whom I am listening. Nonrepresentational, it "aims to rupture, unsettle, animate, and reverberate rather than report and represent" (Vannini 2015, 5; see also Anderson and Harrison 2010). Thus, while allowing the sensible to take shape and addressing how its logics spread out and congeal as form, I also draw out the "insensible" (Yusoff 2013) from adamantly sense-making projects.

I dwell in the vagaries, the gaps—where the formless begins to take on a form yet falters, where the sensible moves back into sense, taking shape as limits or exclusions that nonetheless have physical substance and qualities. As "connections between seemingly unconnected things" (Howe, quoted in

Swensen 2011, 38), gaps (like vacant lots and edge spaces) are not "emptiness" but rather "an active coupling" (Swensen 2011, 38) in which something happens. Gaps include slippages across temporal moments, the writing moving from a discussion of archival documents into recent ethnographic encounters as it traces a particular modality of noise. Some of this happens in a play between the text and the notes, the latter of which are substantive in and of themselves, and I hope will be read as such. There is a serendipity to the material, found in archives across the country, on government websites now devoid of a historical record under the current administration, in interactions with acoustical engineers and airport officials, and encounters with people who experience airport noise or work to ameliorate that experience. The archive resonates as an encounter not only with texts but with people who shared memories and knowledge. Much of the material is from minor archives, the places themselves sites of ethnographic engagement. Archivists—who often had personal experience with the subject—were helpful guides through sometimes opaque collections, at times even providing access to relevant items waiting to be cataloged. Many archives were personal, consisting of boxes of files in people's homes or shelves of reports in offices. And while I engage some sources for their content without situating them, I discuss others in relation to the place in which they are housed, with documents becoming animated objects in their own right, and the ethnographic necessarily emerging alongside the archive.

In tracing noise as it moves across registers, I find myself in dead ends, cul-de-sacs (literally and figuratively, if you know Westchester's geography), and potentially newly productive—and creative—spaces. These are little eddies of matterings in which I dwell, drawing out their qualities, whether as driving desires or undesirable intimacies. Finding ways out of the eddies (or not), I skim across the surface of things, accounting for temporal horizons and circulation, the movement of a concept or a political concern or a sensory experience. I attend to what the concept means, how it matters, how it catches up other things or changes into something else that might be similar to previous things or that is nascent, newly composing worlds and becoming event. Emphasizing concepts in things, I insist on an understanding of theory as being in the world—of the ethnographic as intrinsically theoretical—and the possibility of drawing that out through writing. As "concrete abstractions" (de la Cadena 2018), concepts are emergent in and through the material; they are what Manning calls "eventness in the making" (2009, 37).[16] More like wind than water, these eddies are flurries and gusts. Like noise, they might sound at times as if they do not quite fit.

The chapters hone in on particular moments and encounters, exploring some of the kaleidoscopic ways in which noise draws together humans and nonhumans, matter and air, amplifying modalities of listening, figurations of sound, and im/materializations of the atmospheric. As compositions, each chapter is an assemblage that coheres around a particular thematic concern. Not classical compositions that recapitulate the opening with variation, but improvisatory, the chapters sometimes end up in a place seemingly far from where they began, a place that might inform the whole as it emerges through an unfurling that moves the reader through, without argument, to the end. Atmospheric in form, insofar as noise provides an opening, there cannot be a conclusion in the conventional sense. In this way the writing echoes, or performs, what noise does as it moves through matter and across registers, resonating in concrete specificities even as it does not necessarily settle. Following John Law's incisive model in *Aircraft Stories*, the world is performed in the writing, a world understood as rhizomatic and fractional (2002, 6). This is anthropology as "a fabulatory art" (McLean 2017, 1)—a creative engagement with a world, a practice that is also a worlding.

In Chapter 1, "Aerial Attunements," I consider how air and ground are drawn together through listening as those living around the airport newly turned toward noise from the sky. At the dawn of the jet age, aerial attunements provided the basis for new atmospheric imaginaries—for air travel, for conceiving of air as partitionable territory, and for sensorial entanglements of bodies and air. Noise had already established airspace property rights through a 1946 Supreme Court case, *U.S. v. Causby*, in which a North Carolina chicken farmer charged that the sounds of military jets taking off over his coops had caused his chickens to take fright and die. Newly producing the atmospheric as space, civic mobilizations against aircraft noise around Los Angeles International Airport in the 1950s and 1960s revealed gaps between the federal jurisdiction of the sky and the municipal territory of the ground. The atmospheric coalesces as a listening space in which the experience of airport noise drew residents, FAA officials, and U.S. senators together in a series of legislative hearings. One of these was held in Inglewood, California, where residents were experiencing noise from LAX. "Experience" ultimately provides unstable grounds for law, and even as efforts are made to concretize noise through its inscription in recording and measurement, noise itself falls away.

Chapter 2, "Noise Annoys," examines how annoyance, commonplace and banal, adheres to noise even as efforts are made to excise it. An indeterminate, unstable affect, annoyance signifies the subjective nature of noise while carrying the weight of nuisance law—of noise as a concern of property. Metrics bring annoyance into being and give it shape, whether as an aspect of sensory experience or an outcome. Emphasizing the viscerality of abstraction, it discusses the development and proliferation of PNdB, or perceived noise decibel level, and its bracketing of *annoyance* in favor of *noisiness*, even as the former seeps back in, hanging on graphs and charted against decibel levels. The weight of perception shifts from the experience of noise to its inscription, the sensory rendered as abstraction. Despite a fixity of metrics, the gap between inscription and perception generates a relationship between the two—a dynamic friction in which discussions about the metric, about its relationship to experience, and about experience itself transpire. Inscription emerges as a form of lively matter that is sensory and affective. Heat maps of airport noise levels are a palpable instantiation of this viscerality, bringing into relief the coextensiveness of thermoception, hearing, and vision.

Chapter 3, "Environmental Imaginaries," traces the indeterminate category of noise pollution as it emerges in the mid-1960s and takes hold in American environmental legislation. The category of *noise pollution* both echoes and amplifies environmental imaginaries of its time, which, while increasingly atmospheric in logic and in substance, remained adamantly anthropocentric. The shift of noise from *nuisance* to *pollution* is significant for registering a then-nascent conceptualization of "the environment" grounded equally in an emergent planetary consciousness and a notion of a permeable body. Casting noise as pollution shifts from a relationship between neighbors to a generalized atmospheric condition, in which the noisemaker may or may not be known. And though it is demarcated as specifically airborne sound, the inclusion of noise in the Clean Air Act Amendments of 1970 does not make it a pollutant of air. Of air but not air, noise is pollution in and through its effects on human bodies, which, figured as permeable, become registers of the atmospheric. And while its general and pervasive quality prefigures something like a notion of "climate," noise pollution does not last.

Chapter 4, "Murmurs: Experiments in Glitching," turns to murmurs—soft, indistinct sounds whose indiscernibility risks illegibility. The negative that matters, murmurs are glitches within a glitch. They percolate up from within like a minor gesture that "opens experience to its potential variation . . . from within experience itself" (Manning 2016, 67), or a minor anthropology that "would make small multiplicities proliferate" (Viveiros de Castro 2013, 19). In this chapter, a series of short pieces takes up a physicality of the ephemeral that emerges in productive gaps between the bases of establishing what noise is and what is excluded from noise and its control, what nonetheless continues to resonate, meaningful as its other. Amplifying the murmurs of the case, as fragments recuperating what is otherwise, they are themselves murmurs. A proliferation of matterings, they are about wind and weather, the vagaries of noise metrics and their sensory extensions into touch and thermoception, chicken fright, microphones, and kites. And even as they dwell in what is excluded, they distill some of the central points of the book. They are drawn together in chapter form to give weight to their presence and potentiality within the text. Imagine that they might be lifted out and read as a small book on their own.

Jet noise disrupted the continuity between indoors and out made possible by the Pacific climate of Southern California. In response, residential soundproofing turned urban life inward, closing holes in homes and fortifying an otherwise permeable skin. Chapter 5, "Vibrating Matter," explores how noise brings into being emergent materialities while newly shaping listening spaces. This was the era of a cultivation of a new kind of listening, in which high fidelity audio technologies oriented people toward recorded sound and away from environmental sound—and noise. Soundproofing registers homes as "bubbles," marking horizons of belonging and their limits. While the aim was to diminish the sensorial effects of unwanted entanglements, here I read against the grain to address how soundproofing makes evident the resonance of matter, "lively sound" animating the matter of walls and windows, the atmospheric materialized in the membrane of the home.

Chapter 6, "Indefinite Urbanism," focuses on infrastructural edge spaces that are effects of airport noise. Though thematized explicitly in the last chapter, the notion of indefinite urbanism applies to the book as a whole. Today, planes departing from LAX take off over dunes that, once held in place by the concrete foundations of homes, are now habitat for the El Segundo blue, an endangered species of butterfly. This is a place of "noisy silence," the ambivalence of "terrain vague" instantiated by the chain link fence encircling winding streets of neighborhoods where an ocean view remains, inaccessible without the picture windows that once framed it (Königstein 2014, 135; Solà-Morales 2014, 24). Encounters between people, neighborhoods, photographs, ice plant, and butterflies become atmospheric forms that echo those drawn together by noise, "encounters that have taken form" (Malabou 2015, 49). I dwell in the atmospheric qualities of the material, whether that of a photograph or a story, a finger drawing the outline of a hill, or a butterfly in flight. Noise itself recedes, remaining palpable in its effects.

1

AERIAL ATTUNEMENTS

On January 25, 1959, the first transcontinental commercial jet flight left Los Angeles International Airport and landed at Idlewild Airport (now JFK), returning to L.A. that evening. This flight is credited with ushering L.A. into the "jet age."[1] Those living around what had been a bean field, an airfield, and, since 1937, a municipal airport that would later become LAX began to hear, with increasing frequency, the sound of jet planes arriving and departing over their homes.[2] Newly attuned toward a resounding sky, listening oriented people toward the atmospheric and each other. In the moment of hearing, those living around the airport may simply have turned to their neighbor, covering their ears or acknowledging the noise by pausing in midsentence. They complained about the noise that interrupted the Pacific climate of the Southern California coast and talked about what they could do. They formed organizations and collected signatures. They called on others to listen to them: the airport; their city councilperson; the county supervisor; the newspapers; a priest; congressional representatives; and the Federal Aviation Administration (FAA). They did not always know whom to address, where to complain, where to direct their rights claims. Yet in appealing to those who might be able to do something, they revealed gaps in jurisdiction over air and ground, airspace as territory emerging through noise.

The airport is an ambient infrastructure, its audibility amplifying its status as a port where transportation infrastructure on the ground meets that of the air (Hubbard, McClintock, and Williams 1930; Timmins 1976).[3] Built to be seen (but not heard) from the air, the airport as an acoustic space divides interior from exterior, severing the experience of passengers from the work of flying, the visual from the aural (Reynolds 2003). Double-glazed windows that produced acoustically sealed interiors stand as evidence that airport architects were aware of aircraft noise, even if its significance for nearby residents was denied. This is a different airport than the one we use for travel, the "nonplace" of tannish walls, TV screens, connected seats with metal arms, overpriced shops and cafes, replicated around the world in variations on a theme, a place for which Brian Eno composed atmospheric ambient sounds (Augé 1995; Eno 1978). The airport we pass through and endure, in which we wait or imbibe until boarding a plane whose cabin pressurization creates an interior space sealed from the sensations of the atmosphere. The airport as border zone, a space of mobilities, "jet terminals" built to provide "a sense of movement, transition, and excitement that flight itself no longer provided" (Gordon 2008, 177), a gateway to the condition of being airborne, that strange doubling of moving through air while sitting still.

Instead, this is airport as working machine, its exterior spaces and sounds that make the experience of the interiors of both airport and airplane possible (Adey 2010b; Bednarek 2001). It is municipal infrastructure, in which infrastructure is an assemblage of jurisdictional domains and law that affords their crossing (Anand, Gupta, and Appel 2018; Larkin 2013). It is economic engine for a "globalizing L.A.," figured through trade and regional development, justified, at least initially, by virtue of the postal service and defense (Erie 2004; see also Doolittle 1952). It is the external zone of a site of security, surveillance, and state power (and the protest thereof).[4] Where workplace regulations require maintenance workers to wear earmuffs, where giant mufflers were once constructed to contain the engine noise of idling planes, and where sound shields designed to protect the neighbors from the noise of departing planes were nixed because "it wouldn't work, the airplanes fly up, higher than the wall."[5] This is the airport as infrastructure for planes whose presence was made palpable principally through their noise and, for those who lived along the coast, the occasional crash, when mangled metal, teddy bears, and stray suitcases saturated with onlookers' trauma washed up onto the beach (Torgerson 1969).[6] The airport about which General James H. Doolittle was concerned when he signed off on the 1952 President's Airport Commission report, *The Airport and Its Neighbors*, also referred to as the Doolittle Report, released in the aftermath of three plane crashes into the neighborhoods adjacent to Newark Airport, and less than a decade after the authors of *Airport Planning* had urged that airports "take their place as an intimate, useful, and aesthetic part of community life" (Froesch and Prokosch 1946, 8).

The experience of airport noise mobilized residents, who formed civic groups, lobbied elected officials, and brought lawsuits against the airport and the city from El Segundo to Lennox, Inglewood to Westchester, areas that had been developed around aerospace.[7] Their frustrations and mutterings were amplified as they joined a swell of others concerned about noise: acoustical engineers, composers, elected officials, medical researchers, building material manufacturers, and people who lived near airports in other cities who were also bothered by noise. Voicing a "politics of the sensible" (Laplantine 2015, 82; Panagia 2009), their concerns resonated at a moment in which interest in noise control was burgeoning. Publications on noise as a scientific, environmental, and civic issue proliferated, while congressional hearings provided a space in which residents listened to and were heard by elected officials as they shared their experiences of airplane noise. There, shared experience pitted residents against the airlines, the pilots, the airport, and the city—all those who may be responsible for the noise but had done nothing.[8] They were eager to talk and to be heard. "Experience," however, is an unreliable form of evidence, as neither noise nor its effects appear to last. Anchored in bodies, experience circulates in its inscription in narrative, recorded sound, and metrics. Audio recordings made in public school classrooms and outdoors under the flight path recruited others to listen to the sounds of aircraft, while an environmental noise survey measured sound levels to objectify and generalize the subjective individualized experience of aircraft noise. Yet even as technologies for measurement and recording provided seemingly more reliable modes of listening and inscribing experience, stored deep in archives or shelved in storage, they also fall away.

AMPLIFYING AIRSPACE

When residents felt overwhelmed by the sounds of planes arriving and departing from the municipal airport, they turned toward elected representatives who might do something about the noise. Met with the impasse of a municipality (that owned the airport) lacking jurisdiction over the skies and a federal agency disinterested in (and not required to be accountable for) that which happened on the ground, residents appealed to their local elected officials to *do* something about airport noise. County supervisor Kenneth Hahn's district, which included the area to the immediate east of the airport, spanned parts of Los Angeles County both within and outside the city of Los Angeles. Hence, those living in the city of Inglewood and in Lennox, an unincorporated area of Los Angeles County, turned to Hahn as an elected official who might be able to tackle a problem of infrastructure under the jurisdiction of the city of Los Angeles. Their letters and copies of his responses are now housed in an archive.[9] Noise, stilled in its inscription, remains palpable as an active yet unstable "object," revealing gaps between jurisdictions differentiating airspace from ground as well as between spatial regimes that draw together ground and air—the sensory and flight as it actually occurs. In September 1959, motivated by citizens' complaints, Kenneth Hahn asked the Office of the County Counsel whether the board of supervisors had the power to establish "aerial rights of way" at prescribed heights. County counsel replied, "It is our opinion that the County cannot regulate the noise emanating from jet aircraft or control the flight thereof by reason of the limitations imposed by the Supremacy of Federal regulations and power in this field."[10]

The legal landscape faced by those living near the airport, which they ultimately helped shape, was structured by a confluence of nuisance and property law, and their conflicting "volumetric" geographies (Graham and Hewitt 2013). Rather than closing gaps, struggles transpired over the legitimacy of differential regimes, between experience on the one hand and law on the other. Coextensive with other processes and dynamics, law both incorporates and seeps into extralegal affairs (Greenhouse 1994). Imbued in everyday life, law is at once sensory and sensible, made through practice and procedure. In configuring airspace, territory, and noise, it channels and shapes experience, civic mobilizations, technological developments, infrastructure, rights claims, property, and more. And while law tends toward a logic of rationalization, it is also a space in which new claims are made and categories refigured.

Sound, designated as noise, composes the atmospheric as space. Sovereign space that is legislated, measured, and partitioned as territory and property; a space in motion and of movement; a space whose qualities emerge through sound, sound that in activating airspace draws together atmosphere and ground, technologies of flight and sensation. This is a volumetric territory that is also a listening space. And while noise is not the only grounds for airspace territory and jurisdiction, its status here echoes another, earlier case (Banner 2008). A 1946 Supreme Court case, *U.S. v. Causby*, remains the basis for airspace property rights below the "public highway" of navigable airspace. Thomas Lee Causby and his wife, Tinie, owned a chicken farm near Greensboro, North Carolina. In 1941, military planes began exercises at an airport adjacent to their farm. Awakened in fright, the noise of departing planes drew their attention to the sky, bringing the aerial into their sleep. No longer grounded in their second-floor bedroom, the sound reverberated as they paced for hours into the night. Meanwhile, their chickens died and their farm lost value. As the leaves of a tree fluttered in the thrust of an engine's roar, air was crafted into property, air as property made audible. Of the "five and ten million Americans [who] tried their hands at poultry keeping in the eighty-year period from 1890 to 1970" (Smith and Daniel 1975, 295), Thomas Causby stands out for making chickens the subject of law, amplifying their otherwise ordinary and overlooked presence and grounding airspace territory not only in noise, but in the affect of chickens. Ultimately, he was one among many who closed his chicken farm and moved on to something else, before chicken farming shifted almost fully to a factory model.[11]

Causby's suit was based on the argument that he owned the airspace over his farm, such that the planes flying overhead constituted a "taking" of his property. The U.S. Supreme Court ruled in his favor "to an extent." Dividing the air above the ground into horizontal layers, it maintained the constitutional basis of aviation airspace as a "public highway," or "part of the public domain," as legislated by the Air Commerce Act of 1926 and the Civil Aeronautics Act of 1938. Below that, it created a new category of property rights, an "aerial easement" in which air's physical properties cast vertical territoriality as an effect of measurement rather than tangible ownership (S. R. Hays 1961, 39).[12] This is a volumetric urbanism that is at once spatial and sonic (Adey 2013; Bridge 2013; Elden 2013; Graham and Hewitt 2013). Noise, with its standards definition of "unwanted sound," is nevertheless usually loud, a fact that is inscribed in the metrics of noise management—systems that ground and satisfy law. Hence, when Stuart Elden writes of the importance of attending to the "dimensionality" of volume and the "calculability" of metric to account for the "politics, metrics and power of volume" (Elden 2013, 49), he might equally be referring to sound as to coal mines or airspace.

Over subsequent years, noise as activating airspace manifests as politicking: Kenneth Hahn goes to Washington, the FAA resists prohibiting easterly takeoffs on the basis of anything other than safety, and county counsel studies "Judicial Application of Airspace Theories," finding that "the nuisance theory . . . indicates that the landowner owns some property right, although perhaps ill defined, in the airspace below normal flight altitudes." An earlier notion of noise as nuisance is cast into a domain of airspace territoriality, presenting the possibility that the county or municipalities might make nuisance claims against airlines. Yet, it turns out, nuisance as legal grounds is relegated to cities and counties and cannot be wielded against the territory of the sky, insofar as it is governed by the federal government.[13] Councilman L. E. Timberlake, a member of the city's Noise Abatement Committee, wrote in a memorandum to his motion to control aircraft noise that, while it "will accomplish the control of the noise of jets on the ground," as "the control of this operation is within the jurisdiction of the city . . . , it does not constitute any control of the jets when they are air borne, as the Federal Aviation Agency has complete jurisdiction over air borne traffic, and has so specifically stated."[14]

Between 1959 and 1962, subcommittees of the House Committee on Interstate and Foreign Commerce held a series of hearings on "aircraft noise problems" (U.S. House 1963). House Resolution 420 "authorized and directed" the committee "to conduct a full and complete investigation and study of the problems involved in, and measures to minimize or eliminate, aircraft noise nuisances and hazards to persons and property on the ground." The 1958 Federal Aviation Act had authorized the Federal Aviation Administration as having jurisdiction over flight. While the act included responsibility toward "protection of persons and property on the ground," noise was not specified. The hearings were intended to explore how this protection might be expanded to include noise (U.S. House 1963, 492). An attorney described the problem that resulted from separating jurisdiction of ground and sky: "We may need a two-man board to run the FAA, one man with his head in the air, the other man with his feet on the ground. I say that sincerely to emphasize the importance of legislating from the standpoint of protecting the rights of all the people, the people who fly and the people on the ground. They are one and the same, and they should be treated equally" (U.S. House 1963, 226).

Flight, casting air as distinct from life on the ground, required new imaginaries to address noise. Drawing together air and ground, noise itself was indeterminate, coming into being even as it fell, again, into jurisdictional gaps posed by divergent arenas of authority. Instead of a "two-man board" who acted as one, there was a magician's assistant, her torso sawed down the middle, head and feet no longer joined. Francis T. Fox, general manager of Los Angeles Department of Airports, gave extensive testimony during which he expressed frustration about the airport's inability to enforce rules on airlines due to jurisdictional limits—limits in authority expressed as territorial. Though the carriers "agree to abide by . . . [the] regulations" of the Department of Airports, "there is an area of disagreement where FAA takes over and the Department of Airports has jurisdiction" (U.S. House 1963, 252). He continued, explaining, "We have felt that we have the authority, but it has been recently clarified . . . that when a plane is in the air and off the ground the FAA has the jurisdiction" (252). Hence, the Department of Airports had no recourse when a pilot went off course or departed over residential areas when doing so was restricted by the airport but not the FAA. While the Department of Airports' Sound Abatement Coordinating Committee had prohibited easterly takeoffs during the night, committee members were surprised to find the restriction had been eliminated when "FAA regulations superseded this regulation that was effective April 1, and superseded all our local regulations" (U.S. House 1963, 253). With a gap having emerged into which noise fell as it was excluded from regulation, the Department of Airports, Fox maintained, had "tried within human and reasonable limits to protect the interests of our neighbors here" (253).

Pilots, "captains of the ship" when in the air, were recruited to assist with the problem of noise, to ameliorate the experience of those on the ground. Yet it remained unresolved where their authority began: on the ground or only once in the sky. An exchange conveying this confusion is worth presenting in full:

ADMIRAL ROSENDAHL: The pilot is the last authority. In the last analysis he is the captain of the ship, and it is his decision.

CHAIRMAN: On taking off and landing?

ADMIRAL ROSENDAHL: On taking off.

CHAIRMAN: Well, that is very interesting to me. I had always had the impression that the control tower operator had the final word with reference to where a plane could takeoff and when he could takeoff.

ADMIRAL ROSENDAHL: Well, actually, he does. But if a pilot tells him for safety reasons he wants to take off on a certain runway, I doubt that he is going to dispute the pilot. . . .

CHAIRMAN: I had always thought, and I believe it is correct, the pilot is the captain of the ship. But he is captain of that ship when it gets in the air and gets off and gets down. I had never thought, at least that the procedure was such that the pilot of any ship could do anything he wanted with that ship on the ground, and as he takes off, regardless of what might happen to any and everybody else that might also be coming in or taking off. (U.S. House 1963, 61)

The FAA runs the control tower, but if pilots ask for a specific runway—one that might result in taking off over residential areas—even without giving a reason, they might be allowed to use it. A pilot testified that he and other pilots were in fact greatly concerned about the experience of those living on the ground below. Yet the possibility that their concern about noise might fall away as jurisdiction on the ground shifts to that of the air provides a partial explanation of the signs posted on runways in these decades, alerting pilots to attend to noise.

Also testifying at the hearings, Kenneth Hahn appealed to the federal government to do what he had not been able to achieve on the local level, though he had tried: to provide funds for quieter engine design, to develop rules and regulations for aircraft in partnership with local government, and to assist with city planning related to transportation. Hahn was exceedingly diplomatic and extolled the hearings as a "tremendous lesson in democracy," insofar as members of congress—"with all the power that is invested in you gentlemen as representatives of the people"—came to their community to hear from the people. William Hall, representing a Lennox citizens group, spoke at the 1960 aircraft noise hearings in Inglewood, laying out the jurisdictional gaps and appealing to Congress for relief: "We were ignorant in the beginning of where we should go for help, to whom we should look or ask for help, and now we have eliminated, one by one, through various channels, all of our approaches, and we feel that we are now at the top. We feel that your committee can make realistic recommendations which we feel will be followed by the rest of the congressional committees and then, perhaps, by Congress itself, to really solve our problem" (U.S. House 1963, 228–29). Yet despite the efforts of civic groups and Kenneth Hahn, people living near the airport continued to experience noise. In 1965, Lee L. Sopher of Lennox wrote to Hahn, "We are having a great deal of trouble with the airplane. . . . We had a promise, that we would get relief, Feb. 1–65. We did, for a week. And then back they came, as low, and some lower. It is almost impossible, for T.V. or radio."[15]

EXPERIENCING NOISE

The congressional hearings on "aircraft noise problems" drew people together around the subject of noise (U.S. House 1963). Noise had already motivated the formation of numerous citizen groups in cities across the country with newly buzzing airports: Queens (the site of the first hearing, on September 7, 1959), San Francisco (the site of the third, on April 20, 1960), and Inglewood (the site of the fourth, on April 21, 1960). At the hearings, leaders of community groups, mayors, airport managers, pilots, and others caught up in the problem of noise testified to patient, largely understanding and sympathetic congressmen, who took peoples' experiences seriously, were concerned about jurisdiction and authority (or the lack thereof), and let people speak freely other than excessive applause or (unrecorded) interruptions from the audience.[16] Affiliations of those testifying identify them as leaders of local organizations against noise, members of civic groups, and homeowners. Their status as such grounds sound from the air in property, bodies anchored to beds and living rooms by the gravity of law as technologies of flight newly expand sensation into the air.

At the hearings, people living near a municipal airport describe their experience, situating the body at a "nexus of living meanings" (Merleau-Ponty 2002, 175). The body is drawn into relation with noise, an aerial attunement that, differently than an "object" of vision, is audible, an ephemeral, temporal acoustic force. "Experience" percolates in narrative; told in congressional hearings or to a judge, described in letters to elected officials, it figures a gap between perception and the narrative thereof that renders it unstable and indeterminate (Turner and Bruner 2001). To experience is to encounter in a practical, immediate way. Accounting for experience shifts the immediacy of encounter to discourse, evidence that is requisite for the process of law. And while narratives of experience convey their own physicality—a tremor in the voice revealing the intimacy of affect, or the sure, stable utterance of someone telling a story they have told many times before—in their remove from the encounter itself, they tend to not be trusted. Kim Lane Scheppele elaborates on the role of verbal testimony as legal evidence: "At a trial, actions and harms are converted into accounts and claims. Events are made into texts. And these are texts that, like legal texts, are open to interpretation" (1990, 44). This may be especially true in the case of noise, cast already as indeterminate: subjective, falling away as sound, leaving no trace on the body. A woman describes others' experiences, her husband's, her child's. She might describe her own but in a way that is shaped and filtered for the audience, the congressman, and FAA officials, using language that can hold up as evidence. Experience is described as effect, as what happened when the plane flew overhead: I jumped out of bed, my husband went into shock, the child screamed. Or it is generalized, adjectives left hanging without a clear referent, experience becoming a general condition, "it is horrible." Moving inward, "I feel it in my body" anchors perception in the known, the proximate, the palpable—as opposed to the atmospheric—even as it remains unverifiable as evidence that might be circulated or held in common.

Their testimony resonates on the page, the experience of noise settling into bodies that press on the reader in their weariness, descriptions of how the sound of airplanes flying over their homes has become exhausting in its near constant demand for attention, how attuning toward the sky in this way is disturbing. There is an edge to their stories, if not their now inaudible voices, as physical conditions are described, at times in too much detail, drawing a listener (or reader) close to a body one would otherwise not know. Royal E. Dalrymple, president of the Queens Committee for Aviation Reforms and of the St. Albans Civic Improvement Association, tells members of the Committee on Interstate and Foreign Commerce: "We on the ground, who have suffered night and day, sleepless nights, with sickness—and I may add 7 weeks ago I was taken to my bed with the shingles, followed by chicken pox, at my age." His frustration and exhaustion are audible as he repeats himself, describing, again, his experience: "Many sleepless nights I had, considering these low-flying planes. I am one of the victims of sleepless nights" (U.S. House 1963, 25). Worse even than being woken by the sound of the planes was being woken from a dream. Dreams, fabulations of the psyche during sleep, take a person somewhere else, and, as argued at the time, serve a crucial role for both health and personhood. Louis C. Moser, of the North Queens Home Owners Civic Association of Jackson Heights, speaks for his wife, who "one night when the plane came through . . . was dreaming of something at that moment. And suddenly the plane comes roaring. And it doesn't go above 75 feet above my roof. My wife jumped out of bed completely frightened and it is hard to control her" (U.S. House 1963, 45).

A body affected by noise is all ears and nerves, entangled with air, home, and ground. William Hall, of the Lennox Citizens Group, explains, "It seems that every time one of these jets approaches, your nervous system winds up like a clock, you could say, and then gradually unwinds as the noise fades away in the distance. We simply have to multiply this by the number of flights and we find that there is considerable wear and tear on any individual's nervous system due to noise" (U.S. House 1963, 228). Mrs. C. A. DeWitt had taken her wheelchair-bound husband into the yard, where he might feel the sun and the breeze; the first plane took off, flying low over their house, followed by two more within a period of ten minutes, sending her husband into shock. "He was in shock for at least 6 hours under sedation," she said (1963, 272). Obscuring telephone communication, television, and conversation, noise is figured as signal's other. Thought, rather than an element of the nervous system, was something more like voices in one's head. Inglewood's mayor could neither hear himself think nor hear someone he was talking to "right at the ten thousand block on Hawthorne Boulevard at 1:15 in the afternoon" (204).

Living with the sound of planes, they had learned something about flight—the height of the plane, the model, the specificity of its sound. Dorothy Brown, chair of the Inglewood Citizens' Health and Welfare Council, describes how "the terrible whining of two jets had me with my fingers in my ears and pressured to the floor. . . . [T]hese jets were coming in so low, these jets are three stories high. . . . These planes fly at 180 to 200 miles per hour, then throw their flaps down, shake our homes, and the earth. We cannot sleep, read, relax, nor live like normal people, and we have not for 15 months" (U.S. House 1963, 220). Inglewood's Citizens' Health and Welfare Council was formed by a group of room mothers. A thousand people attended its first mass meeting, and Dorothy Brown had brought petitions with eight thousand signatures to the 1960 hearings (220). Attention turns to the quality of the sound of the plane from the sound of its interference, jets that "have a distinct penetrating shrill and disagreeable sound" (43). In Inglewood, Mr. Jones explains, "It is not the incidence of the takeoffs, but the magnitude of any individual takeoff, Congressman, sir, that is excruciatingly bothersome. . . . You have a feeling that the plane is coming right at your house. It is a terrible thing, and the house begins to shake and everything; just one of those things can upset an individual and a group of individuals emotionally" (212).

Narratives of experience compose a reliable holistic body, held apart and distinguished from noise that intrudes, that rudely deterritorializes a body bordered by skin—skin that, as made evident by noise, is permeable and porous, plastic in its continual decay and regeneration on the cellular level.[17] A milieu "where inside and outside meet and meld," skin vibrates with sound and prickles with cold (Connor 2003, 27). It is the meeting place between the body electric and the atmospheric, a distribution of energy shocked by friction or dryness. The terrain on or through which touch is sensed, skin folds back onto itself; at once touched and touching, a person becomes both "object in the world and a subject giving rise to itself as it advances to meet the world in that object" (Connor 2003, 41; Merleau-Ponty 2002). That which is eaten, drunk, or breathed enters the body along one skinned passage and leaves, as trace, through another. Senses are thus inseparable one from another, with sound vibrating the skin of the eardrum a form of touch. Following Serres, skin is "a variable confluence of the qualities of the senses" across which the "organs of the senses form knots, high-relief sites of singularity in this complex flat drawing, dense specializations, a mountain, valley or well on the plain" that "irrigate the whole skin with desire, listening, sight or smell" (Serres 2009, 52). Skin, once conceived of as a congelation, is now treated as something worn, a suit protecting muscles and sinews and flesh and fat from falling out onto the ground, a (dry and solid) bag holding the wetness in even as it is itself the body, defining it through its contours, the surface it provides (Connor 2003, 12). Skin bends and breathes, shielding a body from melting into a river even as it forms orifices that are openings to wind, weather, water, and noise. Skin folds around and into auricle, into tongue and throat and stomach, into anus and organ tissue, a body's internal organs no longer separable from their surroundings, a body becoming without organs (Deleuze and Guattari 1987). Skin, thus, provides a means of thinking the body anew, for considering how experience mobilizes a sense of a body that also has to be turned inside out, read as glitch. Listening, the ear is continuous with sound and skin, in and of a vibrating, pulsing atmosphere that is sensed across a body attuned, newly, to an airspace brought into audibility by the roar and whine of an airplane's engine.

Sensory experience withdraws into the personal, individualizing and distinguishing one person from another. A lawsuit based on experience becomes meaningful in the accumulation of individual experiences, not in experience rendered common. And while personal accounts of the experience of the noise of aircraft once yielded success in the courtroom, those accounts, transcribed as they were told to a judge in closed door hearings in Los Angeles in 1975, have been expunged from the official archive, not deemed of sufficient significance to warrant saving in the state law library beyond the years legally allotted. Figured thus, the sensory tends to resist or even disallow "entanglement" or "assemblage." Being sensitive to another's pain—actually feeling it in one's body—is a problem for characters of science-fiction novels (Butler 2000). The partitioning of sense across bodies is reiterated by a withholding, or an assertion of the inaccessibility of experience specifically because it is not possible to feel that which another feels.[18] Sense and language are conceived of as standing across a chasm, dividing, yet again, body and mind, practice and representation. This has long limited academic work on the senses. But we understand many aspects of an other that we do not experience ourselves; one can be witness to a murder or hear the story of its happening and know it to be true, observe lives and listen to stories that relay ways of being and knowing that are far from what is experienced in an immediate sense. Why mistrust perception, doubting how a sensory encounter made a person feel, even if we do not feel exactly the same? Events are staged to overcome such divides, to listen together, sing together, vibrate together. Disasters, another kind of event, can also figure a common sociability through experience. And people continue to anchor "the real" in their bodies; in sharing their experience of aircraft noise, they render the perception of noise personal and unquestionable. As long as their bodies are reliable, or meaningful, it is hoped they might be effective as an appeal to another's sense, whether of empathy or justice, even if not physical sensation itself.

A Sense of Rights

The hearings were an opportunity for people who had been living with the experience of airport noise to appeal to elected officials. Not quite "ethical loneliness," their testimony nevertheless conveys their feelings of "not being heard" (Stauffer 2018, 9). Yet they maintain faith in the liberal project— in elected officials as representing them, in the value of regulation, and, ultimately, in their rights as individuals. Complaints become appeals to such rights, the language of "tranquility" from the U.S. Constitution encompassing both sensation and sociability, as those experiencing airport noise claim a right to quiet, to sleep, and to overall health. As Arthur Berke, moderator of the Citizens of Inglewood, California, stated, "Our rights of peaceful tranquility have been violated. The citizens feel that in the preamble of the Constitution of the United States peaceful tranquility is mentioned as one of the predominant factors in developing the Constitution of the United States. Every day, every night, our constitutional rights are being violated" (U.S. House 1963, 199). Such rights are drawn from their disruption or loss, experience that resutures them to a biological body also understood as a body under capital, a body in need of recuperation to be a better worker or student, or a body with rights afforded by property. While this might be a "constitutional right" of religious practice for people "unable to hear services properly," it is more often "health and welfare," a legal category rendered personal (U.S. House 1963, 40, 80). Hence, subjectivity that comes under pressure with the sensation of aircraft noise is already defined in and through law, providing a buoy that keeps it afloat as a condition of experience.

Having told their stories many times before, seemingly to no avail, they hold the congressmen on the panel responsible, telling them directly that "it is your duty to protect our health and welfare, and to insure safety to our lives and property" (U.S. House 1963, 80), representation rendered benevolent paternalism. Fred Jones, an Inglewood city councilman, spoke from a sense of personal responsibility deflected onto the role of government writ large; lacking jurisdiction over airport noise, he appealed to his colleagues on the federal level, drawing out a seven-point argument about their job of protecting rights and providing services (1963, 209). Folding rights into experience, he concluded with a claim to the "constitutional right of domestic tranquility" (209). The language of "domestic tranquility" from the U.S. Constitution is more generally interpreted as referring to civil war, or simply riots and rebellion. In interpreting it as bearing on the experience of airplane noise, Jones shifts the meaning of "domestic" to the home, amplifying the relationship between family, state, and market along with the significance of private property for liberalism. That "tranquility" might be conceived of as "quiet" puts the sensory at the center of governance, occluding the political economic even as the threat to tranquility by the roar of aircraft engines renders the aerial an element of property. At the time of the hearings, others elsewhere were struggling with the acuteness of the body under liberalism. They also aimed to be heard. On the same day that the hearings on aircraft noise were taking place in Inglewood, senators in Washington approved the Civil Rights Act, signed three weeks later by President Eisenhower. The Student Nonviolent Coordinating Committee (SNCC) had been founded a few days before, following two months of lunch counter sit-ins across the country, prompted by the first in Greensboro, a quiet and determined protest to claim the right to be in a place without discrimination based on skin color.

In Queens the year before, a resident of Cedarhurst, New York, described the jurisdictional differences as a struggle over "human rights versus money" (U.S. House 1963, 29). He appealed to Congress to "give back to the people the rights they have," the rights, that is, "of owning land so far down, so many feet down and so many feet high" (29). This is echoed by Fred Jones, who stated, "One reason for difficulty in abating the jet noise nuisance is because somehow or other landowners have been deprived of their above-ground air rights. Property owners will have, for the most part, all water and mineral rights beneath their land, and surface rights prohibiting trespassing, but apparently they own little or nothing of the air space above their land" (U.S. House 1963, 209). Of course, by this time, ancient rule no longer held, already overturned by the Air Commerce Act of 1926 and reinscribed by the Supreme Court case *U.S. v. Causby*. But more crucial were the ways in which noise from the sky came to organize rights claims that, though terrestrial, relied on particular atmospheric qualities: claims to property, to health and welfare, to the home as a refuge, to classroom learning time, to quiet itself. As the urban became aerial, a city airport was echoed in another city figured as airplane (Kasarda and Lindsay 2011). On the very day that Angelenos were appealing to elected officials in Inglewood, Brasília was named the capital of Brazil. "A future that happened in the past," Lispector wrote of the modernist city that it is "located nowhere. Its atmosphere . . . indignation" (2018, 586, 587). Brasília as "in the air" (2018, 586)—a city more idea than actuality, "the air . . . lacking the indispensable support for people to live"—became a condensate of nascent aerial attunements around the world.

ON BEING HEARD

On April 21, 1960, in Inglewood, California, the public crowds the room. Statements that resonate with experience are met with applause, noted in the transcript. Unrealized claims yield indignant outbursts from the audience. Feelings run high, "I feel" prefacing remarks. A congressman asks for order; addressing the crowd, he expresses sympathy with "your feelings, your emotions, and your deep concern" (U.S. House 1963, 253). He is understanding, coming across as sympathetic and on the side of those who live around the airport, those who have been experiencing airport noise. Morgan Moulder, Democrat from Missouri, tells the people gathered that he is there to listen, reminding them that they are all there to listen, and thanking those who have been quiet for listening. "Let's have order in the hearing room, and may I caution those who are here you have been so cooperative with us in the conduct of the hearings and listening to the witnesses. Your attention is appreciated and your behavior is sincerely appreciated. I hope there will be no demonstrations or actions which will interfere with the conduct of the hearings or the testimony and the statement made by the witness" (1963, 248). The outburst, or protest, had been directed toward Fox, of Los Angeles Department of Airports. Moulder continues: "A moment ago when I was making an announcement not to demonstrate in the hearing room, I can understand the intense, sincere desire and spirit of the people in their interest in this problem. I didn't intend it in any way of criticism for anyone who was cheering your remarks" (1963, 200). He emphasizes his sympathy for their experience—"we are here, to hear the people as representatives in Congress" (203). The audience quiets down, and the congressman continues: "Thank you very much. You may proceed, Mr. Fox" (248).

The hearings become a listening space where people talk and feel that they are heard, where comportment matters, but frustration built up over years of hearing, experiencing, fighting, and struggling prompts outbursts. Those waiting to testify applaud in agreement with their neighbors and shout out with anger when an airport manager or pilot or FAA official talk. These are not transcribed, but the congressman's appeals for people to limit "protest" are. Noise as relational is iterated by the statements of those with seemingly oppositional interests: lived experience versus the airport as an economic engine, property values versus pilots' desires for which runway to depart from, children's learning time versus airspace jurisdiction. Antagonism and conflict are ways of coming together, and here sociabilities produced around noise also draw together the interests of those on the ground in opposition to those in the air.

Listening is also about authority, about granting authority to the one who is talking, whether a teacher, an FAA official, or a civic leader describing her response to airplane noise. The acoustic space of the hearings is a space of collective listening, where the person speaking is granted authority, at least for the time they speak, and where the silence of others is important to maintain a relationship of authority. Louis C. Moser, representing the North Queens Home Owners Civic Association of Jackson Heights, says, "I have been listening very attentively to the discussion that is going on" (U.S. House 1963, 43). The subject is airplane noise, but the subject itself is absent. Earlier that year in New York, a resident had said, "There is only one thing involved in this discussion today, and that is noise" (44). Yet most people do not talk about noise as such; instead, they talk about its effects and its causes, which are not only aircraft engine design but also the airport as an economic engine. Moser objects to the latter, insisting on the importance of eliminating noise at the source.

A congressman listens. He engages residents and leaders of civic groups, drawing on their statements to challenge pilots. Captain Hal Gregory, representing the Los Angeles office of the Air Line Pilots Association, goes on at length about the mirage, or optical illusion, that happens when an airplane comes into view, a phenomenon "well known to most experienced pilots."

> I have many times watched an airplane approaching. I would be at possibly 29,000 feet; he would be at 28,000 feet; and all members of my crew would practically take an oath on the Bible that that airplane was higher than we were, and at the last minute the airplane appears to dive and go under us, and all the time he has been exactly at his altitude. Now, these optical illusions are well known in all branches of human endeavor and I submit that that might be the reason that this lady thinks that that airplane might be making a right turn and then a left turn. (U.S. House 1963, 264)

Steven Derounian, Republican from New York, replies dryly, "This lady said she saw the plane go over her house, and I'm sure that wasn't an optical illusion" (U.S. House 1963, 264). "This lady" was Yvette Kovary. A licensed pilot sponsored for transcontinental races, she had served in SPARS, a women's unit of the Coast Guard, during World War II. Kovary was the twelfth speaker of the afternoon. She draws on her expertise as a pilot to give authority to her statements and to her experience: "I hold commercial multi-engine flight instructor's ratings," she begins, before introducing herself as "chairman of the citizens' committee in Playa del Rey" (243).

Telling her story for a local news feature on Veterans Day in 2015, Kovary sparkles as she describes flying for the first time, invited by a navy pilot while she was working as a coder in the Coast Guard. Her eyes open wide in delight and she smiles, remembering how she noticed the dust jumping off the floor and water dripping onto the roof, realizing they had rolled. The plane had drawn her to flight, her desire to be aloft palpable in her determination— joining the Coast Guard at age twenty and availing herself of every opportunity open to women. Remaining land borne, she served as a member of SPARS, a women's reserve unit that worked on coding in Washington state, and was one of sixteen women sent to Atlantic City for "high frequency direction finding for air-sea rescue"; using radio to chart locations for navigation, she drew the aerial of radio waves into a matrix of cartographic calculation.[19] As a 1963 newspaper article on Kovary reported, her job was to "keep track of all U.S. Navy and Pan-American commercial flights from the West Coast to Honolulu. She had to get and keep a 'fix' on planes, by radio communication up and down the coast and, in the air-sea rescue cases, plot courses and radio rescue instructions" (Dix 1963, 7). Sponsored to fly in the

1950 All Women's Transcontinental Air Race, she turned down a job as a policewoman when they would not let her defer. Her love of flight, of being airborne, is coupled with an obvious pleasure in her expertise.

Kovary put her acuity to work on the problem of airport noise, attending meetings of the Los Angeles Sound Abatement Coordinating Committee and writing to the city attorney when she was excluded from their meetings. (The committee included representatives of airlines, jet manufacturers, the FAA, the Department of Airports, and the pilot's union.)[20] She wrote to the president of the board of airport commissioners and the president of the United States; Edmund G. Brown, governor of California; and congressional representatives who might pass on her message to the FAA. The FAA responded to her appeals, explaining that airport zoning was not their responsibility. She was concerned especially with the possibility of the airport rezoning their neighborhood and buying out their homes, which lay between the runways and the Pacific Ocean, and advocated for a new super airport in Ontario. They loved their homes on the dunes, with an ocean breeze if not a view. Berke, who also testified that day in Inglewood, wrote to thank her for her testimony. Dated April 26, 1960, he typed his letter on his office stationery—Arthur Berke, DDS, Dentistry for Children, in Torrance, California—congratulating her in handwritten scrawl: "The congressmen said your testimony was very impressive."[21]

She had brought images with her, their presence noted in the transcript. She points to an image, to what it shows. They look. She describes what they see, while they refer to the object she is holding. These are different images than the ones used in her lawsuit, which she shows me when I visit her, also indicating—her finger pointing to her home, the dunes, the streets, her neighbors' homes (see chapter 6). At the hearings, the pictures portray what is and what will be. Taken from the air, they provide a bird's-eye view of the airport and runways abutting neighborhoods and towns, of the beach just across a street from their homes. Sound as sensed is implied, not portrayed. The runway suggests the presence of the airplane, its movement as it increases speed for takeoff, its flight as it rises in the air or comes in for landing, its passage over homes and their inhabitants.

> MRS. KOVARY: This is a picture [indicating] that I will pass to you later of Los Angeles International Airport. The two main runways at present, the city of El Segundo, Imperial Highway which divided the city of Los Angeles from El Segundo, and the beach at Playa del Rey, the town of Playa del Rey, which extends out to here [indicating],

West Westchester, and Westchester, which you can see is a highly concentrated area; and this is the new north runway about which Mr. De Joseph spoke. There is to be a further runway there [indicating], according to the airport plans. . . .

MR. MOULDER: May we see that picture? . . .

MRS. KOVARY: And I have here some pictures taken in a helicopter that show the area of Playa del Rey looking southward toward El Segundo, and showing the beach. [Indicating] (U.S. House 1963, 246–47).

She describes the infrastructure along the coast: the Hyperion Water Reclamation Plant, which filters sewage from across the region before piping it into the ocean; the Scattergood Steam Plant; the Standard Oil refinery; and the Edison power plant (U.S. House 1963, 246). Her knowledge of flight extends to the wind. With a windmill on her front lawn and "a very good wind sock in the Hyperion smokestack which always has smoke coming out, . . . I can see the drift perfectly." Winds, she knew, might affect the way an airplane flies, changing departure and landing patterns, or, as an FAA official told her, making a plane drift. She is skeptical of their explanation of why planes fly directly over her house. "Prevailing wind conditions are from the west . . . , the wind comes from the ocean." If planes drifted because of wind, they would go south; instead, she describes how she would watch them take off and "turn slightly toward their right . . . and come over the populated area" (1963, 247), suggesting, though not stating, that pilots were intentionally steering their planes to guide them over homes, and that human agency was behind their movement, not the vagary of the wind. And that wind, an atmospheric condition, might also be knowable—perceptible in itself or in its trace.

She appealed to her neighbors, asked them to listen—not only to the planes but to her and to one another. "We went door to door," she tells me nearly sixty years later, showing me the letters she circulated, now yellowed with age. As chair of the Citizens Committee of Playa del Rey, she mobilized others in the area, appealing to them to write their councilman and protest the potential rezoning, to attend an upcoming planning committee meeting. "DON'T GIVE UP THE FIGHT!!!! As long as there is a chance of defeating this issue, we should take it. The alternative is the noise, dirt, and fumes of airport maintenance, with attendant, inevitable lessening of the value of our homes. THERE IS NO MIDDLE GROUND."[22] Aerial attunements are grounded in the solidity of civic life, of homes whose value is ultimately economic. Yet they are also an opening; drawing people together to listen to one another, they expand horizons of perceptibility and make that which is seemingly solid perhaps somewhat less so.

INSCRIBING AIRPORT NOISE

The hearings are held at Morningside High School, and some note that the absence of aircraft sound seems unusual for the area. After a plane flies overhead, a congressman asks Kenneth Hahn, then on the stand, if that was the normal sound of a plane landing. No, he does not think so. After describing how a recent event at nearby Lennox Park had been interrupted numerous times, Hahn muses, "It might be because of the curtains here, or this auditorium that we are not getting the full effect, but the sound today has not been, to my judgment, what normal, everyday traffic will be here. . . . I don't know why, but it doesn't seem as loud today" (U.S. House 1963, 219). The school superintendent explains that it might be because the room they are in is in a sound-insulated concrete building, much different from the wood and stucco buildings of the rest of the school and of the houses in the surrounding residential community (1963, 231).

The voice of the Inglewood school district superintendent can be heard on a recording housed in the Kenneth Hahn Collection at the Huntington Library; untitled, it has no accompanying information other than what is stated in the recording itself (*Airport Noise* 1967).[23] It is the only audio material addressing airport noise in the collection, offering a sonic record of what is otherwise drawn from written documents. An audio recording provides another form of evidence, its immediacy recruiting listeners across broader spatiotemporal horizons. It is also a way of writing sound that is generally perceived as more reliable than memories of embodied experience. Yet this reliability assumes a logic of transparency and fidelity, belying the particularity of how microphones and tape listen, amplifying airborne sound in the range of human hearing and creating an artifact of sound. Transferred from quarter-inch tape onto compact disc, a medium that will soon begin to erode on its own, the sound—once necessarily experienced in time—moved into an archive and then onto a computer. And while its making is inscribed in the recording itself, its social life is not. Seemingly made for PR purposes, where the recordings were stored previously and how they circulated is now unknown. Perhaps, like citizens' letters, they were sent to Kenneth Hahn as an appeal, making him a listener of aircraft sounds along with his constituents.

The recording starts with a whir and a thud, static shifting into a sustained hum of tape as a male voice speaks in a nasal tone with a measured pace. Introducing the topic of airport noise, he makes it evident that this is also an argument, describing noise as a "debit" rather than a "credit" of a major metropolitan airport. The debit, specifically, is "the loss of teacher instruction and student learning time." He pronounces Los Angeles as "An-ye-les" and provides figures about the frequency of flight: fifteen hundred takeoffs and landings a day, with one aircraft flying over Inglewood schools every "one and one half minutes." Addressing the listener of the recording, appealing to that person (a spatial distance now stretched into a temporal lag), he explains that the recordings were made "to help you realize the density and duration of the aircraft noise factor." While the linguistic content of the recordings draws out the significance of communication and its disruption by aircraft noise, the recordings themselves shift from the content of speech to the experience of listening: they are made to help those listening to them understand through their own experience what those who live or go to school under the flight path experience every day.

In December 1967 he visited three classrooms, using, we are told by a third male narrator at the end of the recording, a Concertone 727 to record the sound, and effect, of airplanes flying over the school. The Concertone 727 was advertised at the time for its portability; weighing "only 16 lbs.," it could be plugged in or powered with batteries. With a microphone for recording, it could also be used to play back music, a more apt use for experiencing how it "Really Swings 'cause it's CORDLESS!" The double meaning of "swing" is conveyed in an advertisement by the drawn figures, two men, two women, dancing in their swimsuits as one man holds the recorder in his hand, dangling along his leg rather than held on a shoulder, as people would later do, a certain awkwardness to a sixteen-pound audio player.[24] The microphone that might otherwise have been directed toward the speakers of a hi-fi system was turned toward the acoustic space of a classroom. The tapes, along with the Concertone 727, allow the sounds to travel from the place and time of recording, such that others elsewhere might hear how the sounds of planes flying overhead imbue the space—and how the teacher pauses as the airplane's whine becomes so loud she would not be able to be heard, though perhaps using that pause for another activity that did not require audible communication.

In drawing others into the experience of aircraft noise, the recordings amplify that which is otherwise limited to the experience of those living near the airport to a public concern and, crucially, a public experience. It recruits a dispersed and unknown public to be listeners—to listen and, based on that, to do something, though what that might be remains unstated. And while what is heard is technically sound sensed by microphone and tape, the recording technology does its job as transducer to bring the experience of one set of listeners to another, and for the narrator to make an appeal toward, at minimum, empathy, if not policy. The description of the equipment used at the end of the recording affirms its potential for fidelity at a moment when that was a central achievement of audio technology. Here, as elsewhere, a logic of fidelity is crucial for orienting toward environmental sound, toward sound from the sky that, in and of air, is potentially the full range of sound outdoors (see chapter 5).

The recording as an inscription that lasts allows the sounds to be heard now, in the present. Yet it remains an archive that has lost its signification, buried, as it is, and without any explanation of what it was made for, how it circulated, or for whom it was played. As I listen in the reading room of a library, on the other side of the county fifty years after the sound of planes and its recording, I am brought into a world of voices of another era, of aircraft noise that, while loud and whining and evidently disruptive, is also flattened by the acoustic frequency of the recording. When I play the recording for others, it wavers between the immediacy of experience and its pedagogical framing, its narrators helping the listener learn how to listen even as the high-frequency whine registers as annoying. "We" listening now become another public, become listeners to something that, though palpable, remains indeterminate.

In the elementary school, we listen in on a math lesson; the teacher says, "yup, just as we have been doing it, parentheses and the whole works. We will be breaking it up into what and what and what, class?" "Hundreds and tens and ones," children's voices say in unison. The hum of the tape becomes the whine of an airplane engine. The teacher pauses her lesson but engages the class; something else is happening, someone is writing on the board, "okay . . . so far is it right?" she finishes, as the noise of the plane recedes. In Monroe Junior High School, an English teacher asks, "What about sentence meaning? What about it? Did it change or stay the same? [inaudible response] Stay the same. Okay." We hear the sound of paper shuffling, the teacher saying, quietly, "Would you pass these on?" as an engine noise comes into audibility, its low hum becoming a high-pitched whine. These, as acoustics engineering firm Veneklasen and Associates explained, are the "two types of noise" produced by the jet engines of commercial airlines, the first "'jet noise' . . . produced by the high velocity exhaust gases which are emitted by all present day jet engines." It is "characterized by a broad band spectral content," meaning "it contains sound energy over a wide range of frequency from the very low pitch rumble to a high pitch hiss." The second type is the "high frequency 'whine' or 'screech' radiated either from the engine intake opening or in the fan jet engine from the bypass air exhaust ducts." As Veneklasen and Associates conclude in their 1968 report *Noise Exposure and Control in the City of Inglewood, California*, "Both of the types of noises described have been particularly irritating and a great deal of research and effort have been expended in the effort to reduce them" (1968, 163). The students have been doing something, perhaps writing on papers or on the chalkboard. "All right . . . all right," she repeats as the aircraft sound passes away.

The setting of an English test at Morningside High School starts with the sound of a plane, papers shuffling, and the teacher saying, "Would you pass this behind you? In the first question, in which story does humor depend upon a serious inner struggle in a certain character?" Her voice increases in volume as the plane's engine becomes louder; she pauses, then continues the question, "name the story, the character, and the struggle." The content of speech cannot be accidental, the "breaking up" of numbers, "meaning," already unstable, interrupted, the "struggle" of a character whose story might be taking a high school English test with planes flying overhead. The school superintendent ends the first half of the recording, asking the listener what sounds like a rhetorical question but is an open-ended appeal: "How would you like to concentrate on taking a test with that noise factor involved?" Without suggesting actions, he draws the listener into relation with the students, for whom the interruption of their work, their productivity, rather than the experience of noise in and of itself, is of utmost concern.

Listening is something that happens. As event, it is marked as a particular kind of presence, of attention. Listening as an element of communication is also what is disturbed in homes, when a person speaking has to raise their voice for the other person to hear, or pause in midsentence until the jet passes overhead. The everyday sociability of attuning to another person's voice when they speak is troubled by a sound that draws the atmospheric into the social, that, even as something undesirable, reveals the otherwise taken-for-grantedness of everyday conversation, of being able to hear one another. Noise is understood primarily as interruption, clouding the signal of the teacher's voice or of thought, as it might the fidelity of a recording. We are meant to hear that interruption, to listen to gaps—gaps filled by the sound of an airplane engine, in which any number of things might be happening that may or may not require an attention to audible speech.

The audio shifts to a different quality of recording and of voice, the second part yielding an immediacy that draws the listener into the experience of the planes, the whine louder, impinging on the ear. "I have been trying to get a fix on the noise. I'm standing in an area just east of Los Angeles International Airport on Lennox Avenue and Newport Street between two runways." Don McGrath of HUD continues, "This is a pretty good example of what I'm trying to get at; I have a plane flying right overhead," the high frequency screech of the engine overcoming the volume of his voice. Becoming audible once more, he says, "can't understand why anyone would object to having that kind of an airplane fly right over your head about every three minutes. After all, that isn't all that noisy, is it." The click of an edit, a cut, and a tape, "one more chance . . . DC-8 coming in," which whirs and whines as it comes in over houses to land; another plane flies overhead, and McGrath continues, "I'm talking in a conversational level, this is one minute after the last one . . . and again I don't understand why these people object to this noise [drowned out] I don't see there is any getting used to that in the middle of the night. These people don't seem to react very much, except to clap their hands over their ears, and some of the smaller children fall to the ground." The shift from irony to empathy as he witnesses peoples' non-response is presented without framing.

As if the noise overwhelms his ability to make sense of what he is experiencing, confusion abounds. Which "I don't" introduces his true intention? Why cast the claims and complaints of residents in ironic terms on a recording intended to convey the seriousness of the issue, the veracity of what people have been saying about aircraft noise? The sound of the plane is the subject of the recording, and rather than a narrative that conveys a clear and legible message, the tape is meant to perform the experience for its listener. Here we hear the plane, experience the whine in the ear though not in the body, as one would if standing there then. But then McGrath might pause midsentence, as the teachers do, to ensure his words are heard by a present listener. The Department of Housing and Urban Development (HUD) was responsible for land use around airports, but many things are happening here. More legible than the content of speech is McGrath's struggle to be heard as he continues talking while the plane flies overhead, its sound vibrating the microphone as its roar is inscribed as an electrical signal on the tape in the Grundig EM3 pocket-size model ("pocket" perhaps relative, as it was still reel to reel, with glass vacuum tubes), in September 1967.

FIGURE 1.1 Electronic voltmeter at Western Electro-Acoustic Laboratory.
Photo by author.

The following year, Veneklasen and Associates, an acoustical engineering firm based in Santa Monica, conducted an environmental noise survey of Inglewood. They take credit for conducting the first such survey (though some challenge this claim), a project of attuning toward the atmospheric via microphones and sound pressure meters—of shifting listening onto technology to quantify experience. Ambient noise-level measurements taken at periods throughout the day and night were followed by aircraft flyover noise-level measurements. Engineers sat inside a van with "a sound level meter, octave filter set and tape recorder," a microphone "mounted on an aluminum tube on top" of the vehicle, "approximately 8 ft." above the ground (Veneklasen and Associates 1968, 208). The microphone sensed fluctuations in air pressure, transducing sound into measurement of its volume and frequency, inscribed as an electrical signal on a length of tape. Also an aerial attunement, microphones as sensors draw together sound from the sky with sound on the ground, echoing and, as some may have hoped, amplifying the experience of Inglewood residents, even as the somatic shifts into another mode of inscription that is trusted for its reliability and objectivity. The portable "sound analyzers" developed for this survey sit on shelves at the Western Electro-Acoustic Laboratory in Santa Clarita, Veneklasen's acoustic testing lab, their durability outlasting their technological use (figure 1.1). The tapes themselves no longer exist. Inscribed as experience, whether that of people living near the airport or the microphones of a sound analyzer, noise falls away.

2

Noise annoys. This is a commonplace, even banal. Too broad to have specific, specifiable meaning, *annoying* is the de facto adjective that seemingly everyone uses. So intertwined are the two, that noise seems to have become definitive of annoyance. For instance, noise is the subject matter of two of the first three chapters of the book *Annoying: The Science of What Bugs Us* (Palca and Lichtman 2011), while a gag gift called the annoy-a-tron uses noise to achieve its intended effect. Hidden from sight, it is said to really annoy people with "periodic beeps and sounds [that] make your friends crazy hunting for that ANNOYING NOISE."[1] A mode of sensory attunement or attention, an everyday way of attending to sound, annoyance, like noise and heat, marks a sensory threshold in which perception shifts to signification— signification that composes sociabilities through its everyday unremarkable iterations: we might say to someone standing nearby, "It's hot," or "That sound is annoying." Entirely ordinary, it trips off the tongue, a register of something felt, a pressure to conform or at minimum respond. Less an index of social relationships, annoyance is something more like an index of listening—it conveys, simply, that someone has sensed something. In its repetition, annoyance crystallizes as a thing in itself even as it resists reification, its instability revealing it as an "invention . . . for viewing self and relations with others" (Lutz 1988, 9). Annoyance is a public feeling, a common and shared mode of attention, a means of drawing people together or pushing them apart (Brennan 2004; Cvetkovich 2012; K. Stewart 2007). It percolates and bubbles as ordinary affect, or as a driving dimension of noise metrics that aspire for a generalized and dispersed "public ear."

Annoyance is at once visceral and abstract; a concrete abstraction, it slides between the particularity of any given experience and generalized concept. As language that moves into inscription, "What starts as description fails as it turns into life, as it becomes not a description of something else, but a vital thing-in-the-world in its own right" (Swensen 2011, ix). The Buzzcocks' 1978 song "Noise Annoys" plays on this, the density and volume of a "dirty" electric guitar, a persistent bass line with driving drums and screaming, amplified vocals commented on by lyrics that repeat "noise annoys . . . noise annoys . . . noise annoys."[2] The word *annoyance* sounds like noise. Spoken, read, and heard, it stretches *noise* into an indefinite article that tips into sound, the nasal inflection embedded in *noise* elongated in the *noy* of annoyance, the sibilant weak beat of its final syllable delayed, deflected, deemphasized. Annoyance—annoys—a noise.

Noise annoys. I find myself trying to get to the bottom of this. But instead I've ended up in something more like a swarm or a cloud, "collections of species transforming together in both ordinary and surprising ways" (Lowe 2010, 626)—though "species" in this case is something more like sounds, sites, moods, and various modes and figures of authority and authorization that bring noise and annoyance together, making them seem inseparable. Annoyance, like noise, is atmospheric. It is noise's atmospheric partner, the two entwined in a dance of indeterminacy, (un)grounding each other as they waltz across sensory, affective, discursive, and techno-rational registers of science, engineering, and law. Entangled with noise, annoyance spins a web, a worlding whose references dot transcripts of public hearings and burgeon into metrics, graphs, charts, surveys, and maps. Its circulation yields a swarm of assumption, iteration, reiteration. Occasionally it stops—pausing its circulation, annoyance is questioned, or bracketed from noise metrics. But then it moves on, proliferating, becoming at times so full, so large, so intense, that it tips over, spilling into something else entirely.

Annoyance is by definition the "state of feeling caused by that which annoys" or "disturbance caused by that which one dislikes" (*Oxford English*

Dictionary, s.v. "annoyance"). A "state of feeling" is a curious well, a deep hole that, peered into, disappears into a void.[3] Agreeably neutral, it remains unencumbered by debates over the nature of the senses, human/nonhuman relationships, and the structure of mind. At the same time, it bends toward *emotion*, a loose category of feeling without the solidity of either affect or sensation (B. Anderson 2016; Ngai 2007). Lacking foundation in and of itself, nuisance law anchors a "state of feeling" in property ownership. I begin by tracing annoyance as it adheres to noise through nuisance law, falling away as regulatory regimes shift from hearing to sound, from ground to sky, and from the specific to the general—toward, that is, the atmospheric. Yet annoyance, relegated to the vagaries of human experience, remains a concern for acoustical engineers engaged with the problem of environmental noise. They use the tools they have and develop devices for measurement, do studies, make charts, and develop, trouble, and refine metrics. As engineers listen to how others listen, or listen through others' ears, there is a yearning, a straining to incorporate the expansiveness of experience despite the limits of their tools. In making and remaking metrics, modes of inscription circulate and resonate, their sensory-affective quality amplified. A widening gap between perception and inscription affords new modes of engagement. The airport's noise complaint system includes a flight tracker map; as planes depart and land, dots marking the location of noise measurement microphones change from green to yellow to red. Intended to be engaged by the public, heat maps of noise levels around the airport exemplify the viscerality of abstraction even as they refigure the sensory, thermoception destabilizing a divide between sensation and that which is sensed.

NOISE - NUISANCE - ANNOYANCE

Noise. Nuisance. Annoyance. The three words are said to share etymological roots and a common history in English common law. Yet such suturing is also unstable. While some trace the root of *noise* to *nuisance*, an undesirable object outside a subject, others locate it in *nausea*, an internal, physical response to the abject, the grotesque, the unwanted and expungeable, or perhaps to the movement of a boat at sea (Novak 2015; Serres 1997; Swensen 2011). Hence *annoyance*, *noise*, and *nuisance* "resonate rather than cohere or correspond with each other" (Deleuze and Guattari 1996, 23). Their relationship shifts depending on where, or when, one begins. While presently noise is categorized as a nuisance in municipal ordinances, the notion of nuisance did not always extend to noise. Rather, "Many seventeenth- and eighteenth-century documents use the words 'annoyance,' 'nuisance' (or, more frequently 'nusance') and 'noisome' synonymously," with "noysome" referring to "annoying smells" (Cockayne 2008, 18). Hillel Schwartz identifies the moment when noise in and of itself became grounds for legal claims, and when sensory experience, rather than health, was taken seriously by courts. This, he maintains, is Horace Wood's 1875 *A Practical Treatise on the Law of Nuisances*, which states, "It is now well settled that noise alone, unaccompanied with smoke, noxious vapors or noisome smells, may create a nuisance and be the subject of an action at law in equity or an injunction" on the grounds that it is "offensive to the senses'" (quoted in Schwartz 2011, 659). Nonetheless, Schwartz cautions, insofar as "Noise . . . was so much a function of an observer's referents and attention . . . it seemed paradigmatic of the principle of indeterminacy." And, because of its indeterminate nature, "All along, courts . . . had problems with noise" (2011, 655).

As an element of nuisance law, noise was categorized as a private or more frequently a public nuisance, establishing property as belonging to an individual rather than a collective. Nuisance as pertaining to property is embedded in its definition, its second sense being "a. *Law.* Something harmful or offensive to the public or to a member of it, for which there is a legal remedy; *spec.* unlawful interference with an individual in the enjoyment of his or her rights, esp. those relating to use and possession of land; an offence against private property." It is only in its "weakened use" that nuisance is "a source of annoyance or irritation" (*Oxford English Dictionary*, s.v. "nuisance"). Property as necessarily that of an individual became a means of undermining legal struggles against airport noise. A 1969 class-action lawsuit brought by Inglewood residents over noise from Los Angeles International Airport was dismissed three years later on the grounds that the Inglewood Residents Protective Association "had no property of its own and therefore could not represent the class of residents." As the California Supreme Court ruled in 1975, reversing a successful appeal of the earlier decision, "Damages for noise . . . must be considered on an individual basis" (Oliver 1975, 3).

U.S. law, organized through precedence, finds precedent in common law (Latour 2009). Instantiated broadly as tort law, or the area of civil claims, nuisance law is said to have been sustained first as zoning law (Schwartz 2011, 668) and later environmental law. Both zoning law and environmental law articulate an entanglement of property and policing scaled from an individual body to the human writ large. Yet changes in technology, urban governance, and social relations seek new solutions that draw selectively from existing forms. Thus, the regulation of noise through zoning law, while ostensibly a continuation of nuisance law, also allowed noise to be disarticulated from nuisance. In Clifford R. Bragdon's study of municipal noise law, he writes that Chicago's 1955 zoning ordinance was the first to introduce allowable decibel levels that "placed restrictions not on the type of industry . . . but rather on its performance in terms of noise emission," such that, "For the first time industry was being regulated according to specific acoustical criteria rather than by the more vague nuisance provisions" (1971, 2a). In other words, noise as nuisance shifted from hearing to sound, from the experience of a person who might be annoyed to the measurement of sound pressure at its source. This shift, while driven by a concern about nuisance, nonetheless casts annoyance—and perception—as indeterminate and unstable, and therefore not grounds for systematic standardization.

As noise pollution became a subject of environmental law on the state and federal level, cities rewrote their municipal codes to address this newly significant concern (see chapter 3). In Los Angeles, the Department of City Planning published a 1975 general plan that included a standalone document on the "noise element." It built on the city's 1973 noise ordinance with the intention of establishing "uniformity of policy and direction within local government concerning actions to eliminate or minimize noise pollution."[4] Noise pollution, while integrating noise measurement into its regulation, was also vague, wavering between a dispersed condition and a public health concern. By this time aircraft noise had been established as a concern. Yet, while nuisance law had historically provided grounds for urban noise abatement campaigns, aircraft noise, sounded in the federal territory of the public airspace, is exempt from nuisance claims. As something of a crisis in the context of struggles against aircraft noise, this gap afforded novel modes of engagement with the aerial as an elemental and legal domain (see chapter 1).

Los Angeles's 1975 "noise element" document focuses on modes of remediation on the ground through zoning and soundproofing, appealing to the FAA to "assign cruise altitudes high enough to minimize the impact of aircraft on land use."[5] Inglewood's noise ordinance was drafted in 1971 and presented during congressional hearings on noise pollution the following year (U.S. Senate 1972). Acknowledging the lack of municipal jurisdiction over the sky, it lists aircraft noise along with other more immediate "nuisances," such as drums, construction, amplified sound, hawkers and peddlers, animals and fowl, and radios and televisions. Though "It shall be unlawful for any person to operate or cause to be operated any type of aircraft over the

City which produces levels exceeding 90 dbA within the City," an exception was granted for "any aircraft operated in conformity with, or pursuant to, federal law, federal air regulations, and air traffic control instruction." Also exempt were aircraft with technical difficulties or operating under "the declaration of an emergency" (U.S. Senate 1972, 217; City of Inglewood 1969, 11; Bragdon 1973).[6] While the inclusion of aircraft noise in a municipal noise ordinance moves toward a formulation of noise as environmental—as in and of the air, generalized and dispersed—by making aircraft noise commensurate with noise as "nuisance," it draws the atmospheric into a domain of immediacy, with a known accountable perpetrator: the aircraft operator (or the train engineer who pulls the whistle).[7] The ability to point to a specific perpetrator shifts as noise enters environmental law, when noise pollution is figured as generalized and diffuse (chapter 3).

Noise, still "annoying," drifts away from tort law, nuisance, and property into other evidentiary domains, circulating across a range of areas from workplace to airspace. The first discussion of annoyance in the *Journal of the Acoustical Society of America* draws out its sensory-affective quality. A 1929 study of (unspecified) workers had confirmed the suspicion that annoyance was "a function of pitch as well as of intensity"—an area of inquiry that would be investigated for at least the next thirty years. The acoustical engineers who conducted the study describe it as consisting of "mental reactions . . . in the realm of feelings—mild emotional-like states almost invariably associated with sensory experiences." A "psychological basis of annoyance" was, they wrote, "an elementary affective process, a feeling-element which in our minds is coordinate with sensation and distinguishable from it, but which is nevertheless akin to sensation and derived from the same source." Emphasizing a physicality of sensation, with mind indistinguishable from body, "it carries with it an unpleasant feeling-tone, a tinge of restlessness and tension." And though there might be "personal variation" in response to noise, annoyance was general, a common condition "in the sense organs and thalamus in the mid-brain" (Laird and Coye 1929, 158). Distinct from "loudness," its systematization and objectification remained uncomfortably unresolved: "It has not been possible for us to discover as yet any method for measuring absolute annoyance; this is a pressing and important problem." Most annoying to engineers was that annoyance eluded computation and inscription, remaining amorphous and indeterminate. "The observers are of the opinion that there is a close relationship between loudness and annoyance, but whether this is a straight line or a curvelinear [sic] relationship can only be conjectured" (Laird and Coye 1929, 162).

Extending the engineer's mathematical logic, Jonathan Sterne suggests that annoyance is "an aesthetic category, and one of some refinement, as evidenced by the five-point scale recommended for use within ten decimal places" (2012, 158). While hearing tests (in his case of MP3s) craft a scale of expertise around a perceptual register of audition, if to be annoying is in the domain of aesthetics, "refinement" and taste are perhaps not the best bases—notions that rely on classificatory (and comparative) characteristics rather than qualities of perception. Sensory, affective, and bodily aspects of annoyance might be interestingly engaged in terms of an aesthetics of listening (Feld 1982; Pinney 2004; Shipley and Peterson 2012). Yet, when cast as a mode of classification, annoyance is flattened, transformed from a dynamic twitchy feeling to a scale that is normalized and against which other things—sound, the listener—must also be construed as norms, consigned, in the language of noise ordinances, to "any reasonable person of normal sensitiveness." Moreover, aesthetic philosophy's divide between an object and human perception that has been reamplified as a means of giving agency to the object does not support an understanding of sound as an immaterial object that is immanent in its perception; in other words, figuring annoyance as an aesthetic determination makes sound an object (Harman 2018; Shaviro 2014).

At the same time, annoyance's migration into aesthetics understood as a mode of distinction is in part what limits its grounds in law. In a 1950 article, "Torts: The Nature of Nuisance," R. Makowski writes that "a violation of aesthetic values alone . . . does not result in a nuisance" (1950, 242). Rather, a "nuisance to be actionable must materially impair the comfort and enjoyment of individuals of the use and value of the property. The standard used is substantial annoyance to persons of normal and average sensibilities" (242). A nuisance is thus a "material annoyance," or "an annoyance caused by the act of the defendant" (242, 243). In John Francis Timmins's 1976 thesis "Noise Pollution and the Law," he explains that, in the context of nuisance law as applied in the United States, annoyance is deemed too subjective (1976, 138). Moreover, glossing annoyance and nuisance, he writes, "There is no fixed standard as to what noise constitutes a nuisance" (164). Hence nuisance law finds grounding in "reasonableness," the composition of a general, though not necessarily average, listener, whose experience is nonetheless unique. As the Supreme Judicial Court of Massachusetts ruled in 1933, "Noise becomes actionable only when it passes the limits of reasonable adjustment to the needs of the listener. What those limits are cannot be fixed by any definite measure of quality or quantity. They depend on the circumstances of the particular case" (Timmins 1976, 139). In 1971 the Supreme Court of the United States ruled in *Coates v. Cincinnati* that *annoyance* was unconstitutionally vague. The case revolved around public assembly and freedom of speech, with police claiming they were annoyed by antiwar protesters from Antioch and striking GE workers. With annoyance figured as a general category, the ruling resulted in numerous municipal noise ordinances being overturned (Weiner 2013).[8]

MAKING NOISE METRICS

The visualization of annoyance solidifies and confirms its existence. Yet even in this crystallization, this hardening, something flickers and opens. Metrics meant to stabilize (or bracket) annoyance are often accompanied by discussion of its instability, its vagueness, its fuzziness (Botteldooren, Verkeyn, and Lercher 2003, 1487). Noise metrics are tendencies—temporal, future-oriented inscriptions in process that become objects in and of themselves, removed, in this way, from their aspiration as representation. At once descriptive and prescriptive, their standardization is deemed necessary for regulation insofar as they "prescribe levels or conditions that cannot legally be exceeded, when tested or measured by specified procedure" (U.S. Senate 1972, 345). Widening, rather than closing, a gap between perception and inscription, metrics proliferate into an array of points on which pressure might be put: differentials of place and time, of mode of transportation, of survey method or hearing test technologies, of the duration and frequency of an event, of acoustic frequency and pressure, of the very nature of sound and its perception, of the meaning and location of annoyance, and of the correlation of all these indeterminate issues. As metrics are made and refined, rejected and reproduced, annoyance percolates as intrinsic to noise and as an effect of its perception, as an axis of quantification and an overall framework for interpretation. Annoyance hangs on the side of graphs; pushes into sentences, explanations, and definitions; and lurks under floorboards or in disrupted radio and television signals. Fixed in a rather nebulous field of affect, sound level, and time, inscribed in measurement systems that are more or less opaque, objective, and predictive but perhaps further from experience, annoyance resonates across perception and inscription.

While inscription circulates in often indeterminate and atmospheric ways, its very lines and forms are zones of intensity that flicker and buzz as active objects of engagement for engineers and others concerned with noise and its control (Deleuze and Guattari 1996; Halpern 2015; Latour 2012). Acoustical engineers and physicists—including Leo Beranek, Karl Kryter, Thomas Schultz, Sandford Fidell, Vern Knudsen, and Paul Veneklasen—evince an intense engagement with inscription, a commitment to getting it right. As Karl Kryter maintained, "There is little point . . . in making any physical measures of sound if they, in turn, cannot be interpreted in terms of human reactions to them" (1959, 1423). It is clear from their tone, reverberating even from the page, that there is something at stake: an adequacy of inscription to complexity, to experience, or to what they call "context"—meaning the possible range of environmental (and personal) factors. The "question of criteria," Kryter asserted in his testimony during hearings titled *Noise: Its Effect on Man and Machine*, is "a most complex one" and requires taking "into account the whole system, the whole community's environment," with "many things . . . specified" (U.S. House 1960, 38; see also U.S. EPA Office of Noise Abatement and Control 1971b). These "many things" might include a person's feelings about the sound source itself, anything related to the situation in which a sound was heard, time of day and frequency, the character of the listener, and any other variables that might make someone feel more or less annoyed by noise. And while people might be asked directly about how "annoyed" they were, more often effects of noise—like not being able to sleep, or not being able to hear the TV—were taken as indicators of affect.

Others bemoan the difficulty of measuring annoyance in situ, aspiring for an ethnographic approach even while relying on the stability of the category and an ideal of a universal subject (U.S. EPA Office of Noise Abatement and Control 1971b). Les Blomberg, director of the Noise Pollution Clearinghouse (NPC), also has an idea for new, more accurate metrics.[9] Though his metric "hasn't been studied," he believes it is more fair, more comprehensive than ones currently in use. "My metric would be a reciprocity metric, a net noise metric." The decibel accounts for "just one small part" of noise; bracketing frequency and other qualities of sound, it is, moreover, unidirectional. His metric would include not only the road itself but how noise from the home affects the road. "It would be a better metric than sound pressure level alone; it would explain more of the variation in the data." Like Borges's map, the metric begins to become the world, an expansive and capacious representation that becomes, itself, an intensity.[10]

Deinscribing Annoyance

Perceived noise decibel (PNdB) was a metric that would newly draw perception into noise measurement. Developed in the late 1950s, it was oriented toward the nascent problem of airport noise, providing a measure for tolerable noise levels and a basis for operations. Like other metrics, it was intended as an improvement on the decibel, which, as a scale for the measurement of sound pressure intensity, had been established as a means of addressing "the 'law' governing [the] correspondence of stimulus and sensation" (Chion 2016, 21).[11] The decibel is limited to the frequency band in which most human hearing occurs (though does not encompass the full range of human hearing), thus excluding very high and low frequencies. Through A-, B-, and C-weighting, the decibel had already been refined to more adequately account for the vagaries of human hearing, with frequency incorporated as an aspect of sound measurement. A-weighting emphasizes the frequency of the whine of aircraft noise that had been found to be most annoying, while C-weighting shifts toward low frequencies. Overall, the effect was to limit "noise" to that which is perceived by the human ear via air. Scoffing at efforts to "find the 'law' governing [a] correspondence of stimulus and sensation," Chion, who maintains that he "holds strictly to what we hear," describes the decibel as having an "uncertain status" as "a unit of measure for intensity that is an article of faith when it comes to anti-noise regulation." Emphasizing, though not elaborating on, the weirdness of the metric, he explains that "the creation of such an oddity was" based in "the preoccupation with developing a unit of measure that would take into account the functioning of human sensation," understood to be afforded by the "logarithmic nature of the decibel scale" (Chion 2016, 21–23). Les Blomberg is also critical of the limited nature of the decibel, which is "just such a small subset" and does not capture the range of ways in which sound is meaningful. "All the decibel does is measure the amplitude of a vibration, a change in the air pressure. Vibrating particles in the air measure the change from atmospheric pressure. And that's all it does. You know, we've got language, we've got music. You don't get noise if you don't have language, music, and all the other things." In other words, "sound pressure level did not account for the nonacoustical factors involved."

PNdB continued to rely on the decibel while incorporating perception, widening sensation beyond the physiology of human hearing. With an understanding of perception drawn from psychoacoustics, it excluded annoyance as an aspect of noise, replacing it with a new category of "noisiness"

(Kryter 1959, 1415). Crafted by psychoacoustician Karl Kryter, "the PNdB scale is a measure of the effect of noise without regard to emotional feelings." Kryter described the development of the metric, explaining that "it measures how the ear and the brain as an auditory system respond to sound. We are trying to measure the way the human organism as a filter and a meter reacts to sound, independently of any meaning the sound may have to the listener" (U.S. House 1960, 37). Stripping emotion from listening, meaning from perception, the human is rendered machinic, a purportedly objective rather than subjective measuring device. Having published *The Effects of Noise on Man* in 1950, Kryter was hired by Leo Beranek's firm, Bolt, Beranek and Neuman (BBN), around 1956 to develop its psychoacoustic consulting work. Beranek, a founder and principal of BBN, was an acoustical engineer whose career spanned the twentieth century and included concert hall design as well as noise measurement and control; among other things, he developed fiberglass for the purpose of soundproofing air force cockpits, created the first anechoic chamber, and was involved in the development of DARPA, which became the internet as we know it (Beranek 2008). Kryter had been a fellow in Stanley Smith Stevens's Harvard Psycho-Acoustics Lab, which, in collaboration with Beranek's Electro-Acoustic Laboratory, conducted tests for the U.S. Army during World War II.[12] Stevens's psychophysics project was driven by the question of whether it is possible to measure human sensation as an effect of sensory input. Aiming to overcome philosophy's mind-body split, Stevens was concerned with how "experience, sensation, [and] sensory attributes" might be scaled as functions of "the acoustic amplitude of the stimulus" (Miller 1975, 439, 440; see also Newman 1955). The aim of PNdB was to render noise general and objective rather than individualized and "subjective." Insofar as noise is understood as adhering to the physicality of sound, PNdB draws together sound as sensed and that which is sensed through a metric that inscribes a logarithmic physicality of sound (dB) in its perception. Noisiness, Kryter's substitute for annoyance, is an index of the relationship between perception and sound pressure.

In 1958, employees of acoustics firm BBN were enlisted for Kryter's study of the relative noisiness of aircraft sounds, to determine how much noisier new Boeing 707s would be, planes that would afford longer passenger flights and ultimately usher in the jet age. Because of noise-related lawsuits brought by residents living near Newark airport, Pan Am's plans to launch commercial air travel from then-named Idlewild Airport were on hold. The New York Transit Authority called on BBN to help address noise issues so that the airline might begin operations in 1958. In preparation for listening tests, Leo Beranek and his colleagues made magnetic tape recordings of propeller planes departing at Newark and 707 takeoffs in Seattle, the latter "fully-loaded" with lead bars to replicate the weight of a commercial airplane carrying people and luggage. Photos were used to calculate how high the plane was flying. The tapes were brought back to BBN's offices, where a room was prepared to have "negligible reverberation," loudspeakers placed an unreported distance from the listener (Beranek 2007, 95). Seated in a chair with a knob at their fingertips, ten women and twenty-six men—secretaries and draftswomen, engineers, scientists, and executives—listened first to a recording of the Super-Constellation propeller plane, followed by a recording of the Boeing 707 (Kryter 1959). A second test was held at an air force research laboratory, with ninety-one men and nine women participating. There, "approximately 75% of the subjects were engineers and scientists and the other 25% included administrative, secretarial and maintenance personnel" (Kryter 1959, 1419). While the second test was intended to expand the subject pool, the fact that a still-circulating standard was developed from the responses of a limited number of people largely working in acoustical engineering, a group reflecting the gendered division and distribution of labor of that field, matters—though one can only speculate in what ways.

In a room approximating an anechoic chamber, a room meant to not affect the sound of the recordings as played over the speakers, the test subjects were to imagine themselves in their home, planes flying overhead or nearby, several times an hour. Listeners were asked to evaluate paired recordings of different planes based on how they might perceive the sounds, and whether the second would be "more disturbing or less disturbing than the first noise if heard in your home periodically 20 to 30 times during the day and night" (Kryter 1959, 1418; see also Beranek 2007, 2008). The sound is "perceived" because it "is heard and measured 'in the listener's mind'" (Kryter 1959, 1423), a mind asked now to respond to what was heard in the moment while imagining its body elsewhere. In this way, the listening tests figured imagination as bodily—as drawing together the actual perception of sound with an imagined scenario of its experience to situate their bodies elsewhere, a virtual projection from the physicality of the conditions under which they listened. What would they have imagined as they listened? Would they have imagined not only the roar of the jet engine, but the curtains fluttering in the open kitchen window as they poured cereal for their children or sat and read the morning paper, low frequencies—inaudible to the ear—rattling the china in the cupboards? Would they have imagined being startled from the depths of sleep as they lay in an upstairs bedroom, a plane seeming to skim the roof of their house? Would they, in other words, have placed themselves in their homes as they listened through headphones, supporting Polish psychologist Joseph Segal's 1916 notion that "The imagination is neither a 'seeing' of a mental picture with the so-called 'mind's eye' nor a conceptual thinking, but rather a kind of action, and above all a bodily action," such that "imaginative space is essentially kinesthetic just as perceptual space is" (Murata 1999, 175)?

Acoustic frequency was distinguished from the frequency of aircraft flyovers, actual perception in which frequency was embedded in a sound artifact projected onto an imagined scenario of frequency as a temporal event occurring in a place displaced from where they were at the time. And though the levels of both recordings had been "adjusted downward somewhat, so that they were heard as if inside a typical home, in summertime, with open windows" (Beranek 2007, 95), the recordings, made outdoors, did not capture the reverberation of a home, typical or otherwise. Rather, the acoustic medium heard by the microphone is air—air that in Newark was likely rather different than in Seattle, both in temperature and humidity. Air conditions sound, especially insofar as sound (or energy that becomes transduced as sound) might propagate over long distances, across which atmospheric conditions vary. Douglas Kahn describes this as "transperception"; insofar as sound is always conditioned by its medium, it includes "air, atmospheric currents from wind and temperature, ionized air, rock, walls, electronic circuitry, . . . objects, and artifacts" (Kahn 2013, 170). In the case of these airplane sounds, the microphone and noise measurement device are the sensors, the site where movement, resonance, and listening happens—where transperception is registered. The tape fixes the sensory dynamism of machine listening to aircraft, relayed to people whose listening experience is otherwise shaped as static and neutral, the main activity being their fingers turning knobs to adjust the volume and their imagined teleportation to their living room. They are not, however, meant to be annoyed but simply to register perceived noisiness. Ultimately, through others' listening, Kryter and his associates found that though propeller planes and jets are similar in volume, their "noisiness" differed because of their frequencies, and that the sound of the 707 would have to be reduced by 15 dB to match the level of noisiness of the Super-Constellation propeller plane.

Inscribed as a standard, PNdB circulates across legal and technorational regimes that include environmental legislation and airport noise management systems. "Related to the production of new forms of perception, observation, and governance," standards are applied as a scale measured against another and presented in the form of graphs and charts (Halpern 2015, 25; Latour 2012; see also Bowker and Star 2000; Sekula 1986). In this way, acoustic perception is transduced as visual inscriptions, able to circulate insofar as they are "immutable, presentable, readable and combinable with one another" (Latour 2012, 6). The process of inscribing noise and folding description into prediction in the form of regulation is governance as practice, an abstraction of governmentality rendered concrete. At congressional hearings on noise, legislators affirmed again and again the need for adequate and accurate metrics, for standards that, while best accounting for noise levels, could provide the systematization necessary for creating an even field across space and time, for finding commonalities in experience or accounting for differences, for transducing noise and the experience thereof into inscription that could both scale up into law and regulation and circulate as such.

"Noise is unwanted sound." In Vern Knudsen's unpublished manuscript on noise, the acoustician attributes the definition to the American Standards Association's Committee on Acoustical Measurements and Technology (Knudsen 1955), thus providing a historical basis to what is otherwise taken as transparent norm. Explaining that he prefers the definition of the International Committee—"Noise is sound not desired by the recipient"—because it includes a hearing subject, Knudsen shifts the designation back to sound unanchored in perception, concluding, "It is the unwanted aspect of sound that makes it noise."[13] Based in a historically specific technological consideration of electrical noise as obscuring communication through the telephone, the standards definition of noise scaled from the particular to the general. Today, its designation as "unwanted" is often turned back to an individualized human listener as a means of describing noise as "subjective" (Beyer 1999; Bijsterveld 2008). Thus, while standards in principle require stability and scalability, in practice they are made and circulate in ways that are also messy and indeterminate (Lampland and Star 2009). Les Blomberg mused on the curiosity of such a definition being formulated by engineers; how strange, he said, that engineers would inscribe a subjective definition as a standard. Others, particularly those working in the field of airport noise, use this valence to shift the burden of discrimination onto a listener whose experience may not extend to others.

That PNdB was included in international standards was, for Beranek, an achievement, a validation of the accuracy of the metric and a realization of the aim of metrication. He also described it as a political success, his work affirmed against pressure by airplane manufacturers and airlines to limit the measurement and systematization of noise.[14] Though "out of place and time" and nonsynchronous "with the event it is depicting, translating, comprehending, guiding" (Halpern 2015, 23), as artifact, inscription is continually drawn back into practice. In 1958 BBN worked with Austin Tobin, the director of the Port of New York Authority (PNYA), to set a maximum PNdB level for its airports. Beranek recalled that Tobin "went to a home near the end of the runway in Howard Beach and sat on the porch. Several of us from BBN were with him to make measurements. Whenever a propeller plane flew over the house after takeoff, we would advise him of the maximum PNdB that was measured. He would then consult our chart of figure 2. After a time, he came to a conclusion. He stated that a person owning a house near the airport should be able to sit on his porch and enjoy life. He was convinced that if the noise exceeded 112 PNdB, that quality of life was not possible" (Beranek 2007, 97). Moving from listening to looking and back, the airport official demonstrated the achievement of "visualization" conditioning "physiological capacities" (Halpern 2015, 23). Metrics and other modes of inscription remain active as vibrant, agentive matter. For Beranek, the adoption of PNdB as a metric, and agreement about the maximum PNdB that should be allowed, "made the jet age immediately feasible, preventing the advent of women with baby strollers on the runways to stop the jets" (Beranek 2007, 99).[15]

Though Kryter went to great lengths to replace *annoyance* with *noisiness* as a means of evaluating "how wanted . . . or unwanted a sound is considered to be by the average listener" (Kryter 1959, 1423), it nonetheless proved difficult to detach annoyance from noise. As Kryter himself acknowledged, the "wantedness (or unwantedness), the acceptability (or unacceptability)" of a given sound was previously referred to as "the annoyingness of a sound" by investigators, including himself (Kryter 1959, 1423; Newman 1955).[16] A decade later, he published a paper titled "Annoyance (Perceived Noisiness)" (Kryter 1970). And as Berglund, Berglund, and Lindvall wrote, "Kryter's . . . concept 'perceived noisiness' is ambiguous and covers both the noisiness and annoyance concepts" (1975, 931). Despite attempts to bracket annoyance, relegating it to a realm deemed auxiliary to perception, it remained as trace, percolating within and alongside metrics, including PNdB itself. Beranek recalled, "Further subjective tests verified that when the S-C and jet aircraft were judged by listeners to be equally 'noisy' (annoying), they would have the same perceived noise levels in PNdB" (Beranek 2007, 95). Sanford "Sandy" Fidell, who worked at both BBN and Veneklasen and Associates, recalled the same history on the occasion of Leo Beranek's ninety-ninth birthday. He also glosses "noisier" as level of annoyance, explaining, "It was estimated that jet noise would have to be reduced by 15 dB to be judged no more annoying than the noise of large, four engine propeller aircraft. Karl Kryter and Karl Pearsons developed the 'Perceived Noise Level' scale to represent the frequency-weighted noisiness, rather than the broadband acoustic energy, or sounds" (2014, 42). As Jerrold "Jerry" Fadem, a lawyer in numerous cases related to airport noise and property in Southern California, writes, "The PNdB scale assigns more weight to the higher and more annoying frequencies in the sound being measured than to lower and less annoying frequencies" (King 1973, 11). And Timmins, in his 1976 thesis, "Noise Pollution and the Law," states in a section on "Psychological and Behavioral Effect" that "Perhaps the area in which most work has been done in this context is the question of the annoyance that noise can cause" (1976, 26)—"The annoyance factor has been added to the decibel scale to create the perceived noise in decibels (PNdB) scale" (1976, 27). Annoyance, apparently, is hard to drop from noise.

Reinscribing Annoyance

While annoyance was excluded from PNdB, it continues to be embedded in other noise metrics, whether as a dimension of the experience of noise—that is, as a concern in and of itself—or as a predicted emotion that might also spur various forms of action. The latter is a feature most notably of the Schultz curve (figures 2.1 and 2.2), which exemplifies some of the vagaries of the metricization of annoyance. Developed to "reliably predict the community's subjective response to noise" and determine "a suitable living environment" (Schultz 1978, 377), it was named after Theodore J. Schultz, who, as an employee of BBN, developed the curve for the U.S. Department of Housing and Urban Development (HUD). The curve correlates the percentage of people who are "highly annoyed" to noise exposure, as measured by the average noise level over a year, or DNL. Using data from social surveys about various types of transportation noise in the United States, Europe, and Japan, Schultz found it challenging to transpose diverse survey questions into a category of people who were "highly annoyed," and for which "the intensity of annoyance" was in response to the noise itself. Nonetheless, some consistency was found, or generated, across at least some of the surveys, resulting in a curve named after its maker that circulated widely in its implementation in federal regulation.

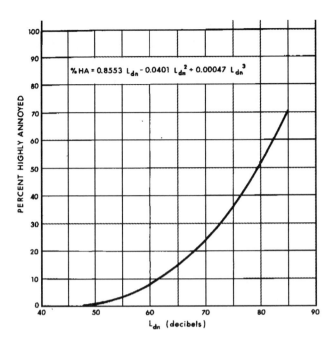

FIGURE 2.1 "Synthesis of all the clustering survey results. The mean of the 'clustering surveys' data, shown here, is proposed as the best currently available estimate of public annoyance due to transportation noise of all kinds. It may also be applicable to community noise of other kinds" (Schultz 1978, 382).

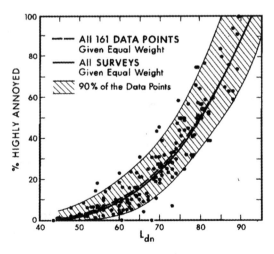

FIGURE 2.2 "Summary of all survey data points" (Schultz 1978, 383).

On the occasion of the Schultz curve's twenty-fifth anniversary, Sandy Fidell, whose first job out of graduate school was with BBN and who continues to be active as a consultant and an author, published a critique on the grounds that it did not sufficiently account for the variability of factors (2003). In an earlier coauthored article presenting a different model for "estimating the prevalence of annoyance with aircraft noise exposure," he offers two graphs. A graph with a field of dots represents "variability in annoyance rates" (figure 2.3). Before charting a line through a field of dots, with a newly added "community tolerance level," he presents the dots as a cloud or swarm of circles bracketed by scales of "Day-Night Average Sound Level (dB)" and "Prevalence of High Annoyance (%)" (figure 2.4; Fidell et al. 2011, 792). The line that makes a cut between the dots is of principal concern. Fidell suggests that his computation remedies Schultz's, which, as acoustical engineer Paul Schomer underscores, shows "significant scatter" (2005).

The first image draws the viewer into an abstraction of particularities, with dots that dance and scatter, cluster and disperse as they find comfort in one other or push apart. Overlapping in darker densities of line, elsewhere they drift outward into irregular constellations. This is the *noise* of the data, which, read against the grain of its intended logic, affords an engagement with what Halpern describes as "epistemic uncertainty and desire" (2015, 25). The graphs require and animate expertise, in both their crafting and their interpretation. Reading against expertise entails reading graphs as image, flattening them into what is presented on the page as a means of drawing out traces of indeterminacy that are acknowledged as present but worked on to disappear or minimize. This is a glitch reading. On Fidell's graph, annoyance is granted its own axis, scaled in its prevalence, though not in its intensity or frequency or other possible threshold; it is detached from yet measured against noise, figured as decibel measured and averaged over time. While the scatter is intended to suggest correspondence, if not correlation, the dots appear as a distribution of the sensible, visualization rendering a sea of affect.

An asynchronicity of visualization draws future potentiality into the present flatness of the graph, here simply of percentage annoyed, but elsewhere moving into other kinds of action. Annoyance becomes agentive; unhooked from the event itself, it factors the risk of various forms of response on the part of listeners, which, as had already been learned, might include complaints, community action, or legal action against the airport. When acousticians emphasize the reliability of their evidence over that of ordi-

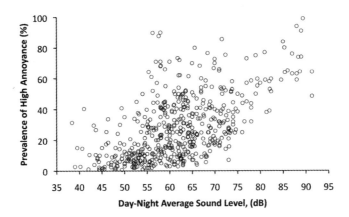

FIGURE 2.3 "Illustration of variability in annoyance prevalence rates as a function of cumulative noise exposure. Each point represents an estimate of the prevalence of high annoyance at a single interviewing site" (Fidell et al. 2011, 792).

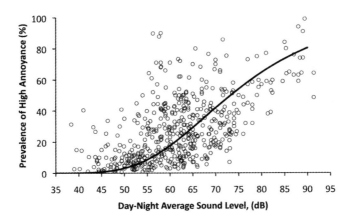

FIGURE 2.4 "Fit of all aircraft annoyance data to effective loudness function for a CTL value of approximately 73 dB" (Fidell et al. 2011, 799).

nary experience, the space between the two palpates. On the conclusion of Veneklasen and Associates' 1968 community noise survey in Inglewood, they wrote, "We believe that legal actions by a multitude of individuals or groups may actually harm the cause, especially if their actions may be ill-advised technically, or inflammatory in nature. This subject of noise is inherently a highly technical one and progress will result only from informed and concerted efforts" (Veneklasen and Associates 1968, 3). As the possibility of legal action is corralled into the objectivity, rationality, and coolness of technical measurement and treatment, there remains a lingering presence of affect, of annoyance as an experience that acousticians are trying to make sense of and account for.

In metricizing perception and potential action, noise control is rendered social control. Responses to airport noise already underway are pinned to the y-axis as metrics are made to do their work of prediction through the line that moves upward, arcing into the right-hand corner of the graph and pointing outward and beyond into an unknown that now seems inevitable. Yet, as forms of "affective measuring," metrics are "'a probe for the improbably,' the indeterminate, or the not-yet of futurity" (Clough 2018, xiii). Community noise response (CNR) was a metric formulated to quantify the results of community noise surveys and correlate experience with action (see figure 2.5). A 1954 National Opinion Research Center (NORC) study of community annoyance levels examined the relationship between a feeling of annoyance and actions described as "overt expressions of annoyance" (NORC 1954, 1). In London, over a decade later, "Items for the annoyance scale proper were obtained by asking informants to rate each kind of disturbance they had experienced, according to how much it annoyed them when it occurred—Very Much, Moderately, Only a Little" (NORC 1954, 6). Yet the reliability of CNR was maybe less certain than intended, insofar as it "supposedly predicts whether a given noise will lead to no response, or provoke a rising degree of protest, culminating in vigorous legal action" (Timmins 1976, 28). Inscribing legal action as a function of noise level undermines the significance of actual social relationships: of neighbors talking to neighbors, having meetings, and organizing letter-writing campaigns; of people living around an area in one part of the country talking to others thousands of miles away; of the possibility people might read newspapers or engage with the airport and its sounds by becoming experts on flight paths, on weather conditions, or on the way sound moves. All this was another means of taking experience and making it mean something, of mobilizing annoyance in the hopes that it would ultimately be ameliorated.

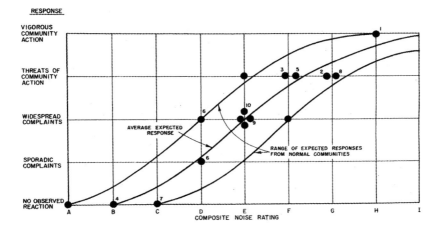

FIGURE 2.5 Community response versus noise severity (Kushner 1958, 52).

A Public Ear

Noise metrics shift the particular to the general; rather than control of one's neighbors, or those who are unruly, noise control is control of the "community," a dispersed and generalized public that subsumes any particular experience. They produce what we might call a *public ear*, an average, general mode of hearing and experiencing noise. This dispersal is atmospheric: a horizon of membership that extends indefinitely, catching potentially everyone in a generalizing net, a community that never materializes. Its field of inclusion is limited only by specificities such as those outlined for PNdB; as Kryter maintained, "The definition of the 'average listener,' and the specifications of the 'conditions of listening and testing,' must be prescribed explicitly for each application of the perceived noise level" (1959, 1425). Manufactured publics, such as those achieved by opinion polls, craft a framework of citizenship and norms, with membership that is at once inclusive of an "average listener" but excludes any particular listener. Noise ordinances sustain this through the legal fiction of a "reasonable person." The "neurotics," however, push through, those who "will be annoyed by many things including noise; even noise that they think they hear, which may not even be physically measurable" (U.S. EPA Office of Noise Abatement and Control 1971g, 184). The "neurotics" as they are here labeled (though elsewhere may be "the mad" or "the sensitives") challenge the very possibility of a general listener and what has been construed as the social order more generally.

A play between specificity and generality is inscribed in noise and its metrics; acoustical engineers speak on behalf of people in general even as they standardize noise as something individualized—subjective and affective. Noise control is understood as an engineering accomplishment rather than a social project. Yet there is a politics to the way in which annoyance continues to circulate. Residents mobilizing against airport noise in the 1960s do not really use the term *annoyance*. They talk about fear, windows rattling, the inability to sleep or have an uninterrupted conversation or hear the television—things that get folded into annoyance by acoustical engineers. Those who use *annoyance* most are engineers, regulators, senators, and lawyers, though always in relation to other listeners. Annoyance as emotion slides back into the personal, an individualizing strategy that divides people, making collective action more difficult. But, as Lutz (1988, 9) points out, this confuses an understanding of emotion as personal with the work it does. As with other emotions, annoyance is relational, attuning people not only to a source of noise but to one another. And if emotion is often feminized, as Lutz suggests, this may have been part of why engineers and medical professionals directed their public service messages against noise toward women, and why airport noise resonated in an era in which mothers were at home during the day—mothers who may have experienced aircraft noise themselves or witnessed their children experiencing it, and who talked to one another about that experience. And some of the women, more politically inclined, mobilized around this noise. In this way, modes of minimizing emotion were in fact bases for its political force.

Inequities emerge primarily around the ways in which the particular pushes up against the general, and in how assemblages that cohere in and through noise result in different modes of mattering. Inscribing *annoyance* either as entangled with or an effect of noise, metrics shift the particular to the general, occluding differences not only in experience but in civic engagement. Hence social inequalities emerge as organizing features rather than already existing or static characteristics. These are the limits of the general public—the exclusions of the particular, of any singularity that does not meet the regulatory dimensions of norms. Moreover, any relationship between demographic category and the experience of noise is structured around political participation more so than what is now bundled under a notion of environmental justice. In an undated report for EPA's Office of Noise Abatement and Control (ONAC; it would have been drafted between 1972 and 1981), Arthur de Vany points out the lack of work relating annoyance to race, and the significance of the latter for the experiences of and responses to urban noise.[17] For instance, NORC's 1954 opinion poll, *Community Aspects of Aircraft Annoyance*, does not correlate for race or ethnicity. It found that "The 'greatly annoyed' tend more often to be middle-aged housewives with a high school or grammar school education, who rent their homes" (95) and concludes that demographic factors, especially age and social status, are "important considerations in influencing expressions of complaint," with "younger, better educated persons . . . more likely to institute some civic action than older and less well educated residents" (10). And though a respondent's income correlated with their proximity to the airport, race was not a demographic category in the NORC study but rather an aspect of other "social problems" that might also annoy residents (67). Distinguishing between "who is annoyed by noise (air craft) and who does something about it," de Vany credits Kryter with suggesting that some groups are more likely to complain even if not affected as much, while others, who have more favorable attitudes toward noise producers, are less likely to complain. Or, as de Vany concludes, "It is not really likely that many high income, well educated folk will live in high aircraft (or car or truck for that matter) exposure areas. However, it is likely that these people will have knowledge of how to complain."[18]

Even if demographics were not incorporated into these metrics, the achievement of a metric resides in shifting authority to those who hold or wield it. Metrics themselves are no longer bases for rights claims—at least not about immediate noise—despite the request of Inglewood residents during 1960 hearings. Metrics are used as the basis for land use, residential soundproofing, and prescribed flight paths. Claims might be made against one of these things, but the regulatory regime as constructed and satisfied by metrics will be used to push back against them. LAWA employees in environmental services say, "That was an allowable flight path." Or, "You are not within the 65 CNEL [community noise equivalent level] contour." At that point, social inequities are evident through differentially weighted complaints. Residents of Palos Verdes Peninsula, a wealthy enclave to the southwest of LAX, were successful in shifting the flight paths by complaining about the turn backs that were happening over their homes. A Hawthorne resident who went to a Los Angeles World Airport (LAWA) Community Noise Roundtable meeting because the airplane sound had, he said, been getting worse, and his calls did not seem to make a difference, seemed less optimistic about the possibility of change. More recently, a Culver City neighborhood association has had airport noise on their agenda and sent representatives to the meeting. They think something might be done.

Between Inscription and Perception

Widening a gap between perception and inscription, noise metrics rely on a play between the sensory and the sensible in which the former is the basis for the latter even as it is ultimately undermined by it. Noise management has been systematized, implemented in a series of microphones mounted on poles around the airport, the data from which are transcribed in the form of noise contour maps, redrawn every three months. Thus, when airport noise management staff say they "want to turn noise into sound," they shift the weight of perception onto inscription: microphones and noise contour maps are the only reliable listeners. The maps, developed as a visualization of metrics intended to accommodate experience, annoyance (or not), or speech interference, now have a life of their own. An immense amount of work goes into maps, which, for LAX, are recalculated quarterly and averaged for the year. Sometimes noise monitors go down—a microphone gets dirty, a wire fails, or a computer crashes—and they have to drive there and restart it, call the company to troubleshoot, recalibrate the microphone. Data are always coming in, some as information, some to tweak, some used to adjust something else—flight paths, sound profiles, easterly departures when the weather is bad. In LAWA's Environmental Services Division, a staff person was assigned to listen to the recordings of loud noise events to determine whether they are aircraft; if not—if the noise is someone mowing their lawn, or construction equipment, or a party—it is deleted from the CNEL data, which only accounts for aircraft noise.

Averages, though, are not what people experience. That this is commonly stated by both noise management experts and people experiencing airport noise reflects the ways in which metrics have become objects of engagement in themselves. Perception pushes up against a public form as noise complaints register the ways in which experience does not match metrics. Yet even if people cannot change metrics of a noise contour, the gap between inscription and perception generates a relationship between the two, which takes the form of discussion about the metric, about how it does not match experience, and about the experience itself. The national airport noise advocacy group N.O.I.S.E. asserts, "As DNL is an average and humans do not perceive noise in averages but rather as individual events, we believe it is time to investigate alternative metrics that could measure impacts" (N.O.I.S.E. 2019). A former manager of an airport community roundtable, to whom I was directed by N.O.I.S.E.'s contact person, underscored this, saying several times, "DNL is an average. People don't hear averages, they hear straight decibels at the time it appears." This causes people to ask why there is a map of average levels, to say, "that's not what I'm hearing." DNL and CNEL are "hard to understand for people not in the acoustics industry. 'That's not what I experience,' they say. There are soft and fuzzy edges to it. You're dealing with perception, with the physical ability to hear sound." This gap is also intrinsic to measurement and regulation; iterated and reiterated, as the achievement of closure is reopened, managers of noise are distanced from the experience of people. Those who experience noise and those who manage it are reconnected as the latter seek remedies for the problem that is now not so much that of noise itself but the gulf between metrics made to model experience and still ongoing and existing experience.

Annoyed by airplane noise, a woman who lived a few miles outside the 65 CNEL line had been coming to Community Noise Roundtable meetings regularly. In part to ameliorate her, LAWA staff had set up a noise monitor at her house, in what is known as an upper-middle-class African American neighborhood. She described her neighborhood as so quiet they could hear birds. LAWA staff had already shown her the flight paths in relation to where she lived and told her that the sound was normal, that there was nothing they could do. But she was quite bothered by the planes and kept pressing. She did not believe the data, they said—she described flights she couldn't see but could hear, which, she insisted, must be different than the ones on the map. They spent an hour in her yard and pointed out the plane she heard each time, explaining the procedure it was following. They described the technical aspect of what she was hearing: the cone of the airplane sound would reach her after the plane passed overhead, as the sound comes in a forty-five-degree angle rather than straight down. Thus, as the plane passes, "a 45-degree cone envelops you . . . like a sound wave that gets pushed out." At night planes might have seemed louder, as the departing planes were mostly international flights, full of fuel and luggage. Yet despite what she may have perceived, there were no planes circling over her house. They left the noise monitor at her house but expected it wouldn't be "anywhere near" 65 CNEL. This was not something they would ordinarily do, but because of her persistence, and because she had been to the roundtable, they acceded. They said she was happy they had come and paid attention to her, that she felt she was being listened to. But what could they do? There was nothing they could do about the noise she was experiencing, or the fact that she was perhaps more bothered by it than others would be.

All they could do was educate her, let her know everything is normal, and hopefully with that, give her some peace of mind to know that someone is watching the planes.

VISCERAL INSCRIPTION

Today in Los Angeles, those who are annoyed by planes flying overhead or within audibility might call the airport's noise hotline to register a complaint. Before doing that, they might consult the airport's website. The LAWA website features a live flight path map for the purpose of logging noise complaints—a highly elaborate system to demonstrate the airport's community relations work around noise. Flights are color coded as arrivals and departures, or as those of nearby airports and flyovers. Their shapes designate type of aircraft: turboprop, general aviation, military jet, unknown, cargo plane. The map uses the visual trope of a heat map, and as planes pass over, colored dots marking the location of noise measurement microphones change from green to yellow, orange to red, invoking, perhaps, the level of irritation and annoyance felt by a listener. The numbers change according to the dbA levels, which are those perceived by the noise measurement device receiving information from a microphone mounted on a tall pole. As the airport puts it, dbA levels are "an expression of the relative loudness of sounds in air as perceived by the human ear." The airport qualifies these levels, which "represent the actual real time sound level at that location at that moment in time and may be the result of an aircraft flying over or near the noise monitor. These noise levels may also be attributed to community-based noise, such as vehicle traffic, lawnmowers, etc. or just the ambient noise at that location."[19]

The map suggests an appearance of something approximating reality itself, with the little icons of the moving planes and their dashed trails marking where they were in the past thirty seconds, differently colored and shaped, the heat map logic of the sound pressure meters giving an immediacy to the level recorded. Listeners become air traffic experts, though much (that may be audible) is withheld from view. The map as mimesis obscures its gaps. The flight tracker, appearing to be live, is delayed fifteen minutes for security reasons, and high-security flights are not displayed. Other things are lost too. As the website explains: "You may also notice aircraft icons sometimes 'dropping off' and/or suddenly doing unusual things. This is especially true in the area immediately around LAX, but could also occur away from the airport as well. These 'ghost' aircraft are due to radar and aircraft transponder reflections from the ground and high rise buildings around the airport, and possibly from terrain and meteorological conditions farther away from LAX."[20] Its gaps are also those between inscription and perception, as noise complaints are folded into already realized management systems. Complainants are warned of the difference between "the actual real time sound level" and the averaged levels that afford residential soundproofing, among other things.

The realism of the map is further undermined by the territorialization of the dots, which are both too large and too small; unlike the sound of the plane, they are discrete and bounded, suggesting a curtailment of the acoustic even as they are themselves much larger than the microphones whose measurements they convey. Yet even as they obscure the lines marking streets and runways, their resemblance to a hole punch casts them as void or absence. They are only loosely related to the noise contour maps that prescribe soundproofing or other forms of "land recycling," with their static lines of annual average and temporally weighted noise levels, which nonetheless convey a gradation of the spatiality of sound in a way that here is lost in the individualization of noise events. And though the dots are obscured by the passing planes, the vertical distance between the source of sound and its perception (and between sound and its metricization) is invisible and hence inaudible. The volumetric—as both a verticality of airspace and amplitude of sound—is projected rather than portrayed. The image is flat and silent.

Sound is perceived via the visuality of the level of heat of the circle, which, in miniature, does not in itself prompt a feeling of annoyance (S. Stewart 1992). The perception of sound becomes perception of the map, which yields its own vitality and vibrancy. A person viewing the map looks down at the planes from above rather than hearing them from the ground. The concrete particularity of experience that makes airplane noise matter happens elsewhere. Watching the flight tracker map, we cannot hear their sound, nor that of the people on the ground. And what is visualized, though not felt, is heat. With heat visualizing noise, thermoception, hearing, and the perception of luminescence emerge as "*the vibration*, which . . . follows an invisible thread that is more nervous than cerebral" (Deleuze and Guattari 1996, 168). Thermoception provides a way of thinking through other senses that shifts from a division between subject and object, hearing and sound, vision and image (M. Peterson 2016b). Insofar as it does not distinguish between sense and that which is sensed, thermoception provides a model for understanding sound and image as immanent in perception. As Vannini and Taggart write, "Thermoception . . . is not like a thermometer. It is instead an atmospheric attunement: an attentive force that manifests itself in corporeal involvement in warmth and in the transformation of living environments." Moreover, as "an interface, and . . . a skill, a hub of activities, a sensibility, and an orientation to modulate the world" thermoception is "a type of *affect*" (2015, 48).

Reading across senses through thermoception draws on a formulation of heat, sound, and light as energy, relying thus on modern physics, while keeping its grounds as "empiricism" at arm's length. Heat maps use a visual trope of temperature—and its sensory basis of thermoception—to convey gradation or scale. The rainbow is coded as cool to hot, blue to red, lower to higher, less to more—heat or noise or some other undesirable thing on the red side of the spectrum. That red means both *higher* and *more* grounds temperature in thermodynamics and a relative level of heat energy, or what Stephen Brush (1986) describes as "the kind of motion we call heat." This maps onto noise—also a kind of motion—insofar as we understand the scale to be one of greater intensity rather than quantity, say, of homeless or gun crimes. At this point the heat map becomes a transduction of thermoception into the visual, another sensory domain, which, though also bodily, is generally cast as that of logic, rationality, reason, and sensibility. From the perspective of modern physics, heat and sound are of an order: low frequencies can be perceived as heat, while second sound is a phenomenon in which heat transfer occurs via waves rather than diffusion. Emphasizing sound as energy disallows an objectified approach to sound and to the sensory more broadly. And though, as Brush explains, "the establishment of the wave theory of light . . . and of the principle of conservation of energy and thermodynamics . . . are generally regarded as two separate events in the history of 19th-century physics," he maintains that "they should be seen as successive and closely related stages of the same transformation of physical theory, in which explanations of phenomena were increasingly based on *motion* rather than on *matter*" (1986, 306).

Critiques of heat maps (also referred to as "rainbow color maps") focus on their inaccuracy, or their inability to present information clearly and legibly, while suggesting ways to use color to better effect, distinguishing one thing from another through perceptual schema that are less likely to confuse the viewer. The problem is cast, principally, as an issue of visualization—of the vagaries of human perception, for which hue confuses less than color. The authors of "Somewhere over the Rainbow: How to Make Effective Use of Colors in Meteorological Visualizations," published in the *Bulletin of the*

American Meteorological Society, discuss the merits and limitations of RGB, or rainbow, visualization in relation to human perception. Similar to the perception of sound, humans have "a logarithmic perception of luminance." Because RGB colors are differently luminescent, their use in data visualization can mislead the eye and the interpretation. To remedy this, the authors espouse "a perception-based color concept called hue-chroma-luminance (HCL)," which "is based on how humans perceive color, in contrast to the RGB color space, which is based on technical demands of TV and computer screens" (Stauffer et al. 2015, 204).

In other words, according to their critics, heat maps are literally vital, vibrant, pulsing figurations, inherently active in their visuality. In affecting, or differently impressing on, perception, heat maps compose a relationship between sensation and communities of interpretation. This is a crucial aspect of their circulation, rendering them as affective—as, that is, "intensities that pass body to body," or "resonances that circulate about, between, and sometimes stick to bodies and worlds" (Gregg and Seigworth 2010, 1). The heat map materializes sensation even as it "*passes into sensation*" (Deleuze and Guattari 1996, 193; see Ingold 2005). Deleuze and Guattari suggest that through sensation—or "contemplation of the world"—"we become with the world"; hence, in its shimmering, resonating, pulsing, and warming, it might be said that the heat map as a visual artifact renders "flesh . . . the thermometer of a becoming" (1996, 169, 179). In this way, the status of the map as representation shifts, along with the very status of representation.

Lefebvre describes maps as representations of space, rather than spatial practice or representational space. Yet the interconnectedness of his spatial triad, and its subsumption to a (social) process of producing (social) space, renders representation as concrete and immediate rather than something removed from spatial practice. A Cartesian divide between thought and matter, between "the thinking 'I' and the object thought about," no longer holds. Rather, the production of space is "a process which subsumes signifying processes without being reducible to them" (Lefebvre 1992, 37; see Massumi 2002). And though spatial practice may not necessarily be coterminous with representations of space, there is a relationship; as Lefebvre puts it, they are "interconnected" though not necessarily "a coherent whole" (1992, 40). Thus the map, like annoyance, is a concrete abstraction, an abstraction that is "visceral" (Holland, Ochoa, and Tompkins 2014; see also McCormack 2013, chapter 7). And while heat maps are not the kind of thing generally thematized in these terms—the domain, instead, of artist fabulations or affective renderings of nonhuman becomings (McLean 2017)—they none-theless *do* something. A gap opened between a feeling of annoyance and the visualization of metrics renders visual media immediate and affective, undoing, in turn, a sensory dualism that posits seeing as detached or ob-jective and hearing as haptic (Campt 2017; Deleuze 2005; Starosielski 2019).

Annoyance is ranked high on the Delft Institute of Positive Design's "negative emotion scale"—it is literally in the red. Invoking a heat map with a gradation of color that spans red to green, emotions are grouped by typol-ogy. Annoyance, like dissatisfaction and frustration, is categorized as a type of agitation; these, along with negative emotions that fall under "personal provocation," are red.[21] The colors used in their schema invoke a sensory-affective continuity across thermoception, hearing, seeing, and emotion. This is suggested rather than explained, and the fact that only negative emotions are included renders the heat map color coding a gradation from negative emotions prompted by things happening to a person (blue or green) to negative emotions that entail a more violent response, whether as agita-tion or action (red). The institute's mission of increasing well-being through design is not part of this schema though ostensibly would include the use of color to affect experience, whether to increase happiness or a sense of pride or "parenting well-being" (Owusu 2011–12). Yet while red might represent annoyance, as a design tool it is used to enhance things like "community well being" (Zuthern 2013–14). According to Nicole Starosielski, researchers testing the "heat-hue hypothesis," or the notion that "the color of an object or environment affects the human perception of temperature," found that people were more comfortable—"warmer" and "more satisfied"—in aircraft cabins with yellow lights than those with blue lights, as are currently used (2019, 152, 153). Marita Sturken, however, suggests that the significance of heat maps in an era of climate change lies in their ability to affect viewers, with red signaling alarm and "the dominance of red trending toward ma-roon . . . a key factor in this sense of anxiety and crisis" (2014, 2526).

As heat maps "make sense" of the sensory, they do so with a visual form that, in its circulation, renders the invisible visible across modalities of sensa-tion (Merleau-Ponty 2002); "not the transformation of one into the other, . . . but something passing from one to the other," this is "a zone of indetermi-nation, or indiscernibility" (Deleuze and Guattari 1996, 173). As the red of the heat map brings annoyance in and out of view, it wavers, falling away as a feeling but remaining, perhaps, as a sense of agitation. Sianne Ngai suggests that annoyance is a negative emotion whose "marginal status . . . is related to the ease with which it always threatens to slip out of the realm of emotional experience altogether, into the realm of physical or epidermal sensations" (2007, 1, 184). Its indeterminacy casts it as a feeling of our contemporary condition, if not the Anthropocene writ large, then a sense of being in and apart from an atmosphere that is increasingly against us (humans and many others as well), in ways that are as yet largely unknown. It is the irritation and irritability in the face of yet to be realized but inevitable atmospheric nuisances, that which gets under our skin in literal and metaphoric ways.[22]

3   ENVIRONMENTAL IMAGINARIES

Noise pollution is a product of the 1960s. By this, I mean that the notion of noise as pollution was formulated and took hold during a particular period. The story of noise pollution in the United States begins in the 1950s, the term seemingly first used to refer to sound inside the home. By the late 1960s, *noise pollution* had emerged as a viable and motivating category, noise as an environmental issue newly coordinating the politics of aircraft noise, work on noise and health, noise control engineering, and workplace safety. Noise pollution is conjured in and through encounters between historically specific experiences and formulations of noise and of pollution—encounters between sometimes incommensurate fields in which their friction is minimized, softened through the suturing of differences, through hierarchizations of matterings. The ability of a notion of noise pollution to take hold relies on also then emerging conceptual fields, political mobilizations, sounds, and sensory experience. These include conceptualizations of pollution, atmosphere, and the environment; a renewed focus on privacy;

the sounds of airplanes, trucks, and household appliances; the annoyance caused by those sounds; and a growing insistence on the possibility of controlling noise on the part of acoustical engineers, building material manufacturers, and urban planners.[1]

In being designated *pollution* rather than *nuisance*, noise shifts from something relational in which the source, and perpetrator, is known, to a dispersed, undefined, and atmospheric condition (Radovac 2011; E. Thompson 2004). As such, noise pollution echoes and amplifies key environmental imaginaries of its time. This was an era of a new "planetary consciousness" marked by "the disappearance of the outside," the atmosphere no longer apart from human life but entangled with it.[2] Conceptualizations of networked holistic ecosystems proliferated in the form of ecologies of mind, nature, and technology (Bateson [1972] 2000). At the same time, *the environment* was defined in distinctly anthropocentric terms: "The natural world or physical surroundings in general either as a whole or within a particular geographic area, esp. as affected by human activity."[3] Noise pollution—generally described as the effects of the sounds of manmade machines on humans—echoes this anthropocentrism even as it undoes the stability of such partitioning, rendering instead a permeable body that is "intermeshed with the more-than-human world" (Alaimo 2010, 2). Though demarcated as specifically airborne sound, noise is not a form of air pollution. Instead, it is the pollution of the sonic environment by noise. Difficult, in this way, to pin down or point to as a concrete and stable thing, its atmospheric qualities and manifestation in experience render it both self-evident and generalized, even as they serve as grounds for its dismissal.

Aircraft noise was crucial in figuring noise as pollution.[4] More pervasive, more generalized, and more of an exteriorized threat than other kinds of noise, it amplifies an environmental imaginary that is fundamentally atmospheric. Though aircraft and airport noise are often glossed, specifying aircraft as the source of airport noise generalizes beyond the geographic space of an airport, shifting from particular political mobilizations. Aircraft noise served as an index for the noise crisis and for antinoise mobilizations. It was generally listed at or near the top of decibel scales, surpassed only by the sound of a rocket or space shuttle launch. R. Murray Schafer's 1970 *The Book of Noise*, like many publications of the time, ranks a jet plane highest on a decibel scale, at 130 dB, with threshold of hearing (0 dB) and rustling leaves (10 dB) at the bottom.[5] Articulating a widely shared sentiment, Schafer describes aircraft noise as the ultimate increase in technological sound; "not localized or contained," it turns the sky into a "big sound sewer."

That "aircraft spreads noise everywhere" marks its pervasiveness, filling the skies—or airspace—with noise that, in its proliferation, seems to be dangerously beyond the control of people experiencing it on the ground (1970, 17, 16). Its increase in frequency and volume by that time fueled fears of its further intensification, the algorithmic logic of the decibel wielded in anticipation of sensory futures. Aircraft noise was at the center of early federal noise regulation, exemplified by a Noise Abatement Office housed under the FAA beginning in 1967.[6] At the same time, as a more general frame of the environment emerged, it began to lose its hold on noise writ large. In *The Politics of Airport Noise*, Gordon McKay Stevenson Jr. (1972) credits environmental legislation with successfully addressing airport noise by scaling up and making it a generalizable concern. Yet the noise of planes, inseparable from their safety, also remained apart; Edmund Muskie's proposal that the EPA have regulatory authority over the FAA was voted down (U.S. Senate 1974b, 120–24).[7] Half a century later, aircraft noise continues to stand on its own, a still unresolved legislative domain folded into yet distinct from environmental regulation.

TRACING INDETERMINACY

Noise pollution deobjectifies sound. Though there may be "sounds of" traffic or aircraft, there is no "sound of" noise pollution. Moreover, those "sounds of" that cohere as noise pollution emerge and come into being through sensation, which, following Deleuze, "is in the body, and not in the air" (2005, 32). Yet sensation falters, its seeming reality allowing noise pollution to take hold even as it remains unstable and indeterminate. The notion of noise pollution runs ahead of its content, a Lacanian signifier anticipating the meaning of the signified (Lacan 2006, 419). There is something that can be pointed to that is noise, and something that constitutes noise pollution. But that "thing"—which is hardly a thing—does not produce its own meaning as such. Lacking specific content or even amplitude, its substance emerges as a factor of measurement that opens a space of negotiation between experience and metrics (see chapter 2). Emerging along with a then-nascent environmentalism, it is figured as its own form of pollution that, though of air, is not air. The instability of the category and its falling away—into gaps of legislation, jurisdiction, experience, regulation, bureaucracy, environmentalism—suggests an immateriality of sound, or the *notion* that sound is immaterial. This is not, per se, an inherent or ontological property of either sound or its signification but a feature that is made in multiple ways.

Of great concern in the 1960s and 1970s, the term *noise pollution* has subsequently declined in its use in print.[8] As with the environment, noise pollution is "a shifting subject which is the product of constant negotiation" (Goodie 2001, 80). Its decline is in part empirical, the result of the development of quieter technology and the implementation of noise management systems. Yet noise pollution continues to resonate in and through its effects. A flurry of legislation on municipal, regional, state, and federal levels around workplace safety, public health, and the environment from the late 1960s through the 1970s is sustained as regulations and their attendant bureaucracies. And while noise pollution remains of concern, it is by now thoroughly naturalized, pollution folded into an understanding of noise. Today when LAWA noise management staff are asked whether they use the term *noise pollution*, they immediately respond: "No! Noise is by definition pollution." Continuing, they explain that "Noise is unwanted sound." This might be followed by a description of the PR nature of their job, and how the management of language is necessary to not give fodder to the ongoing dissatisfaction of people living near the airport, whose complaints are required to be heard as part of the community relations mandate of noise management regulations but no longer affect flight paths or sonic volume. Complaints, which once motivated civic mobilization efforts, lawsuits, noise pollution legislation, and technological developments, are now in excess of a system that folded the subjective nature of noise into noise measurement systems (see chapter 2). Yet, as suggested by LAWA's iteration of noise pollution, there is also always an excess—a wider field that is excised, a quality of that which the metrics rationalize and a qualitative aspect to the metrics themselves.

Making Noise Pollution

It is a curious task to convey the emergence of a term, the ways in which something—an idea, a category, a sensation—that previously did not exist took hold. To capture how something as amorphous and indefinite as *noise pollution* came into being—came, that is, into awareness, audibility, and political attention. And to assess how a multiplicity of experiences and sounds was rendered singular, generating agreement. Tracing the emergence of *noise pollution* from 1964 to 1967 helps historicize a term that is by now fully naturalized. While we have access to references in print, the ways in which *noise pollution* captured a public imagination and circulated in speech are less accessible. Moving from an indoor environment to the outdoors, *noise pollution* was made possible by an emergent environmentalism, even as it stood at the forefront of environmental concerns. As Nicholas C. Yost, then deputy attorney general of California, told a congressional subcommittee in 1972, while "Two years ago 'noise pollution' was an unfamiliar term," it now prompted more complaints "than any other pollutant or threat to the environment" (U.S. Senate 1972, 165). Once established, noise pollution is cast back onto earlier noise controversies that were not conceived of in those terms at the time, lacking, as they did, the environmental framework that made noise pollution possible (Coates 2005; Rome 1996; Smilor 1977, 1980).[9]

In 1966 Republican senator Theodore R. Kupferman of New York gave himself credit for coining the term *noise pollution*. On April 21, he introduced a bill to establish an Office of Noise Control within the Office of the Surgeon General.[10] Beginning his remarks with general comments about environmental concerns, he proclaimed: "Another serious environmental problem which demands our immediate attention is that of excessive noise. I call it 'noise pollution.'"[11] Picking up on a discussion percolating among acoustical engineers and the building industry, Kupferman, who once argued, "It does not take Gertrude Stein to know that a contract is a contract is a contract," was said to have coined the "newest phrase" of "Noise Pollution" (New York State Unified Court System 2014; Delta Democrat-Times 1966). Nonetheless, though Kupferman's use of the term may have moved noise pollution outdoors, he was not the first to use the term. That honor goes to journalist Patricia McCormack, who two years prior seems to have brought the term *noise pollution* into the American public imaginary.[12]

In 1964 McCormack published two syndicated editorials insisting on the importance of quiet for health and well-being. Her rather differing sources attest to a widespread interest in the subject at the time. Readers of the *Logan Herald Journal* in Logan, Utah, were urged to "Take a 10-minute 'quiet break' once a day to overcome harmful effects of noise pollution on the homefront." Drawing on a presentation by Lee E. Farr to the Insulation Board Institute (IBI) symposium on the "deterioration of sound environment in homes," McCormack warned readers of the "psychosomatic illnesses" caused by too much household noise—especially that of one's neighbors (P. McCormack 1964a). Later that year, the *Lubbock Avalanche Journal* in Texas ran a piece on the importance of "quietude." Here her source was Barbara Chapin, a "consultant on peace literature for the American Friends Service Committee," who was inspired to think about "noise pollution" by a young boy "sitting beside her in a bus one day." Pointing out the open window of their "rickety bus," he told her he wanted to "hear all the no-sound nothing out there" of the trees they were passing. With the silence of trees echoing that of a Quaker meeting, quietude, Chapin maintained, was a means of developing an "authentic" self, a centered, grounded person able to function in the world (P. McCormack 1964b).

While Chapin is otherwise silent in the archives, Lee E. Farr's work circulated widely in editorials and congressional hearings on noise, most notably through an article he published based on his 1966 presentation. Titled "Medical Consequences of Environmental Home Noises," it addresses "Noise, or 'unwanted and intrusive sound,' as a pollutant of personal home environment" (1967, 171).[13] For Farr, crowded cities, apartment living, technology, and prosperity had coalesced to make the environment of the *home* a potential threat to the psychic, if not physical, health of its inhabitants. Farr, a pediatrician and chair of the Department of Environmental Health at the University of Texas School of Public Health, also worked as a consultant for the IBI (Hamilton Daily News Journal 1965). Farr's research up to then had focused on another atmospheric concern, that of the relationship between nuclear radiation and pediatric medicine. Later he turned his attention to the risks of smoking and applied his interest in industrial acoustics by submitting a patent for a new double-paned window. Farr's article on environmental home noises is anecdotal rather than research driven, bemoaning consumer culture, apartment living, and loud cocktail parties. There, listening enacts a certain sociability—a new form of professional obligation, a way of being together with neighbors, confirming and solidifying commonalities of class while amplifying differences in age. Though written in a detached, generalized way, Farr's description of the sensory experience of a cocktail party comes across as entirely personal. "When heterogenous background noise becomes significant, . . . the problem of discrimination and selection of conversational sound from an adjacent person speaking may require a major effort in an older person. The inability to clearly distinguish what is said then can result in a rejection of participation in such gatherings by this individual, despite the fact that invitations to such affairs within some circles are a measure of success" (1967, 173). The annoyance resulting thereof, experienced while in the throes of the party, disperses and spreads, the atmosphere of the event generalized as an atmospheric condition—a condition of the time, or of an "environment."

Farr anchors his perspective on noise in Samuel Rosen's study of the Mabaan, another widely circulating article that is frequently referred to in legislative hearings and publications on noise. The Mabaan make an appearance in R. Murray Schafer's *The Book of Noise*. In a section titled "Why the

Africans Hear Better," he explains that Samuel Rosen "attributed the superior hearing ability of the Africans to their noise-free environment. The loudest sounds the Mabaan heard were the sound of their own voices singing and shouting at tribal dances" (Schafer 1970, 11–12). The Mabaan were an ethnographic fantasy rendered real through metrics and calculation, as well as through their displacement from an industrialized present. Not exposed to "the cacophony of modern civilization," they offered an opportunity for studying the relationship between noise and hearing loss. In Rosen and colleagues' "Presbycusis Study of a Relatively Noise-Free Population in the Sudan," they describe traveling by Jeep down a "narrow, rough dirt trail" that was "sometimes difficult to find and to follow" to arrive in a village "650 miles southeast of Kahartoum," where their trip had started, "a few miles from the Ethiopian border, and 10 degrees above the equator" (Rosen et al. 1962, 727). We learn little of how the Mabaan listened. Instead, Rosen and his research team listened to the pulse and rhythms of Mabaan bodies and activities, measuring their heart rates and testing their hearing. A projection of American norms and desires broadly construed, the study circulated in support of a range of concerns.

For Farr, less concerned with hearing loss, the Mabaan study provided evidence of the effect of noise on a person's "emotional status" (1967, 171). Rather than causing health effects in and of itself, noise proliferates into sensory-affective registers that in turn might cause psychic or physical effects, or that might disturb aspirations of domestic harmony, the home a sanctuary, at least for men.[14] Sounds within the home were newly audible (and gendered): the kitchen appliances, the shrieking kids, the nagging wife—all of which require control, dampening, and acoustic treatment to avoid angering a husband who was at the office all day and for whom, a former president of the Acoustical Society of America suggested, noise might cause "circulatory troubles, hearing loss, fatigue, emotional disturbances, nagging and wife-beating" (New York Times Service 1965). As visualized by *The Blue Marble*, the first image of Earth as seen from space, there is no longer an outside, an other, a horizon of difference; instead one's own home, indeed one's self, was now a threat. Apartments—with thin walls that allow the noise of others to seep in, reverberating materials of tile and glass and inhibiting conversation—had become the problem rather than the neighbors. And while noise had moved from nuisance to environment, the latter remained that of the acoustic space of the home.

From noise pollution's origins in the home, it began to move outdoors. The Acoustical Society of America's 1965 meeting focused on the subject of noise (Acoustical Society of America 1965). Although the term *pollution* is not used in the abstracts, *environment* appears numerous times. And though hundreds of papers were presented at the ASA meeting, and dozens specifically on noise and noise control, one on traffic noise was taken up by the press to cast noise as pollution. The *New York Times* covered the meeting under the heading "Noise Pollution." "Engineers Find U.S. Gets Louder," the headline proclaims. "The talk centered around 'the noisy environment,' in which the air is being increasingly polluted with more and louder cars, the shriek of jet planes, the clatter of construction and automated equipment and the harsh crackle of transistor radios" (New York Times Service 1965). A columnist in Tyrone, Pennsylvania, picked up on a paper presented by a Canadian acoustical engineer whose work focused on traffic noise; drawing noise together with other forms of pollution, Dick West opined, "We here [*sic*] a lot about air pollution and water pollution, and the measures being taken to control them. But sound pollution has been largely neglected" (West 1965). The Society for Science and the Public reprinted *Science News-Letter*'s report on the same talk with the title "Noise Pollutes Air." "The world around us is filled with noise, noise, noise. Unwanted and unnecessary sounds are a form of air pollution not receiving the attention their high nuisance value deserves" ("Noise Pollutes Air" 1965, 389). The brief article is in the corner of a page that features pieces on acoustic technologies for perceiving—for bringing into focus, or audition—that which is unseen and inaudible: "Ultrasound 'Sees' Tumors" and hydrophones that "Aid Underwater Hearing" (Ewing 1965, 389; "Aid Underwater Hearing" 1965). The "inaudibility" of noise resides in the "schizophrenic" attitude of people who want their cars to audibly index power yet would also "like to enjoy an evening out-of-doors in peace and quiet." To achieve an "integrated attack on . . . traffic noise," public attitudes must change ("Noise Pollutes Air" 1965, 389). The title proposing that "noise pollutes air" reflects some instability about what kind of pollution noise might be, which is only lightly or loosely stabilized in the following years, as noise pollution becomes a subject of federal legislation.

The year Kupferman is said to have coined the term *noise pollution*, its use burgeons, gaining stability in its diversity. By this time, the range of things that compose the "hybrid" of noise pollution include public health, annoyance, progress, jets, decibels, residential noise, deafness, anxiety, cities, technology, and progress. There is little criticism of it. Humor columnist Harold Coffin is unique in his skepticism. Though he suggests the newfound problem of noise pollution might be masking ulterior motives, he turns toward its potential as something he seems to have experienced himself (Coffin 1966).

> "Noise pollution" is the new hazard in our big cities. Seems the smog is getting so thick the residents can hear it.
>
> Among other offenders are noisy autos, jet airports and television commercials.
>
> They used to tell us it wasn't the heat but the humidity. Now it's not the smog—but the racket.
>
> City slickers sure can dream up a lot of excuses for moving to the suburbs.
>
> It's almost impossible to hear yourself think these days, but this could be a blessing when you consider some of the things there are to think about.

His critique is not that of noise pollution per se but of white flight and suburbanization, of a privileged politics that can take up something like noise pollution at a moment of more pressing concerns. And though noise pollution might obscure other issues, it also joins a cacophonous atmosphere of crisis and change. A journalist questioned Kupferman's timing in calling for legislation addressing noise pollution. It was an election year, and he suggested that there were enough causes already. "However, if it's something different you want, you might try the crusade against 'noise pollution' which is being spearheaded by Theodore R. Kupferman, a New York congressman" (Long Beach Press-Telegram 1966). There does not, however, seem to be a question about whether noise is in fact pollution. A news piece with the headline "Is Noise Pollution?" is in fact an argument for it as such; though, anticipating subsequent negotiation over its nature as pollution, the article suggests that a better term might be "auditory pollution," or the pollution of that which is heard (San Rafael Daily Independent Journal 1966).

Noise pollution persisted, and by the following year, it had arrived as a worldwide crisis grounded in an international geopolitics, as marked by the publication of an issue of the UNESCO Courier dedicated to the subject. Its nine editions—English (United Kingdom), French, Spanish, Russian, German, Arabic, English (United States), Japanese, and Italian—map the problem of noise, as articles address ways in which noise is being dampened, abated, curtailed, legislated, regulated, studied, and experienced in Switzerland, the USSR, the United States, Germany, France, and England. Images convey the negative experience of noise, whether the "noisiness" of a given situation or the auditory-emotional experience of hearing, or living with, such noise. Scooters turning a city corner reverberate in the narrow street of a medieval city, the volume of sound metamorphosed as a "feeling of power" ("Noise Pollution" 1967, 7). A photo of the interior of an early anechoic chamber, with long soft tubes of stuffed fabric lining walls and ceiling, a man holding something, perhaps a sound pressure–level meter, is a warning against total silence. Images from a wind tunnel test of supersonic aircraft shows whirling white lines—their sound also unfathomable. Three children hold their ears while a commercial aircraft flies overhead, clouds lit by the sun from behind; one boy smiles broadly, another more slightly, the third following the photographer's direction to gaze toward the sky with a look of concern. This photo is staged and likely a composite. Argentina's "noisy" city is conveyed by a tangle of signs hanging in a street, visual "noise" substituting for the sonic. Dust flies in front of an apartment building demolition—"noise" ("Noise Pollution" 1967, 9, 12, 15, 21). Another photo, titled "A Piece of Noise," realizes noise as object. A little mountain scene, it is "what sound would look like if it were solid instead of vibrations in the air" ("Noise Pollution" 1967, 23), the black shadow it casts in the circle of light behind it evoking Wagner's Valhalla. Figured as an iceberg, noise is cast into a future of climate change, icebergs melting, noise falling away.

Becoming Atmospheric

Noise pollution enters U.S. federal legislation as Title IV of the Clean Air Act Amendments of 1970. Emergent environmental imaginaries took shape in and through air and noise, attunements toward an atmospheric that, in orienting away from the durability of soil and water, moved above and beyond the surface of the Earth. In constituting noise as specifically airborne, humanly audible sound, environmental legislation gave noise an atmospheric—and indeterminate—status. Newly figuring attunements to the sensory, the audible, and the aerial, noise pollution is conceived of as something in need of regulation, a problem to be controlled, a risk from which people should be relieved. Performing what Foucault calls "governmentality" and Latour describes as "inscription," senators and experts come together and talk, governmental agencies are formed, bills are scripted and circulated, regulations are developed and enacted as law, bureaucratic scaffolding configured for their enforcement. Citizen experts and experts in acoustics, law, municipal governance, and the environment share their expertise, trying to make something of noise. Noise pollution draws together a public and its representatives, amplifying a relationship between elected officials and their constituents in which the latter appeal to the former to do something, and the former make government a protectorate of the people— a people in need of protection and education. Noise pollution is a PR campaign to help the public understand what it risks from a newly imagined environment that is, because of their own actions, already against them.

Noise, which began 1970 categorized as a concern of health and quality of life that might best be addressed through the Surgeon General's office, ended the year as an environmental concern. 1970 was in many ways the year of the environment. Highlights include President Nixon signing the National Environmental Policy Act (NEPA) on January 1, passage of the Environmental Quality Improvement Act on April 3, and celebration of the first Earth Day on April 20. The Environmental Protection Agency opened its office on December 2, and on the last day of the year, Nixon signed the Clean Air Act Amendments of 1970, Title IV of which addresses noise pollution. Over the course of the year, a flurry of noise control legislation was introduced, backed by Democrat congressman William Fitts Ryan and Republican senator Mark O. Hatfield.

Between January 20 and March 26, Ryan introduced three versions of the Noise Control Act of 1970 to the Committee on Interstate and Foreign Commerce.[15] The bill proposed an Office of Noise Control in the Office of the Surgeon General, which would issue grants to governmental agencies "for noise control and for research into the causes, effects, control, and abatement of noise."[16] It would also provide funds for demonstration projects and establish the Noise Control Advisory Council in the Department of Health, Education, and Welfare to oversee the activities of the Office of Noise Control. This would move the existing Noise Abatement Office from the FAA, shifting the emphasis from the source of noise to its experience, and from a particular type of noise, that of aircraft, to noise as a general concern. Ryan included an article that had been published that week in the *Washington Evening Star* on the problems of noise, which makes a case for its significance, if not on the level of pollution, as a "menace to health and well-being" that "if it does not threaten the environment, lowers the quality of the environment." From this perspective, "Noise, unlike ugliness and blight, can be measured with great precision."[17] Hearings on the proposed Clean Air Amendments were held concurrently by the Senate Subcommittee on Environmental Pollution (then the Subcommittee on Air and Water Pollution), a subcommittee of the Committee on Public Works chaired by Senator Edmund S. Muskie (U.S. Senate 1974a, iii).

By November 24, the noise control bill had moved to the Senate, where Mark O. Hatfield introduced the Noise Abatement Act of 1970: "A bill to promote public health and welfare by expanding, improving and better coordinating the noise abatement and control services of the Federal Government; to the Committee on Government Operations."[18] The EPA had recently been formed, and noise was now squarely pollution, in the domain of the environment rather than public health.[19] Hatfield had recently given a talk at the organizational meeting of the Noise Abatement Council of America titled "Noise, the Gathering Crisis," touching on topics that spanned urbanism, health effects, metrics, law, and labor (U.S. Senate 1974b, 127–32).[20] Insisting that pollution was *the* pressing concern of the twentieth century, Hatfield argued that noise "is reaching crisis proportions in the United States," its cumulative effects conveyed by what Leo Beranek called "'acoustic fatigue'" (U.S. Senate 1974b, 127–28). When Nixon signed the Clean Air Amendments of 1970 on December 31, it included the Noise Pollution and Abatement Act of 1970 as Title IV.

All discussion of why noise pollution was included in the Clean Air Act Amendments of 1970 is absent from the record. A note in the bill's legislative history states only, "Materials dealing with noise pollution have generally been excluded from this document. (Separate legislation dealing specifically with noise pollution has since been enacted, Public Law 92-574)" (U.S. Senate 1974a, vii).[21] Yet traces remain, providing hints about the inclusion of noise pollution in an act addressing air quality. It states: "The growing public awareness over the quality of the environment has spotlighted another form of pollution. Noise may prove to be the most difficult of all pollutants to control. Evidence regarding the effects of noise has been accumulating at a rapid pace, and Federal action has become appropriate" (U.S. Senate 1974a, 445). That noise is "pervasive . . . [and] omnipresent in our technological society in urban areas" (U.S. Senate 1974a, 446) indicated a need for regulation. Accordingly, bureaucratic concerns are addressed—the office to be formed (at this point named the Office of Noise Pollution Control and Abatement), its oversight (the secretary of health, education, and welfare, to be moved to the Environmental Protection Agency), and its work ("comprehensive study of noise, including its causes and effects, and to make recommendations to the Congress for appropriate legislation"; U.S. Senate 1974a, 446). The Noise Control Act of 1972 initiated the formation of the Office of Noise Abatement and Control (ONAC) under the EPA, with an immediate mandate of research. That ONAC did not include the word *pollution* in its name reflects a shift toward a more generalized notion that "all noise is pollution," a formulation only possible after noise had already become pollution.

Of Air, Not Air

The inclusion of noise pollution in the Clean Air Amendments suggests it is a dimension of air—air figured as a holder, carrier, or container of other things, air that might be either polluted or clean. Vibration is occluded conceptually, as the propagation of sound in and through materials other than air is excluded in practice (see chapter 5). Yet distinguishing the two as exclusive is a curious operation that is in itself productive. As Steve Goodman suggests, "By zooming into vibration, the boundaries of the auditory are problematized" (Goodman 2010, xvi). Hence *airborne* is produced as a singularity that is not coterminous with general acoustics: air becomes agent, carrying sound, as it were, rather than enmeshed with sound as a vibrating conductive medium. Air figured as such was crucial in shaping modern environmental imaginaries. Not only did air pollution drive environmental policy, air articulated a unique conceptualization of the environment (Dewey 2000). The dispersed nature of air made it impossible to contain, its pollution at once specified as "aerial contamination" and generalized as an "atmospheric condition" (Dewey 2000, 37, 40). While smoke had long been a problem in industrial cities from London to Pittsburgh, Los Angeles was the birthplace of a form of air pollution consisting of myriad, inseparable sources—of, that is, smog, a mysterious mixture whose components only became known after a decade of oil company–funded research by the Stanford Research Institute, which intentionally obfuscated both source and solution (and where psychoacoustician Karl Kryter later worked; Jacobs and Kelly 2008; also see chapter 2).

Taking at face value the title page of the Clean Air Act Amendments of 1970, it appears that noise is a pollutant of air. The list of air pollutants in the amendments runs from *A* to *X*. "Acetaldehyde, Acetamide, Acetonitrile, Acetophenone." I scroll down to the *N*s. "Naphthalene, Nitrobenzene, 4-Nitrobipheny, 4-Nitrophenol, 2-Nitropropane, N-Nitroso-N-methylurea, N-Nitrosodimethylamine, N-Nitrosomorpholine" (U.S. Environmental Protection Agency 2017). No "noise." Noise, it turns out, is not a pollutant of air. *If*, however, noise were an air pollutant, as its inclusion in the Clean Air Act Amendments of 1970 suggests, it might instantiate air, "materializing" something immaterial yet ever present, even in an immaterial form. Noise could be what Irigaray calls air's "entry into presence," its manifestation

(1999, 9, 14); however, noise is absent from air, and only wind and smoke bring air into human awareness through sensation. This is a different air than that of the Clean Air Act Amendments. Irigaray's air is absence; withdrawing from perception, it is "impalpable, imperceptible, invisible, insensible, unintelligible . . . while remaining the condition of possibility, the resource, the groundless ground" (1999, 5). Conversely, the Clean Air Act Amendments bring air into being as a kind of chemico-material mush, full of stuff that cannot be seen but can definitely be breathed, and that might be disarticulated through testing. Noise, however, is not rendered substance in the same way as the chemical but is cast in its own domain, a sonic environment whose amplitude might change, its aerial status implicit.

At the same time, Irigaray's discussion of air's instantiation points to something of what is at stake in the Clean Air Act Amendments, and in the relation between noise and air as figured in their categorization around pollution. While wind and smoke are air's "entry into presence" (Irigaray 1999, 9, 14), air is singular as a *medium* for light and sound: "No other element carries with it—or lets itself be passed through by—light and shadow, voice or silence" (1999, 8). Thus for Irigaray wind/smoke and light/sound differ in their relationship to air, the former a manifestation of air, the latter a substance differentiated from air.[22] This distinction is crucial for the status of noise pollution in the Clean Air Act. Smoke, an early way of understanding air pollution, is a substance that imbues air; inseparable from it, smoke pollutes air—it is a pollutant. Sound, however, is conceived of as independent, carried along by or moving through air without becoming or manifesting air, a conceptualization that is sustained as *noise pollution* is formulated in congressional hearings, EPA documents, and publications.[23]

Noise, ultimately, is what Theodore Berland in 1970 called "the third pollution"; its own form of pollution, it is considered comparable to yet distinct from air and water pollution. Perhaps most obviously, noise pollution differs from air and water pollution in its very formulation, with noise itself the pollutant. For the EPA, the differences between forms of pollution lay in the nature of an unpolluted atmosphere and the capacity for measurement. In 1972 noise pollution hearings, an EPA official explained,

> There are some fundamental differences between "air pollution" and "noise pollution." These are, in the main, the following: (a) We know the chemical constituents of a "normal" atmosphere, and (b) our sensing devices (because they respond to separate contaminants) can tell us how much of each given contaminant there is in the atmosphere at

a given point, as a function of time. . . . In noise pollution, however, (a) there is no such thing as a well-defined "normal atmosphere," and (b) the inputs from various sources cannot be separated by our sensing devices—the microphones—since there is only one "contaminant," the pressure waves. And not all pressure waves are even noise: some may be music or other desirable sounds. (U.S. Senate 1972, 357–58)

A sense of confusion percolates in the addled prose. Proliferating into contingencies, its author seems to be thinking through what noise pollution might be rather than making a definitive statement. Noise pollution begins to take shape in its difference from air pollution. It is defined principally through lack: a "normal atmosphere," differentiated contaminants, and social agreement about its value.[24] Each negative is indeterminate, without ground, a shifting atmosphere held steady only by the microphone. Noise pollution evinces a kind of weird realism of escaping forms of matter, of matterings that are in the air. Atmospheres proliferate across air and sound. The "acoustical environment," measurable as "ambient" sound levels, is what noise destroys or corrupts. It is, everyone seems to agree, vague, indeterminate, difficult to define, and even more difficult to measure—shifting sands on which noise pollution lies. The EPA recommends avoiding the term *ambient noise* entirely: "The problem of criteria for noise is complicated, and the effects are not as readily perceived as for air and water pollution. A criterion describing a 'cause and effect' relationship. Ambient levels of noise, unlike air, change and dissipate rapidly. The problem of 'ambient' noise is when and where?" (U.S. Senate 1972, 541). At the same time, the general formulation of sound as "pressure waves" and its measurement by the microphone as "sensing device" betrays a slippage across registers of perception, conveying how the specificity of noise pollution is crafted out of its potential meanings, and how something that is not air is nevertheless of air.

"Not air," noise pollution falls away as a legal category. In 1981 Reagan closed ONAC; the act remains but without an enforcing agency, a source of some anxiety to this day.[25] As of 1990, titles of the Clean Air Act Amendments are:

I   Air Pollution Prevention and Control
II   Emissions Standards for Moving Sources
III General
IV   Noise Pollution
IV-A Acid Deposition Control

V	Permits
VI	Stratospheric Ozone Protection

The list is Borgesian, evocative of the nonsensical categories (or modernist-rational categories of nonsensical things) of the Museum of Jurassic Technology. Following Foucault, Borges's "Chinese Encyclopaedia" breaks "up all the ordered surfaces and all the planes with which we are accustomed to tame the wild profusion of existing things" ([1970] 1994, xv). The order of material structured by the section titles of the Clean Air Act Amendments does not need to be rational—these are legislative acts addressing issues related to clean air as they arise. As the titles tell us, sometimes the issue is the pollutant (moving vehicle emissions), sometimes a part of the atmosphere that is threatened (ozone), sometimes a climatological effect of pollutants (acid rain), sometimes regulatory processes (permits) or just "general" issues. This arational list also does not provide many clues about the meaning or nature of noise pollution, other than its status as a category that was of concern at a particular moment. As an index of process, the act itself takes on structural curiosities. In 1990, Title IV-A: Acid Deposition Control was added to the Clean Air Act, without repealing existing Title IV.[26] There are now two section IVs.

Noise as Environmental

Meeting the mandate of Title IV of the Clean Air Act Amendments, in the latter half of 1971, public hearings were held across the country on sources and aspects of noise: construction noise; manufacturing and transportation noise; urban planning, architectural design, and noise in the home; standards and measurement methods; legislation and enforcement problems; transportation noise (rail and other); urban noise problems and social behavior; physiological and psychological effects; agricultural and recreational use noise; technology and economics of noise control; national programs and their relations with state and local programs (U.S. EPA Office of Noise Abatement and Control 1971a–h). An investigation into the scope of the problem of noise, the hearings ultimately led to the formation of ONAC in 1972 through the Noise Control Act. Coordinated by the EPA, the hearings mark a moment in which diverse and divergent issues and interests related to noise come under the umbrella of the environment. With a range of subjects, interests, engagements, and modes of attention, the hearings were spaces of attunement, where people came together to form something that is inherently formless. Noise pollution comes into being as something identifiable if indeterminate through encounters and exchanges, prepared speeches opening into questions. The hearings reorient ways of being in the world as some share their experiences, others their analyses, and still others their expertise or their ability to control the indeterminate. These are *public* hearings, and a speaker thanks the EPA for listening to them, and for listening to (acknowledging, taking seriously, doing something about) noise (U.S. EPA Office of Noise Abatement and Control 1971c, 24). People, interests, research, and experience coalesce. Distinguishing between sources and spaces of noise, the hearings draw together those who have made noise and its control a concern with others engineering modes of transportation and those hearing its noise. Speakers include acoustical engineers, urban planners, public health officials, lawyers, and medical doctors.

In July, the director of ONAC chaired a panel with an acoustical engineer from Bolt, Beranek and Newman (BBN); a professor from Clemson University; the director of Citizens for a Quieter City; a representative of the Governor's Council of the State of Virginia; and an environmental engineer from the School of Public Health at the University of North Carolina.[27] Addressing the subject of noise in construction, they heard from representatives of building material companies, contractors and machinery manufacturers, police, architects, the FAA, and citizen groups from Atlanta to Illinois. Someone spoke from United States Gypsum, a company that was also a member of the National Noise Abatement Council, a lobbying and PR organization principally comprising companies manufacturing building materials for acoustic treatment.[28] The Sierra Club sent a representative, as did the airport noise lobbying group N.O.I.S.E., formed by residents around La Guardia and Los Angeles International Airport. John Glenn represented Citizens for Clean Air. And there were citizens, members of the public speaking about their own experience, speaking for themselves and not on behalf of an organization, complaining of truck noise on recently built freeways and arguing for zero population growth.

Though the hearings were listening sessions, they were not open to comments from a general public. Instead, citizen experts—people bothered by noise who had learned an immense amount about its production, measurement, and control—were there as laypeople. A few of these, some of whom testified and served on the moderating panel asking questions of those testifying, founded civic groups on either the local or national level and authored books about noise directed toward the general public, educating readers of the threat of noise and urging them to lobby their elected representatives to do something about the burgeoning din.[29] In Dallas, a woman read a poem about trees. She argued for their use as acoustic treatment, only to be told that the study she referred to had been debunked; trees do not in fact lessen decibel levels, though their appearance makes people perceive a decrease in noise.

San Francisco hearings, ostensibly addressing the topic of standards and control, end up focusing on the specific and pressing noise concerns of Californians. Airports and freeways loom large as areas of concern. Los Angeles city councilperson Pat Russell, whose district included the airport and communities to its north and northwest, suggests that the definition of blight be expanded to include the effects of airport noise on homes. "In my district, we have really beautiful homes which are blighted in every way except physically." Shifting a definition of blight would, she claims, allow homeowners to take advantage of zoning changes rather than selling to the airport for a potentially devalued amount. A citizen group whose members include aerospace engineers lurks behind her proposal, an "organization . . . signing up almost every house within a group of about 800 houses to take part" in a project of changing "single-family residences into multiple use and into a commercial use." They are stymied in their project, however, by their inability to condemn property and by their lack of authority to enact eminent domain (U.S. EPA Office of Noise Abatement and Control 1971d, 69–73).

Noise as an environmental concern sharpens during these hearings. Randall Hurlburt, environmental standards supervisor for the City of Inglewood, and a regular speaker at federal noise hearings, is also there. He reports on their noise ordinance and on levels, precedents for other airport-adjacent areas. He lobbies the EPA to adopt policy related to community noise levels and noise standards for airports and other forms of transportation (U.S. EPA Office of Noise Abatement and Control 1971d, 369). As his testimony attests, airport noise had become pollution. "Although located near the Los Angeles International Airport, noise was not considered to be a severe problem until the advent of the jet aircraft in 1959. With its high-pitched scream during approach to landing and with the great increase in number of flights that has taken place during the last ten years, the jet airplane has made Inglewood today an extremely noise-polluted city" (U.S. EPA Office of Noise Abatement and Control 1971d, 366). Ellen Stern Harris of Beverly Hills, an environmental activist instrumental in the creation of the California Coastal Commission, repeats testimony presented at hearings in Los Angeles the previous year (Oliver 2006). She focuses on airport noise, a problem for Beverly Hills. Admitting her own sensitivity, Harris explains that she has very acute hearing. She calls out the ineffectiveness of LAX's Noise Abatement Commission—people were not calling its hotline anymore, they were calling her. But she rejects an offshore airport as a solution, contending that a different population would simply be exposed.[30] Moreover, the dredging required for the project would likely pose a similar risk as that of nuclear plants at sea—another threat to human health and the health of the Earth's resources that was atmospheric in both its physicality and its uncertainty.

THE MATTER OF NOISE POLLUTION

Noise had arrived. There was agreement that it was a problem and that it was pollution. Yet in these processes of fixing noise—as pollution, as a problem, as able to be regulated, as a subject of federal concern—something seeps out. In discussion of what, precisely, noise pollution is, it wavers. Acknowledged as emergent, it was also already a growing problem; a form of pollution, it was unlike other defined forms, its newness as a term related to its sonic quality. Senator John Tunney from Riverside, California, opens his 1972 hearings on noise pollution by describing it as a pressing problem that was growing louder every year. An effect of urbanization and of technological progress, noise was affecting as many as 80 million people. With most noise legislation related specifically to aircraft noise and sonic boom, he proclaims the need for comprehensive research and control of ambient noise (U.S. Senate 1972, 95).[31] *Noise pollution* designates something already "worsening" even as it opens a space for complaints—for a new mode of attunement toward an amplified atmosphere entangled with a listening self. All of this is channeled into noise as a legislative concern, a machine generating regulation, bureaucracy, and concepts.

At the noise pollution hearings, there are no dissenters among those testifying. Everyone is there to address noise as an environmental problem, to solidify noise as pollution, to treat noise pollution as a public health concern, and to regulate it through legislation. All are in agreement that noise is negative, a stance confirmed by its designation as pollution. Even its "subjective" nature does not lessen the overall problem of noise: of noise in general, of noise generalized, of noise as pollution. The doctor who loves the unmuffled roar of his motorcycle also argues that noise in general is bad. This is noise as "matter out of place," a contemporaneous notion of pollution that, in a generalizing logic of structuralism, continues to hold as a definition of noise (Douglas [1966] 2002; Serres 2010). And yet, while noise is assumed to be bad, or unwanted, how much, why, and how to systematize are points of discussion and debate. "Noise is hard to measure," one speaker says. There is a need for standards, though such standards have to be practical to apply. Police, for instance, were unused to working with standards, and one-hundred-foot distances for measurement of traffic sound were untenable in urban areas (U.S. Senate 1972, 101). And then, which metric? "The decibel scale used for measuring and evaluating sound is just as important as the procedures," but "in the area of noise we are confronted with conflicting schools of measurement" (U.S. Senate 1972, 102). Should ambient levels be the basis, or "single spiked noise events"? (102). Defining noise as pollution (or as any given thing) fixes noise, even if as a "relative" notion. Yet when treated ethnographically, noise comes into being in its definition.

Materiality surfaces in the regulation of noise pollution, physical qualities serving as defining principals. "Noise is not subject to easy regulation. Unlike the common air and water pollutants, noise does not accumulate in the environment. Noise is not subject to collective treatment and reduction processes" (U.S. Senate 1974b, 89). Noise's ephemerality casts it as pure negative, a negative that must, however, be given substance. As Dr. Belt, motorcycle aficionado and frequent speaker at legislative hearings related to noise, notes: "In dealing with the problem of environmental noise, we must make some very basic assumptions about what constitutes a healthy environment. The absence of observable effects of environmental noise does not constitute scientific proof of a safe environment as some would have us believe. The absence of proof proves nothing" (U.S. Senate 1972, 160).

The EPA presents a chart comparing air and noise pollution as a means of stressing why standards for air quality measurement do not apply to noise (table 3.1). The agency is the most expert witness in the room, in the position of smoothing over discrepancies and addressing misunderstandings. It stands above the fray, drawing together and synthesizing (or excising) the perspectives of engineers, politicians, medical professionals, and more. Air pollution had by then known and measurable substance and effects. "Made up of potential chemical substances that are both cumulative and residual, and subject to meteorological dispersion/diffusion laws," it could be measured in the environment and by its effects on humans; a high incidence of respiratory effects was evidence of air pollution as a public health concern. Yet, along with the difficulty of measuring ambient noise levels, the only verifiable effect of noise on the human body was hearing loss. Its

TABLE 3.1 Comparison of Noise Pollution with Air Pollution Regarding the Feasibility of Using "Ambient" Standards for Controlling Noise

Differences between Air and Noise Pollution, Which Lead to the Infeasibility of Using the Promulgation of National Ambient Standards as a Valid Federal Procedure for Controlling Noise

	Air pollution	Noise pollution
Characteristics	Made up of potential toxic chemical substances that are both cumulative and residual, and subject to meteorological dispersion/diffusion laws.	Physical energy characterized by sound pressure level and pitch (varied frequency). These sound energies are additive, decay with distances as a function of the inverse square law, and leave no residual after source termination.
Measurement in the environment	Measurement of time-concentration dose are [sic] easily accomplished with present equipment technology, since air pollutants do not vary rapidly with time or at short distances between monitoring stations.	Ambient measurements are extremely difficult, since noise is subject to rapid "on-off" source relationships and can vary appreciably at short distances from monitoring stations and in time at the same point.
Measurement of the human body	Presence of the polluting toxicant in the body is directly related to easily measurable ambient concentrations, and can be readily identified through physiological changes (e.g. large incidences of population respiratory attacks during high ambient chemical concentrations).	Other than for hearing impairment, there are no readily identifiable permanent physiological changes that can be solely related to noise exposure. Annoyance, on the other hand, can not be correlated with ambient noise levels alone, since it depends on time, frequency, and intensity relationships at the receiver along with socioeconomic factors.
Geographical control	Air quality regions were established to control ambient air pollutants traveling great distances and crossing geographical and political boundaries.	Noise travels only short distances from its source (i.e. sound energy decays as the inverse square of the distance from the source). Therefore, it can be controlled at or near the source and in most cases within existing political and geographical entities.

Source: U.S. Senate 1972, 356.

other effect, annoyance, depended on factors in excess of ambient noise levels—time, frequency, and intensity, along with, some suggest, socioeconomic factors, thus making annoyance too individualized to scale to the level of public health (see chapter 2).

At stake is the specific physicality of noise, described as "physical energy" that "decay[s] with distances" and "leave[s] no residual" (U.S. Senate 1972, 356). Noise pollution is mathematical, while air pollution is chemical, substantive. Because noise only travels a short distance, unlike air pollution, which crosses geographic and political boundaries, it is best controlled at the source under the authority of existing political entities. Air pollution, conversely, drew new geographies, and air quality regions had been organized to address it—governmental agencies like California's South Coast Air Quality Management Agency, whose job was to work with and across existing city and county offices to regulate and control air quality. Such comparison is not, it turns out, an argument against the legitimacy or existence of noise pollution. It is simply the precursor to a discussion of the specificity of noise as a factor of sound energy and human perception, such that "To affect the human environment perceptibly, reductions of 5 dB or more are required (or major reductions of exposure time)" (U.S. Senate 1972, 362).

Noise pollution is ultimately construed as a relationship between perception and measurable levels of environmental noise, a dynamic entanglement of sensory immediacy and externalized techniques of inscription. The EPA leans on the logic of the decibel, explaining that "The human ear . . . responds logarithmically"—facts that are relational, that draw out discrepancies between human hearing and sound measurement as coextensive dimensions of noise control. Thus, "the amount of decrease in sound *level* will be of subjective importance to human observers rather than the corresponding amount of decrease in sound energy." This logarithmic entanglement of perception and sound pressure is sustained in the EPA's "Operational Conclusions":

(a) When a noise environment is caused by several sources operating at once, (1) If the sources are at all approximately the same level, it does no good to abate one unless you abate them all. (This differs from the case of air pollution, where removing one of three equal sources would remove one-third of the contaminants.) (2) If one source is clearly dominant (6 to 10 dBA higher than the others), no perceptible reduction of the environmental level will result unless the dominant source is abated first. (U.S. Senate 1972, 362)

Noise, both in its perception and environmental measurement, is a factor of complex mathematical operations. It is relation rather than substance, an immaterial force for which vagaries of human perception rather than definable quantity provide the bases for measurement. This is at play in the statement, "It is the policy of the United States to promote an environment for all Americans free from noise that jeopardizes their health or welfare" (U.S. Senate 1972, 62). Noise pollution is thus a dynamic relationship between an environment "out there" and human health.

Atmospheric Bodies

Noise pollution composes the atmospheric even as it is itself atmospheric—invisible yet pervasive, persisting not in the air but in bodies, always and inherently subjective. Formulating noise as pollution casts the atmospheric as an entanglement of air and body. Across this continuum are both physiological effects of noise and "noise effects." A notion of a permeable body at the center of twentieth-century environmental imaginaries is captured doubly in noise pollution. The body subject to noise is described as "immersed in a sea of noises" (U.S. Senate 1974b, 556).[32] That immersion might be a problem relies on a permeable body, at threat from noise surrounding, and imbuing, it. At the same time, noise pollution helps stabilize the very notion of a body as permeable. As Linda Nash elaborates, "The notion of the body that has underwritten environmental activism since the 1960s . . . juxtaposes an awareness of the body's permeability and susceptibility to environmental change with the modernist desire for bodily purity" (2007, 212). In Los Angeles this proliferates across homes and neighborhoods, the permeability of the skin extending to the walls of the house through which aircraft noise might be heard, and the boundaries of a neighborhood newly porous to people no longer restricted by covenant or school segregation (see chapters 5 and 6).

In Silent Spring, a book credited with launching the 1960s environmental movement, Rachel Carson describes a body whose entire surface is now at risk.[33] Humans (and other species) do not simply inhale pesticides with their respiratory organs; rather, pesticides can be absorbed in and through the skin, permeating bone, blood, tissue, sinew, and organs. The body's largest organ, considered protection from that which is not-body, is newly figured as something that exposes a person to toxins or pollutants, invisible and potentially ever present in the atmosphere. "Dieldrin," Carson writes, "is about

5 times as toxic as DDT when swallowed but 40 times as toxic when absorbed through the skin in solution." Like radiation, chemicals cast "a shadow that is no less ominous because it is formless and obscure." The skin— and nose and ear—are not so much in air as of air. This body-air entanglement means that forces or chemicals in air are equally in bodies, within which there is "an ecology of the world" (Carson 2002, 25, 188, 189). In Carson's posthumously published children's book *The Sense of Wonder*, she draws out the permeability of a sensing body as she describes the scent of low tide, "seaweeds and fishes and creatures of bizarre shape and habit, of tides rising and falling on their appointed schedule, or exposed mud flats and salt rime drying on the rocks" that is "drawn into one's nostrils" or the whippoorwill's "monotonous night chant, rhythmic and insistent, sound that is felt almost more than heard" (Carson and Pratt 1956, 66, 69). Following Timothy Choy, "Thinking about the materiality of air and the densities of our many human entanglements in airy matters also means attending to the solidifying and melting edges between people, regions, and events" (2012, 128).

Noise pollution amplifies an atmospheric imaginary in which human bodies are porous, "melting edges" casting a division between flesh and air (or "sonic environment"). And while noise, like air pollutants and nuclear radiation, is invisible and pervasive, it is understood as uniquely impermanent, both as a quality of sound and as a social designation. During EPA hearings, noise was described as an "invisible, weightless, non-toxic pollutant" (U.S. EPA Office of Noise Abatement and Control 1971d, 86). "A Silent Pollution Affecting Us All," as an editorial headline proclaims, is perhaps a metaphor gone awry, an unruly extension of the senses continued in the piece itself: "There is a form of environmental pollution which is invisible. It is tasteless and odorless" (Eureka Times Standard 1972). Thus noise pollution does not offer itself as the floating cloud encountered in Don DeLillo's *White Noise* (1985), a visible threat everyone tries to escape by car as it might, if inhaled, cause illness. Noise is more insidious, albeit like pesticides, variable, unquantifiable, and unknown, with potentially unfelt effects that nevertheless persist or accumulate.[34] As such, it resonates with other invisible threats of its time. This was the era in which cigarettes became known as hazards to one's health, and letters from readers warning of the risks of smoking followed articles about the threat of noise (Rosen 1974). More recently the detrimental entanglement of bodies and atmosphere has been characterized as the chemosphere, amplifying the problem of "exposure" (Mitman, Murphy, and Sellers 2004; Shapiro 2015).

Noise differs from other forms of pollution in which the modifier is that which is polluted. Suturing such discrepancies, a notion of persistence based in an additive logic affords commensurability across divergent forms of pollution. This logic grounds an urgency about the problem of noise even as it defers the crisis to the future. Variations on acoustical physicist and antinoise campaigner Vern Knudsen's statement circulated widely: "If the noise we make keeps increasing at the present rate, it will be as deadly in thirty years in some of our downtown cities as were the Chinese tortures for executing condemned prisoners" (U.S. Senate 1974b, 133).[35] Elsewhere, in an alarmist tongue-in-cheek statement, he extrapolated that, at current rates of increase, noise levels would reach 225 db in 2029, far exceeding 160 db, which "will burn the hair off your head and chest or raise the temperature of your body to a lethal level," or "the 193-db barrier when you have complete modulation of the environment" (Knudsen 1955, 11). At the same time, noise is differently additive in bodies than other pollutants. As James Tunney stated at hearings on noise pollution that he chaired,

> Although noise . . . does not last in the environment for a long period of time, there is no question that the person who is the recipient of that noise, if it is excessive, and a danger to public health, can have lasting results, and can be permanently affected, and as a result of the noise he has received. So you are in a sense dealing with a similar problem to air and water pollution, and in that sense, the impact on the individual can be permanent. (U.S. Senate 1972, 441–42)

Crucially, it is not noise, or sound, that builds up in a body (which would parallel chemicals, and which is usually challenged); instead, it is the effects of noise, and, if this is annoyance, the effects of annoyance. These have consequences for things that do build up in the body: muscle tension or blood pressure (with pressure a somewhat different notion of "building up"). And though epidemiological studies of the health effects of noise tend to be serially dismissed, generally on the basis of poor correlation, there remains agreement that noise is "annoying."

With noise cast as pollution having entered the lexicon and legislation, another lawyer revisited *U.S. v. Causby* to argue for the legal grounds of noise itself on the basis of a metrics of annoyance. Joseph J. Alekshun Jr. writes, "the law's reverence for the tangible and concrete has made it insensitive to the growth of such invisible agents of disruption as noise. Early judgments of nuisance value remain in authority for today's noisemakers." Maintaining that the property line in the air is "elastic," he shifts the grounds of that line from jurisdiction to annoyance, from governmentality to perception. Drawing on (by then developed) metrics for noise measurement, Alekshun explains how this can be standardized: "The level of aircraft noise and the number of flights are both factors in the production of annoyance. In principle then, a consistent application of the *Causby* rule makes the property line elastic and jointly subject to the two factors" (Alekshun 1969, 741). Annoyance thus serves as a means of registering "noise itself" rather than extra-noise effects, casting the atmospheric as an airbody continuum in which sound is immanent in its medium, its perception significant as a register of sonic presence, a materialization of its immateriality. *Annoyance*, and more generally *the subjective*, continues to ground noise pollution as a category as it is taken up in legislation, regulation, and management. Though on the one hand this serves to make noise pollution a fundamentally unstable category, resting, as it does, on perception and thus unreproducible in its immanent immediacy, when fixed in metrics, *annoyance* is not challenged as grounds (chapter 2). Drawing noise as nuisance into noise as pollution, annoyance becomes a register of "the environment," establishing the latter's anthropocentric basis while casting human affect as entangled with external phenomena—in this case audible airborne sound whose simultaneous intangibility and pervasiveness make it most threatening.

Sounds of bird song, or the "quietest" place on Earth, are increasingly indices of climate change, marking disappearing habitats, species loss, and fantasies of a nonanthropogenic world (Krause 2015; Schafer 1994).[36] Noise's atmospheric qualities are equally significant to understanding how sound registers environmental thought in an era of climate change. As that which mars nature recordings, the wind noise in the microphone, and the driving concern for R. Murray Schafer's soundscape project, noise is also productive in and of itself, crafting the atmospheric conceptually and physically. The pervasive and systemic nature of noise pollution prefigures an atmospheric conceptualization that affords a generalized concept of *climate*. As a sensory experience, noise prepares us for the unwanted, undesirable, and unpleasant sensations of climate change—an atmosphere becoming too hot for human habitation, in which the comforts of contemporary life are potentially lost, smog hanging in air increasingly difficult to breathe. Moreover, like noise, climate change is inherently uncertain and indefinite. Yet the spatiotemporal scale of noise limits its perdurance as a concern both in itself and for environmental imaginaries. This has consequences not only for the parameters of "noise" that count as noise pollution but for the import of the category and its relation to environmental thought. If noise pollution had been based on something like "whistlers" (Kahn 2013), its status as an invisible, and generally inaudible, threat might have taken on a hemispheric scale. Instead, noise pollution falls away: there is no place for it in a totalizing rubric of climate change.

4   MURMURS: EXPERIMENTS IN GLITCHING

Amorphous

Origin: from the Greek a-morphe: without form, or shapeless (Dictionary.com, s.v. "amorphous"; *Oxford English Dictionary*, s.v. "amorphous")

"Having no determinate shape, shapeless, unshapen; irregularly shaped, unshapely" (*Oxford English Dictionary*, s.v. "amorphous")

Formless (Bataille 1985)

"having neither definite nor apparent structure" (Dictionary.com, s.v. "amorphous")

Vague (Fara 2000)[1]

"Belonging to no particular type or pattern; anomalous, unclassifiable" (*Oxford English Dictionary*, s.v. "amorphous")

Indefinite (Solà-Morales 2014)

"Unshapely" materials include chocolate mousse, shaving cream, mayonnaise, and mud, whose "particles jam collectively" (CNRS 2008). Oobleck—or "goop"—made of cornstarch and water, fills the sensory tables of preschools across America. Its surface appears solid, but slide your fingers into it at an angle and it wobbles and oozes across your palm, dripping off in blobs that meld seamlessly back into the substance below, entirely indistinct.

ATMOSPHERIC CONDITIONS

Air density—the relative amounts of nitrogen and oxygen. Humidity—the amount of water in the air. Wind—the atmosphere regaining balance. Weather disrupts noise measurement. For LAWA noise monitors, wind at Ontario Airport—Santa Ana winds—"corrupts data." L.A. County Public Health Department engineers bring a weather station along with their noise-monitoring equipment and will throw out data "if marred." For the sake of noise measurement and mitigation, objects block sound. Atmospheric conditions, on the other hand, might amplify it; clouds, for instance, send sound waves back to the ground, "like water waves against Jello," an environmental engineer said. A July 8, 1952, account of complaints received by the airport explained that "the reverberation of the aircraft taking off in low pitch, flying under the overcast in a Westerly direction, intensified the noise, which lead people adjacent to Imperial Highway area, to believe that the aircraft was actually flying over their homes."[2] This is a common occurrence around LAX, where fog is a regular atmospheric condition because of the airport's proximity to the ocean.

A meteorologist explained that fog *refracts* rather than *reflects* sound, bending and distorting sound "waves." While significant as a dimension of experience, such atmospheric interactions with sound are excised from noise measurement, the objectivity of which is based on the least varying bases of perception and atmosphere. Veneklasen and Associates' 1968 study, *Noise Exposure and Control in the City of Inglewood, California*, presented eighty-eight rather than one hundred samples because "twelve recordings of Boeing 727 aircraft were made on a day in which weather conditions resulted in large sound attenuation at high frequencies." The relative humidity of 18 percent was sufficiently less than the usual 70 percent humidity for the area, which skewed the decibel readings lower for the two higher-octave bands tested. Because a relative humidity of 18 percent occurred only 1.3 percent of the time, they "felt justified in deleting this data as non-representative of the noise in these two octave bands" (42).

Maintaining atmospheric conditions that do not alter sound too much can be a messy endeavor, both mathematically and materially. At the Western Electro-Acoustic Laboratory in Santa Clarita, when testing materials for sound absorption, it is important to maintain the humidity level throughout the process, and to maintain a level that affects sound absorption the least. Previously the lab was at the firm's offices in Santa Monica, where, closer to the ocean, it was more humid. And because humidity affects sound absorption unevenly, they need to maintain humidity around the range where its effect is "flatter." As the engineer said, "the test standard requires that for the transmission loss test it has to be at least 30 percent. For this test it has to be at least 40 percent. So we have a humidifier." Laughing, he says, "We often end up just throwing water on the floor."

The industrial hygienist for the Los Angeles County Department of Health told me that the desert—at least when it is not windy—is the ideal place to take noise measurements.

THE MATTER OF AIR

According to Malcolm C. Henderson, Vern Knudsen's study of the effects of temperature and humidity on the absorption of sound and air "made it dramatically evident" that "sound, like light and electromagnetic radiation in general, became a tool for the investigation of the properties of matter" (Henderson 1963, 28; Knudsen 1931). In other words, the quality of matter mattered, and it mattered on the molecular level. Though limited by physical properties—"No one can boil a kettle by shouting at it, whether watching it or not!" (Henderson 1963, 29)—Knudsen's discovery was significant for materializing air through sound. Air newly mattered, becoming matter.

The air of the laboratory was distinguished from the "open air," where "a whole battery of unwanted effects arises to obscure measurements that would lead to understanding the logical, regular, and predictable behavior of the molecules. In the laboratory, we can neglect thermal inhomogeneities and turbulence, which cause refraction, the presence of fog or dust, reflection from the ground or other objects, scattering and diffraction around buildings or trees, and, of course, also the inverse-square law that spreads the sound beam" (Henderson 1963, 30).

Around the time Knudsen was studying how temperature and humidity affected sound in air, he drafted an essay, "Proposed Standards for the Control of Noise" "for *American Standards Magazine*" (as scrawled on a corner of the title page). "The value of quiet" has been demonstrated: workers are more efficient and less annoyed, profit lost to the company weighed against the cost of acoustical treatment. And though there were noise meters, there were no standards, making their measurements relative. Subcommittees of the Acoustical Society of America had been formed to tackle four dimensions of this problem: "fundamental acoustical measurements, nomenclature and definitions, the absorption and insulation of sound, and the measurement of noise."[3] And so it began.

AIR, SOUNDED

Toshiya Tsunoda's field recordings are "pieces of air" (2001). An airplane is heard "crossing the sky both by its reflection on the ground, and by the original sound wave undergoing mixing and interference," suggesting, "Perhaps this airplane could be interpreted as tracing geographical features with its sound." His field recordings reconceptualize the work of the microphone as a sensing perceiver of airspace. They emphasize sound as atmospheric, with specific qualities shaped by air. Air is produced as space by sound. Air is *sounded*. Sound is *aired*. The microphone is a *sounding* device.

PINK NOISE

I watch silently as an engineer holds a noise measurement device in the air, moving it slowly around the room at shoulder height. The loud SSHWSSS-HSHSHHH of the pink noise blasting from the speaker dangling off the basket of the cherry picker that had been audible through the door is now diffused in the bedroom in which we stand, a teen girl's room with cheap perfumes on the vanity, a graduation photo, an Elie Wiesel novel under the bedside table. The room is small and messy. I am directed to be quiet. We stand still in a clear area and do not touch anything. Outside, another microphone is detached from the monitor, attached to the top of an extension pole with gaffer's tape, the monitor secured closer to the bottom. The microphone is held against the stucco of the exterior wall to avoid the unpredictability of sound's "bounce" off a surface. It is as if the microphone, in an intimate alliance, listens with the wall, hears what the wall hears. This is not so much the sound of the wall but that of airborne sound as it encounters the wall. Later the pink noise will be adjusted by mathematical calculation to replicate the sound of a jet. These fly over as the test ensues. Also loud, their high-frequency whine distinguishes them from the wash of sound from the speaker.

With noise measurement metrics grounded in human audibility and the microphone as basis for noise measurement, the ear is the physiological access point for annoyance, the (anti)foundational basis for noise pollution. Similar to gas warfare (Sloterdijk 2009), one organ is the gateway for both the medium and the pollutant. In this case, the ear is figured as the singular organ through which the body experiences sound. Kahn writes that the tympanic model is "incompletely anthropomorphic" insofar as it excludes the nervous system. As he elaborates, the ear is a transducer that not only registers sound but transforms it through its own acoustical vibrations, or "otoacoustic emissions" (Kahn 2013, 57). Hence hearing entails not only a process of transduction-in-degree but two moments of transduction-in-kind. "The first transduction-in-kind occurs when the mechanical movement of the inner hair cells of the cochlea open ion channels that excite electrochemical signals in the nervous system and brain. The second transduction-in-kind occurs when the nervous system, in very rapid response to an incoming sound (and sometimes on its own, unprovoked), sends signals back to motile cells on the cochlea that create vibrations in the fluid of the inner ear, setting up subtle dynamics beneficial for pitch discrimination and amplification" (Kahn 2013, 56). Thus what humans hear is specific to the process of perception, as any sound "out there" is shaped, added to, and altered by a physiological mesh of flesh, hair, bone, energy, nerves, and brain. What we perceive as sound is its bodily immanence.

The noise measurement microphone sustains an atmospheric logic. Registering (exclusively) airborne sound, it limits "noise" to the "tympanic," modeling acoustic technology on the ear and reducing the ear to the eardrum (Sterne 2003, 31–35). A notion of sound as pressure draws together air and ear through a common register. To objectify (though not replicate) a messy variety of human perception, the microphone used for noise measurement is one with "very even calibration"—a half-inch microphone with a stainless steel diaphragm, originally developed at Bell Labs. These devices might be installed on poles around an airport, set up on tripods, or mounted alongside an airplane engine.

Though the eardrum is the only "skin" the microphone models, the ear has a more expansive meaning for divergent aspects of noise. Even as the noise-monitoring microphone—and hence metrics of noise measurement—is reduced to the tympanic, the inner ear and cilia remain significant insofar as hearing loss is cited as the primary and principal health effect of noise, and occupational safety concerns contributed heavily to the formulation of noise pollution.

Yet the project of objectifying the subjective was not to make a micro-phone that better matched the transductive work of the cilia of the inner ear and the translation by the brain, but to ground the category of noise in the physiological range of human hearing and the relative annoyance of noises.

SOUND ANALYZER

The formulation of sound as pressure waves and its measurement via the microphone as sensing device betrays a slippage across techno-rational registers, conveying how the specificity of noise pollution is crafted out of its potential meanings, and how something that is not air is nevertheless of air.

The microphone transforms sound into signal, now calculable by a noise monitor or measurement device. This sound analyzer (or one like it) was used for a 1968 community noise survey in Inglewood, California, by Veneklasen and Associates (figure 4.1). One of the engineers was murdered as he was monitoring overnight noise levels. His co-worker's voice breaks as he tells me this, almost fifty years later.

FIGURE 4.1 Portable sound analyzer, Western Electro-Acoustic Laboratory. Photo by author.

A FOLD

"The bandwidth of human audibility is a fold on the vibratory continuum of matter" (Goodman 2010, 9). In discussions of noise measurement and control, sound is defined as waves, pressure, and energy, used differentially to create links with other domains: the ear, the microphone, other forms of pollution. Documents explain that sound travels through air, water, and buildings. Yet only airborne sound is registered by sound measurement instruments, and only airborne sound is accounted for in acoustics testing of sound insulation and sound absorption—of materials (doors, windows, wall panels) used to make quieter architectural interiors.

Nonetheless, vibration is a central feature of noise complaints, and of lawsuits against airport noise, which list cracks in walls and ceilings, tiles that have fallen off walls and patios, cracked windows. Bodily ways of hearing and sounding shift listening from the ear and extend beyond the audible.

A residential soundproofing program around San Francisco International Airport had to be adjusted to address low-frequency vibration, following sustained complaints of residents living in the wake of the flight path. An acoustics engineer explained, "We've done some work near railroads, a train passing by you get vibration, it transmits through the ground into the structure, reradiates, so you can actually get airborne noise produced by vibration transmitted into the structure." And when you say "airborne sound not vibration" to a sound artist or acoustician, their immediate response is, "all sound is vibration."

BETWEEN VIBRATION AND PRESSURE

Noise wavers between vibration and pressure. The decibel is defined as a metric of sound pressure. Francis Fox, Department of Airports, insisted that there was a problem with the decibel. The airplane manufacturers had used it to measure the noise (volume) of the propeller plane and the jet engine and reported that they were the same. Yet he—along with airport neighbors—had learned from experience that they were not. Instantiated in the membrane of the noise measurement microphone, sound as pressure also suggests a notion of sound as touch. Insofar as touch is distributed across the body's surface, sound as pressure does not presume an ear as the organ of sensory perception but expands to an auditory beyond the ear. That "the vibration sense may also mediate information as to the material of the stimulus-object" (Zigler 1926, 336) adds a sensory, haptic dimension to Mary Douglas's discussion of the difference between one thing and another (1994). 1971 EPA public hearings on noise pollution emphasize "citizen pressure," a subject, also, of the 1968 novel *Airport* (Hailey 1968; U.S. EPA Office of Noise Abatement and Control 1971c).

EXPERIENCE

The experience of airplane noise recedes, withdraws. Not because one cannot access another person's experience. Most of us can experience the whine of a plane engine departing or landing, hear the roar as the giant planes used for international flights seem to hover over Lennox Park, just for a moment, before continuing their descent toward the airport runways. A conversation pauses until the plane passes overhead, attention turning away from sky and toward the other person. Sometimes the air shakes, the ground buzzes, the tiles lift off the roof of a house. Children continue their games, not even glancing up. On the beach, as the planes depart, it feels dirty more than noisy, the soot of engine oil blackening the sand, dots of soot like those found on plants near freeways, next to highly trafficked streets. And one can listen to others' experience and understand something of it. But accounts of residents' experience are largely lost. Studies are shelved. Transcripts of closed-door hearings before a Los Angeles judge in the mid-1970s, the only lawsuit that awarded damages for the effects of aircraft noise on bodies—sleep, stress, sex life—have been destroyed. Past the decade they are required to be saved and lacking greater significance, they are not to be found in any city, county, or state law library in the state of California. The trial surfaces as trace. Yvonne Brathwaite Burke refers to it in congressional testimony, in papers now buried in her archive.

Noise composes a tangle of affect, unraveling into feelings that falter and threaten to fail, reforming in narrative. Jan Dailey woke with a knot in her stomach every morning with nerves over telling her personal story to a judge—the story of how her libido had suffered. She is undone, exhausted. A letter she sent to a prominent sexologist describing an article she was planning on submitting to the magazine *Sexology* on the effects of stress on sexual health can be found in her papers in the special collections of a local university. In it, she wavers. Perhaps, she suggests, the stress came from the long and involved struggle against the airport on the part of her neighbors, a struggle in which she was ostensibly involved and that made many mothers feel guilty for neglecting their families.

I tried to find her testimony and that of her neighbors. Day after day I sat in a basement corridor of the Los Angeles County Hall of Records, waiting my turn to look, again, at the microfilm records of the trial's preliminary findings. I stared at graying paint and flooded carpet; old, itchy mismatched office chairs; an occasional roach ambling about, impatient, as I envisioned the rolls of microfilm held for me on the other side of the counter. Each time I took a number and waited my turn, after the man requesting his divorce papers who was there with his father, the professional dog trainer, after others waiting for property deeds, birth certificates, marriage licenses, all the stuff of life that is filed with the county and deposited in the bowels of a building staffed by women who know exactly where to find what they're looking for but will not give anything up. Each record requested is given a long thirty minutes by bureaucratic workers whose job was not to answer questions but who finally told me that the microfilm they had would not contain court transcripts, would not contain the testimony of neighbors describing their experience of airport noise.

The family annoyed by aircraft sound also watched television, which, as of 1960, was found in almost every American home and was reportedly watched, on average, five hours a day (Spigel 1992, 1). Not being able to hear the TV or radio was, for those surveyed, the most frequent and annoying effect of aircraft noise (National Opinion Research Center 1954; Wyle Laboratories 1970b). Less frequent but still annoying was the flickering image, a cancellation effect caused, as *Audio* magazine explained, by "different transit times of direct and reflected signals" (figure 4.2), a problem that could be resolved by having "two or more tuners connected together" (figure 4.3). Moreover, "It is the reflections from flying man-made objects (as opposed to flying saucers) which are the major factor"—namely, airplanes (Von Recklinghausen and Borish 1960, 50, 48). Even as TV required the closure of the home, bolstering its fortification against the outdoors, its technology of radio reception situated it in the air, drawing a continuum across indoor and outdoor atmospheres in which new risks might arise. And, as Spigel reminds us, watching television, or listening to audio recordings, whether on LPs or radio, made people viewers—and listeners—of electricity.

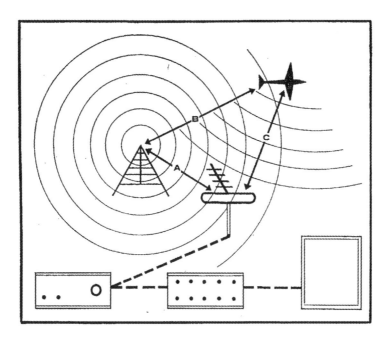

FIGURE 4.2 "Cancellation effect due to different transit times of direct and reflected signals" (Von Recklinghausen and Borish 1960, 50).

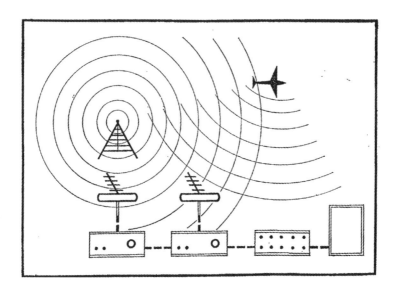

FIGURE 4.3 "With two spaced antennas and two FM tuners, connected as described, only the output from the viable signal is fed to the amplifier" (Von Recklinghausen and Borish 1960, 50).

TOUCH FROM A DISTANCE

"Hearing is a way of touching at a distance" (Schafer 1994, 11). R. Murray Schafer's love of sound is conveyed through a poetics of perception interwoven with a bluntly normative rejection of noise. A notion of "touch from a distance" suggests an intentionality in the relationship between a sound source and its perception, as if a long finger stretches from an airplane engine to tickle an eardrum: a pleasurable caress of the takeoff whine, a nail scratching the cilia of the inner ear. Schafer draws together senses of touch and hearing, the former informing an understanding of the latter, emphasizing the immanence of perception rather than a difference between sense and thing sensed, a difference amplified by the object form of recorded sound and by a physics of acoustics that divides sound and hearing.

Touch, like hearing, is coextensive with somatic senses of proprioception, kinesthesia, and vestibular sense, as the "haptic expands the reach of touch from cutaneous surface to more inwardly-oriented senses" (Paterson 2007, 4). These are bundled under a "sixth sense," along with other senses European modernity did not have room for. Proprioception and thermoception are coterminous with hearing: the former a state of the inner ear, the latter a sensation produced by low frequencies. Thus sound as touch is a dimension of bodily orientation in the world. This is at once a vestibular sense and Lefebvre's assertion that space is heard before it is seen (1991, 199–200).

In 1928, acoustician Vern Knudsen published an article titled "'Hearing' with the Sense of Touch," the results of a study testing people's ability to distinguish differences in volume and pitch with their right index finger (or in the case of a man whose right hand had been injured in the war, their left). Knudsen distinguishes between vibration and pressure, stating that the finger's sensitivity to variations in the intensity of vibration is not the same as the "feeling of pressure, or any of the other cutaneous sensations." That the finger's ability to feel vibratory variations is of an order similar to the ear suggested, for Knudsen, that the sense of vibration is prior, genetically, to the sense of hearing. Moreover, he remarked as an aside, his findings had potential consequences for a general theory of sound—a perceptual rather than communication model, sound energy rather than electromagnetic energy, "the 'resonance' theory of hearing" rather than the "'telephone' theory" (1928, 336). Forty years later he became a vocal campaigner against noise pollution, unique in his field, as often when asked about noise as pollution, acoustical engineers say, "I don't get into that, I'm just an engineer."

A SENSE OF VIBRATION

That distinguishing between rough and smooth surfaces is a sensation of vibration led psychologists in the early part of the twentieth century to argue for a *sense* of vibration. They were challenged on the grounds that the human body lacked an organ specific to the perception of vibration. Yet a debate lingered over whether nerves have a singular sense for vibration, or whether they always "mediate several different qualities of sensation" (Zigler 1926, 335). The vibration of a finger moving across differently textured surfaces and the ability of deaf people to "hear" music by putting their hands on musical instruments as they are played draws together senses of touch and hearing. "The vibration sense is designated by some writers an independent form of sensibility. Others identify it as a form of stimulation of deep sensibility, or as a peculiar form of stimulation of cutaneous pressure (von Frey). As early as 1846 Weber designated these experiences intermediates between touch and hearing" (Zigler 1926, 334).

INFRASOUND

Ione Maxwell worked in a federally funded research lab, where she found joy in her quiet job "fabricating complex custom-built glass apparatus." Maxwell testified in the fourth set of public hearings on noise held by the nascent Environmental Protection Agency, describing the low-frequency infranoise generated by "motors, generators, boilers, ventilators, positive displacement blowers, air conditioners, ducts, compressors" in areas beyond the quiet area where she worked, sending her glass rods vibrating "in constant, varying, erratic motion. . . . [S]trange patterns appeared on the surface of a bottle of mercury—as though it were being squeezed." Trying to find relief, she wore headphones that had the effect of amplifying low-frequency sounds. At the time of her testimony, she was on medical leave, "bone weary" due to the cumulative effect of this noise. It had, she explained, affected her depth perception—her head rang, her ears filled and popped, it was "impossible to think or concentrate. Or escape." The doctor said it was all in her head. So she investigated, reading European studies on low-frequency sound. She began to understand its effects on her body, rendering the sensory sensible as she became an expert in acoustics. A doctor on the panel was sympathetic: "She's a human being and she shouldn't have to suffer just because her own body is more sensitive perhaps than others to this particular pollutant" (U.S. EPA Office of Noise Abatement and Control 1971d, 111–14).

In the court of claims hearing, when they are not talking about the value of Causby's property, or interrogating neighbors' memories about when precisely the runways were extended, or debating whether the leaves on the trees were moved by the planes flying overhead, or asking Tinie Causby whether she can distinguish an army plane from a mail plane, or calculating the economics of eggs, they talk about the chickens. What did the chickens experience, did they really fly into the wall, could they have exploded upon flying into the wall, were they truly frightened, how might fright be evident in their bodies? They describe watching their chickens running as a plane takes off just above their building. They describe seeing them fly into the wall with such force that they die. They describe this as "exploding." They carry them away, dead, silent. Their lawyers report, "Plaintiffs have picked up at times as many as 6 to 10 chickens a day killed by flying into the walls from fright caused by the planes."[4] Tinie testifies, "I have stood and watched them jump against a wall and saw when they were bursted and I have seen him carry off half a dozen at a time when they had died."[5] And a neighbor recalls, "The chickens were jumping and splashing and going up against the side of the house and so on."[6] The intimacy of their account registers an interspecies entanglement in which chickens shift from commodity to companion species. The touch of the dead chicken is weighted with care and remorse, tinged with worry in the face of financial cost yet pregnant with empathy for the chicken's experience, so close to their own. And even if Thomas Causby used a shovel, scooping them up in a heap, their weight would have weighed on him, impressed itself on his arms and shoulders, his back stooping and straightening, removing the chickens from the coop and relieving the still living poultry of the presence of their now still companions.

The head of the Poultry Department at North Carolina State College in Raleigh takes the witness stand. He says it is possible for a chicken to fly against the wall "with enough force to cause death" . . . "but not to burst them open." The egg can burst and, if in the ovary duct, it will cause death. And though "fright would leave no lesions whatever," and "It is not like a disease, no abnormalities you could pick up," nonetheless, he concludes, "fright is detrimental."[7]

I find myself searching the internet for what a frightened chicken sounds like. Someone has posted "26 Sounds That Chickens Make and What They Mean" (Damerow 2019). I wonder if an airplane would be considered a predator, provoking a "Kuh-kuh-kuh-kuh-KACK!" Or if it would be mistaken for a raptor, causing a rooster to make a loud warning sound that tells the other chickens to run for cover. Or would the noise of the plane, not just the dark mass flying above, cause the hens to make "help me calls"—loud, long calls of distress that a chicken makes as it is being captured and carried away. In other words, was Thomas Causby also listening to—not only with—his chickens as they flew against the wall of the building in fright?

The Causbys' experience is also described as "fright," an emergent "affective relationality" apparent in the slippage between their experience and that of their chickens (Lien 2015, 6). Tinie Causby says, "I have just scringed for it time and time again since that baby has been there." Though their experience is given the same name, their response differs from that of their chickens. They pace during the night. They do not throw themselves against the wall. Their eggs do not break in their ovaries. They go to a lawyer. They sell the chicken farm and move. He becomes a barber, she remains a house-wife.[8] Fright, like noise, is atmospheric; an amplification of listening as affect, the force of an encounter registered with the physicalization of fear, ultimately it falls away, its externalization in action called into question.

SOUND AS TOUCH

I want to recuperate sound as touch, own it, dwell in it and in its possibilities, potentialities, openings, frictions. Sound as touch is not "touch from a distance." It is a molecular entanglement, an intermeshing of energy and flesh. Considering sound as touch, rather than vibration, draws sound into flesh, flesh into air, air into glass, glass into hand, as energy that is audible becomes felt (by its absorbing matter) as heat. Ear cilia meet sound, and, as both are moved, "it is difficult to say just where I end and world begins" (Ihde 1973, 99). Though I prefer physics over phenomenology—different ways of getting at a phenomenon.

Sound as touch disallows a separation of sound as thinglike, able to be represented in fixed drawings of squiggly lines, the solidity of a cone. There is no object to sound as touch, there is only sensation, proximity, the coming together of differently moving electron fields that do not actually touch but rather repel one other with different levels of force (Barad 2012, 209), as all electrons do, even within what we understand to be finite, contained, differentiated forms of matter.

We are "always touching something," a five-year-old says—with the punchline "air!" There is never a *between*—in which "Between our touch and being touched lies the organization or the 'constitution' of space in its concrete experiential form" (Ihde 1973, 100). That this touch, of human-air, human-sound, sound-air is a field of swarming, resisting electrons is both "the indeterminacy at the heart of being" and "the inhuman that therefore we are" (Barad 2012, 219, 218).

WIND NOISE

I make recordings of wind noise: the *always* unwanted sound, the "noise" that disrupts, obscures, erases content. (*Everyone* uses windscreens.) The recordings are an engagement with the transparency of the microphone, as common to both noise measurement and field recording. They are an effort to reveal the microphone as technology by disrupting it. Wind noise is sound as touch—this is the sound produced by touching the microphone, whether by finger, breath, or air.

These recordings do not capture the sound *of* wind, but the sound wind makes on the microphone, the sound the microphone makes when touched by wind. Though electronic, the sound is not uniform. Wind is a force with variation. Wind masks but not fully. We can hear sounds connected indexically to their source: Cars pass by. Planes fly overhead.

These recordings are process, methodological: an investigation of the microphone.

They are a way of learning about microphones and the recording devices to which they are attached.

They are a way of experiencing sound as subjective sensation and objective measurement.

They are about atmospherics and im/materialities—forms and forces of energy.

INTO THE WIND

September 11, 1974. Mothers declare war on the FAA. They propose a kite-flying competition, with an award for the child who can fly theirs highest, even, perhaps, into the path of an incoming airplane. The noise inside the school is excessive, and the mothers are tired of waiting for some relief for their children. Theirs is a struggle over the skies, fought from the ground, a struggle over noise generated from the sky though experienced on the ground. Imagine a kite with a two-hundred-foot string. Let out slowly, the string rubs against a girl's finger as the kite tugs and pulls away, ascending into the sky. It's nearly out of sight, a speck against the clouds—did it brush the enormous belly of the plane? All the anger and frustration of residents annoyed by airport noise is carried in this fragile child's toy, paper and wood and string, aloft, coming to life on the wind. A line of flight, an opening, a worlding, the kite is a "trajectory of movement" (Ingold 2010), the air, the kite and its flyer a *"sound body"* of atmospheric "nests that disperse with the wind" (Kapchan 2015, 39).

5

First the holes in the homes had to be closed. The opening for milk delivery. The mail slot. Vents. Windows that opened to ocean air. Cracks that allowed in light and breeze, gaps around windows and doors. Aircraft noise drove people indoors, to spaces newly turned inward. Between 1967 and 1969, Wyle Laboratories conducted a home soundproofing pilot project around Los Angeles International Airport. The twenty houses were "typical of Southern California single-family homes," built of plaster, wood, composition shingle, Spanish tile, with "beamed ceilings and extensive glass areas" (Wyle Laboratories 1970b, 6). They were modest, mostly one-story homes, with windows in every room and multiple exterior doors that ensured fluidity between indoors and out. The first homes designated for soundproofing, those in the trial study, were near the coast. Breezes from the Pacific Ocean wafted through windows left open most of the year. The coastal climate kept the temperature at a level that was pleasant, not too hot in the summer, a nip of chill at night during winter, relieved by a crackling fire or a gas or electric heater. Though this was already the era of smog, the ocean breeze blew the settling haze inland, where it was trapped by the San Gabriel Mountains on the northeastern edge of the county. The climate granted a sense of ease only newly disrupted by the departing jet plane, which roared and whined as it ascended, dropping glops of fuel on the ground, on laundry hanging to dry, and on oranges dangling from a tree branch.

Despite the newly annoying noise of the airport, residents did not want to move. They were content in their homes on the dunes, where, as developer Fritz Burns once explained, there was little political protest. Playa del Rey, to the west of the runways, had been built as the upscale Surfridge in the 1920s, drawing movie stars and directors to the beachfront development. The area, along with Westchester to the north of the airport, was further developed to house those working in aviation during and following World War II. These were not the grimly gridded streets of Lakewood, described by D. J. Waldie in all their uniformity and conformity. Rather, winding roads followed the contours of the dunes, or, in Westchester, serial parcels of concentric cul-de-sacs meant to foster both security and community (Cuff 2001; Hise 1997; Waldie 2005). At a moment in acoustics that included the dawn of the jet age, the study and control of noise, and the introduction of high-fidelity stereo sound, residential soundproofing emerged as a possibility for ameliorating the experience of environmental noise for those living or attending school near the airport. And while many reportedly found their homes more livable after soundproofing, the annoyance of aircraft noise diminished, those closest to the airport told Wyle that they could no longer enjoy their yards or patios, despite the newly added walls. This in a city built on the premise and promise of the single-family home, the yard, and the coastal climate, where a continuity of air was also one of sound and where residential soundproofing included treatments for patio areas.

More than weather, or seasons, Los Angeles has climate. Variations in temperature and humidity are factors of the jet stream, time of day, month. Climate is defined first as a region of the Earth characterized by its weather and second, as the weather of a place, or figuratively, attitudes or conditions—an atmosphere understood as mood (*Oxford English Dictionary*, s.v. "climate"). The turn in the word's definition from the distance of the objective to the proximity of the subjective allows weather and politics to be drawn together, as literal and figurative meanings of climate collide and collude. Thermoception and affect coalesce in metaphor. There were other things in the air at the time, taking form as protests, marches, mobilizations against war and for racial equality. Lines drawn around hue were different from those of the noise contours that mapped microphone measurements; they were *red*lines designating swaths of the city as ineligible for mortgages.

In a climate of change, closing windows to drown out the noise of aircraft might also have seemed to make the home feel more like a fortress, protection against an atmosphere that pressed on its inhabitants—that made the skin crawl, the heart race, or annoyance percolate into an explosive condition. Against a *sense* that something was bearing down, challenging, if not threatening, a precariously maintained scene of domestic bliss. Noise divides inside from out, the skin of the house newly figured as fortification rather than the porous membrane it had in many ways been (Pallasmaa 2012; Sloterdijk 2011; see also chapter 3). Yet, I suggest, what emerges is not so much a divide as a continuity across differently vibrating matter that extends from the skin of the body to that of the house and beyond. There is no between; rather, matter is continuous, air and skin entangled in various ways despite—or as part of—efforts to control, demarcate, and condition.

EMERGENT MATERIALITIES

During soundproofing, noise gets pushed into and away from things. When the builders seal the gaps between the window frames and the walls, they drive noise into silicone gel. When they add a turn to the ventilation duct, they send noise bouncing back where it came from. When they install a second pane of glass three inches from the existing window, they create an airspace where noise ricochets between surfaces. Concerned with the materiality of sound, Wyle's acoustical engineers describe noise as a moving force, mobile and agentive (Wyle Laboratories 1970a; see also Bennett 2010). They delineate the shifting status of sound from airborne waves to material vibration as it moves from an airplane engine through air and into a house, where it is heard in the living room, the bedroom, the kitchen. There, if it is too loud, it interferes with conversation, makes it difficult to hear the television, and is, perhaps, annoying.

Soundproofing encapsulates the full range of meanings of *proof*—gathering and making evidence, testing or treating a room or a building, aiming to render impenetrable or impervious.[1] Yet similar to Sloterdijk's soap bubble, the inside and outside are equally captivating, equally of air, equally acoustic (Sloterdijk 2011). Both factors of a wobbling, shimmering membrane, their distinction from each other relies on a material fragility assembled through the motion of air, breath, or sound. The skin of the house is both armor for and an extension of the body's, its permeability and porosity not limited to windows but extended across the surfaces and depth of walls and doors, window frames and thresholds. Skin as "symbolic boundary between the self and the world" (Benthien 2002, 1) is formed under pressure—whether the indeterminacy of matter registered by quantum physics or the slow on-slaught of an anthropogenic atmosphere in which the relationship between a body and its milieu is increasingly itchy (Barad 2012). Skin, whether of an arm or a kitchen ceiling, is a horizon of pressure *and* permeable, entangled with air in a dynamic of force and motion, of energy and matter (Alaimo 2016; Nash 2007). It is, as Manning (2009) puts it, "leaky."

The materiality of walls, vents, windows, and air emerges in and through encounters with noise (Latham and McCormack 2004). Cast by acoustical engineers as distinct in relation to forms of matter, sound—the matter of noise—makes materials differently durable. Described as a wave in air, sound is said to vibrate the matter of the wall—stucco, shingles, gypsum—emerging again on the other side as a wave. At 1960 congressional hearings on aircraft noise problems, Bartholomew Spano, director of acoustics firm Polysonics and formerly of the FAA, drew out the resonant materiality of wall-sound-air (U.S. House 1963, 109):

> Let's consider noise going through a wall. Literally noise cannot go through a wall. Even though you may hear it on the other side it can't go through, of course, unless there are holes on it but if you have a large wall and it is relatively light and relatively flexible, as houses are in the approach paths of many of our major airports, a low frequency sound having its basic quality of, first, a compression wave and then a rarefaction is a very real pressure. *It actually pushes and pulls on the wall* until the wall is set up in motion at the same frequency as the exciting sound. Then, the wall radiates on the other side that same noise. The heavier the wall, the harder it is for the sound to move it and, there-fore, the sound will come through weaker. (emphasis added)[2]

In a vibrant entanglement of energetic forces and agentive objects, sound moves walls, setting in motion matter that radiates the sound energy that was not caught up in, or fatigued from, its work of pushing and pulling. The subject of that day's hearings was what the FAA had done thus far to ad-dress the noise problems at airports, and Spano was there to explain noise. Training senators as expert listeners, he played sounds for them: pure tones demonstrating frequency; music played at 75 (actually 78) and 90 (actually 88) decibels to provide the experience of noise levels inside and outside a house; a DC-7 and a jet at 100 decibels to convey the peculiarities of human hearing and its attunement to higher frequencies.

"Transmission" of sound through the skin of the house, the "building envelope," is the amount of sound that will pass through a given material. Wyle engineers describe how the "action of a sound wave" produces "vibration in it." Sound is lively, animated, "vibrating" and "exciting" material. While a more massive panel resists vibration, a "thin light panel" will vibrate "readily when excited by the same sound wave." There is an animism in their language, in which building materials are affective sensors that are excited by sound, vibrating in perhaps not unpleasurable ways, while variously allowing sound to keep moving, keep moving on, an agent even if not a "thing." Agency shifts from "the interaction between sound waves and the materials with which they come into contact" to the material that does things to sound, "attenuates" a sound wave. The more excited, the more that passes through; less excitation or vibration reduces "intensity." Absorption is treated separately, as the "frictional resistance" to sound waves "as they pass through the material." Acoustic tiles reduce the "amount of incident sound energy reflected by the wall," causing the "amount of sound energy in the room" to be reduced and "in turn lowering the sound level" (Wyle Laboratories 1970a, 4, 5–6).[3]

While the sound transmission levels of building materials can be altered, air is treated as empty, its materiality not addressed in relation to the movement of sound even as it is the matter of openings in the home and, in this way, the most potent conduit. Drawing on an interview with Elizabeth Caudra, who was "overseeing the project for Wyle," the *Chicago Tribune* reported: "Mrs. Caudra said the most crucial elements in soundproofing a house were the windows and doors, then roofs and floors. Walls are the least problem. But then there are the cracks." "'You don't dare to leave a tiny crack,' she said. 'You can get almost as much noise thru 10 per cent of an area as you do thru 100 per cent'" (Chicago Tribune 1968, 15). In air, the sound wave itself materializes as metaphoric liquid: "Because noise acts like water—if it finds a hole, it will leak through" (M. Payne 2001). Air, as a form of matter moved by the energy that is sound, is absent, an absence, as distinct from its earlier figuration as "ether" (Connor 2010; Trower 2012). Yet with soundproofing, as with environmental noise in general, the noise that is measured and mitigated is limited to airborne sound. Sound in and of air is nonetheless always coming into being in relation to differently resonating sound-energies that appear to the eye as wall or windowpane or ear. As Les Blomberg told me, while the emphasis might be on airborne sound, structure matters: "the noise is always emanating off some structure or thing" or being transmitted through your home; "even what I hear of my own voice is structure-borne through my bones and ears." Structures, understood as blocking sound, extended outside the home and into the neighborhood. Brick walls were built around doorways, creating outdoor entryways that could be accessed only on one side (Veneklasen and Associates 1968, 189). Designing a neighborhood to coexist with noise, or, as architect Sean Lally proposes, harnessing forms of energy as "walls" (2014, 121), was beyond the imagination of people whose desires remained grounded in the conventions of a built form that had already promised the sensory pleasures of a good life.

Glass, an Amorphous Solid

Attending to the sound transmission levels of building materials with an ear toward disallowing the movement of sound from exterior to interior was also an attuning toward the resonant qualities of matter—lathe, stucco, plaster, glass.[4] Glass, characterized in terms of its "low attenuation" (Wyle Laboratories 1970a, 5), is unique in its material properties. Glass resonates with sound. This is the wine glass made to sing for a child at the end of a dinner, or extended as a wine glass "orchestra," filled with different levels of water for variations in pitch. The more water, the less air, the higher the pitch, or frequency. Air between two panes of glass has a similar effect, such that a smaller airspace resonates at a higher frequency (Soundproofing Company 2006). Though window designers are aware of this, the high-frequency whine of a departing airplane—the main cause of human annoyance—is not specifically treated with soundproofing. The resonant frequency of glass is the pitch that, if played, or sung, loudly enough, may cause it to break. The apocryphal opera singer.

Mutable, glass is a solid that "contains in its liquid properties the trace of its previous state and the conditions of its making" (Kalas 2007, 175). It is, technically, an "amorphous solid," its chemical structure that of liquid rather than a crystalline solid, atoms and molecules not organized in a definite lattice pattern. High temperatures will change its state from solid to viscous; cold will render molten silica into something seemingly solid. When heated to its glass transition temperature, it is said to be in its glassy state. In glass, we hear the "real force of the immaterial" (Latham and McCormack 2004, 704). Like concrete, another material that moves between liquid and solid, glass "is a particular aggregate organization of process and energy"; thus, "to argue for the importance of materiality is in fact an argument for apprehending different relations and durations of movement, speed, and slowness rather than simply a greater consideration of objects" (Latham and McCormack 2004, 705). Composed primarily of silica, glass is material cousin to sand, whose granularity is another kind of liquid solid marking indefinite, moving margins. Capable of altering the territory of nation-states (Chua 2018; Comaroff 2014), sand is blown by wind into dunes—mobile, migrating formations on which homes that had been built for their ocean views were, in 1959, suddenly under the flight path of newly noisy jet aircraft.

With windows considered "apertures of enlightenment," glass, "to the early modern imagination," was "an important medium of civilization, permitting enclosure yet translucence" (Comaroff and Comaroff 1997, 290). Generally considered in terms of its properties of visuality—transparency, reflection, refraction—glass is less often discussed in terms of its acoustic qualities. The resonance of glass is suggested but not articulated by the Wyle reports that recommend a three-inch gap and separate installation of each pane of glass rather than a manufactured double pane window. That glass resonates "with" sound is crucial: sound is not an external agent or object; it is only and always in and of. Sound, in other words, is immanent.[5]

I meet a Larson Doors sales rep and a window developer at a hotel near LAX, on the strip of big hotels where single-family homes stood before it was subject to "land recycling," rezoned for "compatible" use. The two men are in town consulting on the FAA's changes to its soundproofing program. We find a table in the bar area, all golden-brown wood with tan and burgundy and brown carpet. I order an iced tea but let it sit, ice melting into a clear layer above the brown, condensation forming large drops on the outside of the glass. Larson Doors sells a window technology that challenges the "mass/airspace" model. It uses a hybrid frame of aluminum and vinyl, which vibrate at different frequencies, allowing the materials to dampen each other's vibrations. This moves the focus from the expanse of a sheet of glass to its margins, where another material takes on the vibration of sound. They responded to the desires of those materials, their vibrational proclivities, playing them off each other, confusing and lulling sound. When "the aluminum wanted to vibrate at certain frequencies, the vinyl would absorb it, and when the vinyl wanted to begin to vibrate, the aluminum would absorb it." Because the two materials "resonate at different frequencies . . . it took the ability of those products to vibrate at the frequency they would normally vibrate at and calm them down by adding them together." The window developer's explanation moves seamlessly from the physical property of window materials to STC (sound transmission class) bands—a visual abstraction of sound inscribed on computer printouts—and back.

> The airspace now becomes not as important, because as soon as that frequency hits that glass you have what they call a coincidence dip in the glass. That's what they call a product failure. That's when you max out your product, and if that frequency dip in the STC band—have you been through testing quite a bit? I'm assuming you have?—almost in every curve you're going to see that dip somewhere along that curve, and it's called a coincidence dip, and what that is is that's when you're beginning to max out the material.

At first I am not sure what he is talking about; then my memory is jarred, and I recall the computer screen I was shown in the window testing room at Western Electro-Acoustic Laboratory (WEAL), the jagged lines crossing the x-axis, a series of vertical lines showing time. The visualization of STC bands comes into focus as they become the principal matter of concern. He continues: "So what you try to do, when I look at that curve and I see the coincidence dip, I say, oh, that's where I max the material. I do one of two things, either change up the materials to . . . make the dip not quite as great, or change the materials to shift it, one either side of the STC curve, outside that band, move it up, move it down, to get it out of the band of frequency to level that out." We're sharing a mental image of a computer reading that visualizes the relationship between sound and matter; as material and line move together, abstraction is rendered visceral, and matter becomes inscription (Latour, Woolgar, and Salk 1986; Latour 2004).

Larson windows may have been tested at WEAL, one of a handful of acoustics labs in the country. WEAL uses a building in what is now an office park in Santa Clarita; formerly owned by Lockheed, the building had been the aircraft manufacturer's acoustics lab since the 1950s. There is a room designed specifically for testing windows for manufacturers. Divided in two by a wall with a hole into which a window and frame can be installed, on one side, "just noise" comprising all the frequencies is played, while on the other, revolving microphones send sound to a computer that measures it, breaking it down into each third octave band. They measure from 63 Hz to 5000 Hz, the middle range of human hearing that, I am told, is most sensitive. *Sound* and *energy* are used interchangeably. Higher and lower frequencies have less "energy" in them, and "your ear's less sensitive so it's not as critical." The engineer's voice is overwhelmed by the reverberation of the room—it sounds loud, though at a distance. He turns the noise on for me, which measures 120 dB on the source room side. I hear it through an open door and am warned I would not want to be inside the room when it is on. While they only measure airborne sound, the engineer tells me that if you put your hand on the window that is being tested, you can feel it vibrate. Vibration is felt rather than heard, hearing distinguished from other senses—from touch, and from the body in general.

The Libby-Owens-Ford Glass Company had been able to "draw glass from a molten pool in a continuous sheet" (Isenstadt 2006, 198–99) since the 1930s. It actively marketed the picture window afforded by such technology, based on, among other things, its sound reduction capabilities (Isenstadt 2006, 205). Yet the picture window—which Beatriz Colomina describes as a window onto "a public representation of conventional domesticity," a "shop-window selling the middle-class American dream" that nonetheless made the passerby "suspect, an intruder" (2007, 168; see also Daniel Boorstin quoted in Isenstadt 2006, 214)—was not a feature of the homes in the pilot soundproofing study. Instead, the floor plans delineate the solidity of walls from windows as gaps, unmarked spaces in the line of the wall, holes whose presence makes it appear as though the house cannot even hold together. The materiality of the windows is signified only by the letter *w*. Here, as sustained across decades of soundproofing, a "window isn't much more than a hole in the wall where noise will enter freely" (M. Payne 2001). Only one of the gaps appears large enough to be a picture window. The rest, though running one after another across the side of a house, are small. These are not the glass houses of modern architecture, or even their adaptation into the vernacular, in which windows abutting at corners make the right angles of a building seemingly disappear. They were, as Dana Cuff puts it, "flavored: Ranch, Cape Cod, and Suburban" (2000, 248), modern as a result of the mass production of their materials and form rather than in style.

VOLUMETRIC LISTENING

Though on concluding the 1967 pilot program the airport deemed soundproofing cost prohibitive, it was nonetheless implemented as a means of addressing the problem of noise around the Los Angeles International Airport for both homes and schools. Cities run their own soundproofing programs, and unincorporated areas fall under the county's jurisdiction. Eligible buildings are those inside the 65 CNEL noise contours. These are mapped quarterly, based previously on measurements taken from microphones located at key points around the airport but now calculated using flight data and a formula for engine noise. Noise contour maps inscribe noise metrics geographically. They are an outcome as much as a tool, another mode of objectification that congeals experience into concentric amoeba-shaped outlines inscribed on a map, each line marked with a decibel level: 75 dB CNEL, 70 dB CNEL, 65 dB CNEL. They are both regulatory regimes in and of themselves and means of meeting regulatory requirements.[6]

As contours, they are the outline of a volume—of the sound of an airplane departing or landing, sound that engineers draw for me as a cone-like shape registered on the ground as lines that decrease into a rounded point like the nose of an airplane. They connote volume and volumetric urbanism. Contours are an outline of something that is ordinarily solid, though a shadow could also be said to have contours. They register shape, mass, and density, the contours of a face that are not an edge but an expression of interior matter: skull, flesh, sinews, nerves, organs of eyes and brain (Deleuze 2005). Rounded and smooth, contours are the perimeter of resonating matter, drawing a relationship between flesh and air, ground and atmosphere. Through its contour, noise is materialized, turned impossibly into an object. Soundproofing happens for homes inside this volumetric space, or the space of volume. Contour lines bisect property lines and blocks, their impassive evenness corrected by a gridded extension intended to promote equity. The contours map time and energy, sound events averaged over an hour, a day, a year.[7] While the FAA provides software that calculates the contours based on set paths and known noise metrics for each aircraft, LAWA uses a program called Real Contours that uses actual flight track data to generate the contours. Noise measurement microphones located around the airport provide daily logs of sound pressure levels, with loud sounds automatically recorded; as their mandate is only to register aircraft sound, they use these recordings to delete noise from sources other than airplanes.

In summer 2017, new maps had just been completed: *LAWA's 2020 CNEL Boundary*, a projection generated for its aircraft noise mitigation strategy. Computerized flight navigation aids that allow planes to fly closer to one another and technological advances making planes quieter have shrunk the previous boundaries. Where soundproofing programs have not been completed, some people who had once been eligible are no longer. The county soundproofing program is trying to get the FAA to let them include full blocks rather than follow the line that makes one house eligible and its next door neighbor ineligible. They are pushing for parity, against an equalizing system. A supervisor for the L.A. County residential soundproofing program gave me a tour of their work. He was sympathetic to the community and wanted to do something for people who had otherwise not been given much. He doesn't have to tell me that they are mostly low-income, Spanish-speaking immigrants, as the signs I encounter as I exit the freeway convey as much. He knew they did not trust government, had heard their stories about the county hospital placing liens on homes for unpaid bills. As we drive around, he shows me a house where roofing shingles had been lifted by the force of landing planes. He stops to wait for a jet to fly overhead so I might witness the fronds of a palm tree waving in its wake. I do not see it, but the possibility of what this might look like lingers in my imagination. He points out the new windows on apartment complexes, and we visit a home that was soundproofed a decade ago. The homeowner shows him the condensation in the front double-paned picture window. Termites are eating the wood. She tells us that they used to have red oak window frames, but they had been replaced with a different kind of wood. He acknowledges that the window was sealed improperly and tells her that the county will send someone out to fix it. She is grateful, saying the soundproofing was a "blessing"—a gift, to not have to pay.

When we first arrive, he tells her that we would like to see whether they added a box inside the mail slot. She apologizes profusely because dirt catches there, and bees come in; she had not taken the mail in that day yet and kept a paper towel in the slot so that the mail would not get dirty. We are there to see the soundproofing treatments, but as we wander through the house, she points out renovations done over the years, some related to soundproofing, many not. We are immersed in a "phenomenal object world through which human subjects circulate" (Brown 2003, 18), sound shifting into matter as soundproofing folds into decorating, acoustic experience entangled with more visible manifestations of taste. A small table with a guestbook greets us as we enter. Framed pictures cover tables and are hung in clusters on walls, objects among them; an ornate wooden cross hangs over the picture window in the bedroom, the window suffering from condensation. The piano and its bench are covered with family photos, rendering it silent in a corner. The sensory expands into a sense of home that resonates across the clarity of sound and the orderliness of its clutter. The house is filled with objects, everything spotless, all white and cream. Scalloped trim runs around the edges of the living room, a rhetorical flourish drawing together ceiling, doorway, and dining room. Its dance is halted by a rectangular outcrop intruding into the corner of the dining room, housing for the HVAC ventilation that had been installed as part of soundproofing. She does not like this, though she loves the cover for the fireplace. "We don't use it much. It smells. The neighbors use theirs and the smell comes in." Nevertheless, "this is much nicer than it was before."

She invites us into the kitchen, explaining that it is "pretty much the same," with off-white tile counters, the sink set at an angle in a corner. All the rooms have new windows, but she is not showing me these; instead, she is showing me her home, soundproofing only an element of the things they had changed or still want to. Under the new program, bathrooms will not get new windows; only "habitable rooms" will—living room, kitchen, bedroom. "The ceiling still looks bad. We had acoustic tiles. But there is so much to do in a house." Grapes grow on the arbor on the patio, and fruit trees bend with the weight of guavas and apples. "My husband's hobby," she explains; or, as D. J. Waldie suggests, an expression of "appreciation for the climate" (2005, 172). A couple of years ago a man knocked on the door, wanting to see the house where he had grown up. His parents had planted the two trees in the front yard. She let him in, and he was delighted to see that the house was just how it had been when he was a child, where, he said, his mother had been the happiest in her life. I computed the years and could not guess whether this was before the beginning of the jet age or amid its beginning, when the newly experienced roar of aircraft engines bore down on these neighborhoods. It seemed likely it was the latter, in which case this anecdote confirmed the stories told in soundproofing guides and congressional testimony, that foremost for residents was a deep love of place, an affective attachment to the bungalows and neighborhoods of southwest Los Angeles.

Planes fly overhead, and when we are outside, we have to pause midsentence, starting up again after they pass. But before, she said, it was so much worse. Especially when they were on the phone, and especially to Mexico or Costa Rica, when noise played its historical role of blocking the signal of telecommunication; it was so hard, she exclaimed, it was "like the 1800s!" The army planes were the worst, the roar of their engines vibrating air, roof, and ceiling, transduced in the tinkling rattle of the chandelier's glass crystals, sound drawing together an assemblage of air, house, and body, such that "to sense is always to 'sense with'" (Anderson and Wylie 2009, 326). A rustic rock wall grounding two sides of a room had sold them on the house. The room, an addition serving as a kind of den, where four grandsons watch television on a weekday, is reminiscent of the grotto architecture found across L.A.'s movie set landscape, from the Disney compound in Los Feliz to Clifton's Cafeteria downtown. Her husband still regrets letting the soundproofers replace the two-part door with its rounded top, a top that opened separately from the bottom like the one Snow White looks through to talk to the dwarfs in the animated film. This is a cared-for house, where care for family crystallizes in the choice of flooring and the style of every decorative cover. The exterior vent covers had been replaced with something she liked, though not as much as the white doily cover they had had before, a style her husband had found. She tells us that the soundproofing makes the house a bit hotter. Because, the soundproofing officer explains, it seals all the places that used to let air in.

GOOD VIBRATIONS

Brian and Carl Wilson of the Beach Boys grew up a little further inland, listening to planes from Hawthorne Airport fly overhead. In Brian Wilson's memoir, he recalls that "all day long there was nothing but airplane noise. I didn't really like airplanes, even then. . . . Planes were a problem even if you weren't up in them. The noise got in the way of our singing. We had to shut the windows to keep it out" (Wilson and Greenman 2016, 47). The Beach Boys recorded their "Good Vibrations" in 1966. As surf music it evokes the coastal climate experienced by residents around LAX and the actual lifestyle of teens who carried their surfboards down the street and across the dunes to an ocean essentially in their backyard. The song expresses a sentiment of its time, the pleasure of attraction and commingling with others carried in the tone of their voices, and in the close, resonating harmonies. As with the Beach Boys' work in general, the song creates an atmosphere of its own, a sound that draws a listener into its timbres, into the space of its creation. Their "studio sound"—perhaps in fact an outcome of living with airplane noise—echoes soundproofing's efforts to distinguish interior from exterior, to create differentiated vibrating environments, with vibrations distinguished as "good" or "bad."

This was an era of high-fidelity sound and stereo recording, the space of the home amplified by speakers positioned just so, its acoustics newly mattering for audibility. Nascent audio technologies imbued listening practices in a range of settings both indoors and out, emerging in musical composition and shaping expectations of the "soundscape." Moreover, as people became audiophiles of both recorded and environmental sound, listening was largely conceived of in terms of ear and air. "Easy listening" LPs flaunted covers that portrayed the good life—whether cocktail parties or family leisure time—providing background music to "life" as an echo of an image. The home as a space of pleasurable conviviality was set to saxophones in stereo, two-channel tracks created, newly, with two sets of microphones played back across separate speakers, creating space through sound and, as was touted, bringing the experience of a live performance into a living room. The resonance and reverberation of residential building materials newly mattered in a listening experience that was at once lifestyle.[8] "HI-FI & STEREO," "SPACE AGE SWITCHING CONSOLE," "CUSTOM STEREO HIGH-FIDELITY" scream from the microfilmed Yellow Pages that I look at in the Los Angeles Public Library. "High" is found a few pages before house moving companies and just after "Hearing," where companies like Beltone and Zenith offered bone-conduction glasses and "living sound" hearing aids. (Also serendipitous, the local listings for Airlines bled into Air Conditioning in the As).

The "fidelity" of hi-fi was the seeming mimetic capability of audio recording, which nonetheless needed to be constructed through technological means. Hi-fi recording created a listening experience conditioned by the same metrics used to account for and control environmental noise—though here the noise was in the recorded artifact. Parameters of noise measurement became openings, "The ideal recording medium" capturing "the entire range of frequencies audible to humans, with minimal distortion of the signal, and without adding any extraneous hiss, hum, or other noises" (Morton 2004, 131). The microphone was rendered transparent by virtue of acoustic treatment. "Eliminating a room's natural reverberation removed one source of uncertainty for the engineer, since the microphone sometimes 'heard' reverberant sounds differently than the ear" (Morton 2004, 142). Recording outdoors, Wyle used a two-channel tape recorder to measure the sound pressure level of aircraft outside and inside homes. To measure the "free-field sound levels from the aircraft," one microphone was mounted on a twenty-foot pole "attached to the roof of the measurement van, and away from the house under investigation." Placed in the air, the condenser microphone would register sound as it moved air. Atmospheric listening casts air as neutral or empty, a form of matter that would not affect the sound as hard surfaces would. The other was placed inside the house, in "the room under investigation" but "away from the walls and furniture" (Wyle Laboratories 1970b, 70), another acoustic atmosphere of sound spread evenly, not bouncing off walls or being absorbed, not moving in unpredictable ways and becoming louder or softer.

The "noise" of a hi-fi system or television could also be channeled to test "acoustical leakage." Veneklasen and Associates outline a DIY method for acoustic testing and home soundproofing that uses a hi-fi system as a noise-making machine—a glitch method. They explain that, while acoustical engineers would use a random noise producer inside a room, a resident can reproduce the steady noise necessary by "tuning between FM stations," where "a hissing noise is produced which is sufficiently constant and of broad frequency content to be ideal." Moreover, "The noise must be steady—not music—to make the tests valid." TV receivers might also be able to be used if tuned to an unused channel, though "the volume of sound may not be sufficient, and occasionally the audio from an adjacent channel is picked up." With the loudspeaker placed inside the room, the listener goes outside and "listens closely to the building surfaces—roof, windows, doors, ventilation openings. Any acoustical leakage will be immediately evident by an increased noise level over a relatively confined area" (Veneklasen and Associates 1968, 155).

While a hi-fi stereo system is generally not noted on lists of things interrupted by aircraft noise, it amplifies things that are, especially anxieties around the decibel level of domestic appliances that might make women lose their hearing, but more than that, would disrupt the home as a sanctuary, a place where a new mode of listening was emerging. This was an era of easy listening, with music used in the service of soothing, creating an atmosphere of pleasure and relaxation (T. Anderson 2006). Listening, thus, was an aspect of a nervous system affected by sound, its vibrations making a person at ease or not, annoyed or not, challenged or not (Trower 2012). Muzak, or "mood music," was piped into offices and elevators to increase worker efficiency. In the home, easy listening was highly gendered (Keightley 1996). Despite the fact that women were the ones primarily involved in mobilizations against aircraft noise and consulted about its effects on everyday life, the noise of the home was cast as a problem for men, or projected by male engineers as a problem for women (chapter 3). Veneklasen and Associates' 1968 list of the PNdB level of domestic appliances includes the garbage disposal and vacuum cleaner (90), dishwasher (78), floor polisher (91), and shower (96), but not a stereo system or television (143).

This newly attuned listener is "The Two-Eared Man," a man with "stereophonic hearing," as described in a 1965 Life Science Library book, *Sound and Hearing*, edited by psychoacoustician Stanley Stevens (see chapter 2). With ears rendered as twentieth-century acoustic technology, the range and depth of human hearing is reduced to the division of audio channels across multiple speakers, which had recently opened new auditory worlds for the listener of recorded sound (Seaver 2011).[9] The two-eared man takes on shape and dimension as a husband, all thumbs, agrees to hang a picture and proceeds at once to drop the nail. As the nail hits the wall he does not look—he listens. From that moment his ears are on the hunt. The nail bounces against a table leg: the man recognizes the characteristic sound and spots its location. Finally, the nail rolls on the floor and comes to rest under the table—a new source of sound, this time a moving source. Guided by hearing alone—by two-eared, or binaural, hearing—the hunter reaches unerringly for the nail. (Stevens 1965, 99)

A domestic narrative of audition unfolds, following the sound of a falling and then rolling nail, as it brings into being subjectivities situated in domestic spaces and entangled with the furniture and furnishings of a postwar middle-class home. A world comes into being in the sound of a nail falling on the floor. A world of everyday practices composing and inhabiting social norms and conventions, of orientation to a place and its inhabitants. The absent presence of a wife. A solitary husband, alone in a dining room, "agrees"—already another person's presence is palpable in the recent past, in a future judgment of the precise height at which the picture is hung. Furniture has been selected and organized—by whom? We must imagine the material of the home. Wood, against which a nail might resonate. Wood chairs, a wood table, a wood—not carpeted—floor. Or perhaps a kitchen nook, a yellow Formica table with chrome legs, matching chairs with yellow vinyl seats, a linoleum floor. The husband becoming "man" and then "hunter," his ears orient him in the manner of microphones made to replicate human hearing. The man knows where the nail falls by listening. There is no "sound of" the nail dropping—we are not told how it sounds, as an externalized description by an absent narrator, but how it orients a person who hears and listens.

And while the two-eared man listens as part of a household task, his mode of listening veers toward the acousmatic, a form of attentive listening in which sound is detached from its source. Listening to "sound as such" figures sound as nonrepresentational, cultivating an interior self that resonates with sound heard via the ears (Nancy 2007, 5; see also Schaeffer 2012). Jean-Luc Nancy asks: "What does to be listening, to be all ears . . . mean? What does it mean to exist according to listening, for it and through it?," for sense to not make sense, but to resound, "sound and sense" resonating "in each other, or through each other." In listening thus, rather than for extra-sonic signification or meaning, "a resonance meaning" emerges "whose sense is . . . found in resonance, and only in resonance" (Nancy 2007,

5, 6, 7). This is the sound of musique concrete, of sound recorded on tape that could be cut and retaped, which, beginning in the early 1950s, allowed Pierre Schaeffer to advocate listening to sounds as abstractions, detached from their source. An "acousmatics," it is "the perceptive reality of sound as such" with "listening itself . . . the origin of the phenomenon." Sound, thus, emerges in and through perception, rather than existing "out there" as an object or, in Schaeffer's words, "'reality'" (Schaeffer 1994, 77; Schaeffer 2012). Something of this listener emerges in a mid-twentieth-century attunement toward acoustics, in a person whose ears are understood as models of and for recording technology and its playback, whose ears attune toward the amplitude of sound inside their home as they resonate with the windows and walls; once again, "there [is] no clear-cut division between the body and its environment" (Erlmann 2010, 49). Yet, as Erlmann cautions, "the ear troubles some of our most entrenched clichés. . . . It is connected to the deepest layers of our experience, but it is also articulated to science and reason. It is a physical reality, but it is also a cultural construct" (2010, 24). Such listening is learned, its achievement entangled with historical figurations of sound. Just as architectural acoustics turned away from vibration and toward higher frequencies more easily dampened or subdued by building materials, the hi-fi stereo listener was someone who listened principally through or with ears now cast as discriminating.

Silence, newly desirable in and of itself, was equally a means of controlling unwanted sounds (Kahn 1999; Ochoa Guatier 2015; Schwartz 2011). In a confluence of events that resonates with the scope of this book, John Cage recorded his oft-repeated anecdote about a 1951 visit to an anechoic chamber for Folkways Records in 1959—the year Los Angeles entered the jet age—under the title *Indeterminacy* (Cage and Tudor [1959] 1992).

> It was after I got to Boston that I went into the anechoic chamber at Harvard University. Anybody who knows me knows this story. I am constantly telling it. Anyway, in that silent room, I heard two sounds, one high and one low. Afterward I asked the engineer in charge why, if the room was so silent, I had heard two sounds. He said, "Describe them." I did. He said, "The high one was your nervous system in operation, the low one was your blood in circulation."

Cage's anecdote about the anechoic chamber, ultimately published in *A Year from Monday* (1967, 134), continues to circulate as an apocryphal statement undergirding his conclusion that "there is no such thing as silence." Anechoic chambers are lined with acoustic wedges on walls, ceiling, and floor.

They are built to be fully isolated from the rest of the building in which they are found, so that vibrations do not move into them from elsewhere. At WEAL, the anechoic chamber is large—it can hold an engine, loudspeakers, or a siren. The *First Federal Aircraft Noise Abatement Plan*, published in November 1969, features a close-up of a wall of an anechoic chamber on the cover, "lined with pyramids of sound absorbing material to prevent reflections and echoes." It explains that they "are used by government and industry research organizations to determine sound distribution patterns of various noise sources."[10] Designed to dampen reverberation as much as possible, they are not silent. Rather, when talking to another person or snapping one's fingers or clapping hands together, there is a lack of reverberation or resonance. When the door is closed, a sense of pressure bears on one's ears. Leo Beranek helped develop them and also named them: no echo (Beranek 2008; Lyon 2009).[11]

A year after he recorded *Indeterminacy*, Cage appeared on *I Have a Secret*, a then popular television game show, playing domestic appliances: blender, fan, but not the radio because, as he laughed, there was a labor dispute at the time and the union whose members had jurisdiction over plugging in radios was on strike.[12] It seems that it is not an accident that 4'33" was roughly the length of a Muzak song, such that silence was not only a way of attuning toward everyday sounds but also a mode of silencing; this is also said of Cage's dislike of radio, which he used as instruments in compositions. Others turned the play between noise and music—the former represented by jackhammers and domestic appliances, both targets of antinoise efforts—into humorous, palatable music packaged as stereo LPs for domestic listening. Dean Elliot and His Big Band recorded Cole Porter's "You're the Top" using bowling pins, a cement mixer, a hand saw, a telephone, "and more" on the album *Zounds! What Sounds!* (Elliott 1962; Taylor 2001, 79). The album cover features women with saxophones and bongo drums posed on a cement mixer littered with other sound-making devices: a trumpet, a tennis racket, a clock, a cat.

This was also an era of acoustic indeterminacies, electronics as instruments and "difficult music" that intentionally disrupted the status quo; free improvisation turning song-based bebop inside out, often with an accompanying politics of belonging (notable examples are AACM, AMM, and Cornelius Cardew's Scratch Orchestra); sounds played against the resonant qualities up to then emphasized by acoustic instruments; the crisis of the electric guitar; an attunement toward atmospheric noise. Cage insisted that his favorite sound was that of traffic, which, always changing, does not "mean" anything and is not composed. The sounds of 6th Avenue traffic came through an open window, and he listened in a Kantian, disinterested way from the un-air-conditioned loft he shared with Merce Cunningham. Ambivalences and indeterminacies were worked out through recordings that were intended to be listened to: everyday sounds; Moses Asch's unrealized project of recording everything; Cook's recordings of nascent technologies, including his 1960 *Sounds of the Sky*, featuring celebratory recordings of newly developed aircraft. Thus hi-fi listening also attuned listeners to the sky, conditioning new modes of engagement with environmental sound.

R. Murray Schafer's notion of "soundscape" was developed as a way of turning an aversion to noise pollution into something positive by treating environmental sound as material for musical composition. He uses the language and logic of acoustic technology to draw a normative distinction between hi-fi and lo-fi sounds, the former that of a pastoral rural where discrete sounds can be distinguished one from another, the latter an undesirable mixture of indistinct sound, technological advances, and people.

> A hi-fi system is one possessing a favourable signal to noise ratio. The hi-fi soundscape is one in which discrete sounds can be heard clearly because of the low ambient noise level. The country is generally more hi-fi than the city; night more than day; ancient times more than modern. . . .
>
> In a lo-fi soundscape individual acoustic signals are obscured in an overdense population of sounds. . . . The pellucid sound . . . is masked by broad-band noise. Perspective is lost. On a downtown street corner there is no distance; there is only presence. Everything is close-miked. There is cross-talk on all the channels, and in order for the most ordinary sounds to be heard they have to be monstrously amplified. In the ultimate lo-fi soundscape the signal to noise ratio is 1 to 1 and it is no longer possible to know what, if anything is to be listened to. (Schafer 1994, 32–33)

The distinction between interior and exterior sounds, between the interior of the home (or concert hall) as an acoustic space and environmental sound as figured by soundproofing makes a notion of *soundscape* possible. The World Soundscape Project, founded by Schafer and others, cultivated a new kind of atmospheric listening, attuning toward an environment that was also coming into being. Their work is embedded in the concerns of the era—noise pollution and its control, audio technologies and listening practices. Its normative thrust circulates across organizations emphasizing the value of quiet in cities, from the nationwide Quiet City network of mayors to the National Noise Abatement Council, composed primarily of representatives of building material manufacturers. In relying on terms and norms of audio technology for his project, Schafer casts the soundscape as something that might be controlled with the turn of a dial or measured and recorded, its listener called on to use what had been learned through technology to compose the sonic environment writ large.

AIR CONDITIONING

Soundproofing, like air conditioning, is an exercise in climate control (Banham 1984). Yet soundproofing, in closing off the home from unwanted sound, disarticulates sound from air.

The ear is disentangled from skin, hearing from thermoception. In closing the home from sound, air had to be brought inside by other means. This was particularly acute in schools. When windows were sealed closed to shield children from the noise of departing aircraft, the breeze that cooled the rooms could no longer move freely. Indoor air was compartmentalized, contained. The rooms would now be hot. Recently developed technologies, air conditioners were loud, and there was much discussion over the best ones to use. One noise supplanted with another. An issue of public health remedied with an energy cost acknowledged as both financial and environmental. They decided on units that would be set on the roof, blown into classrooms through newly installed ductwork (Los Angeles Sound Abatement Coordinating Committee 1971). Even as "comfort" has been "the measuring stick for success," with "Comfort control span[ning] an array of variables, from light, temperature, humidity, and scent, to the speed of air moving over the body and the range of sound decibels carried through that air" (Lally 2014, 105), the technology of air conditioning only addresses sound in terms of something it makes. Air, conditioned for temperature, is not conditioned for sound.

Air temperature determines an area's climate zone and the need—or not—for air conditioning inside the home. Though the 1967 pilot soundproofing program was completed a decade prior to the designation of climate zones, in what is now climate zone 6, windows were made to open, and homes and schools relied on them as a source of fresh air. Wyle's pilot study acknowledges this: "Although it is not specifically known which windows the owners were accustomed to open in their normal mode of living, it is a virtual certainty (based on their comments) that in summer they nearly all lived with many windows open, since one of the major attractions of the area is the cool sea breeze in summer." In the late 1970s, the California Energy Commission divided the state into sixteen climate zones based on energy use, temperature, and weather. These are not the climate zones of garden books or agriculture but zones by which energy budgets were organized, providing a basis for "energy efficiency standards" for buildings. Though Los Angeles is the designated city for the climate zone that lies along the coast, the city in fact spreads across three climate zones (California Energy Commission 2017). Los Angeles's climate zones are characterized by relative proximity to the ocean. While Westchester, to the north of the airport and near the coast, is in climate zone 6, Inglewood, to its east, is in climate zone 8. This difference determines whether soundproofing requires a forced-air ventilation system (6) or central air conditioning (8, 9), which is the difference between a home being cooled by ocean breezes or a refrigerant. Of the thirty-nine homes in the pilot soundproofing program, only two had central air conditioning; nineteen had an existing central forced-air heating system, while twenty did not. Homeowners were warned that "the effectiveness of the soundproofing will depend on your keeping the doors and windows completely shut, even though each room will have at least one window that *can* be opened if need be. For this reason, it is necessary that we install forced air ventilation to bring in a fresh air supply from outdoors" (Wyle Laboratories 1970b, 10, 93, 94). At the same time, none of L.A.'s climate zones require protection from the cold. This is reflected in the architecture and in its acoustic qualities. While "in other areas of the nation where the climate is less mild and where the typical house structure is more oriented toward the retention or exclusion of heat, the methods and materials used in this project may not be suitable and in some cases, certain minor modifications may not even be necessary." In fact, "it is not considered necessary to make any modifications to the more massive types of walls such as brick or concrete which occur in other regions of the nation" (Wyle Laboratories 1970a, 2, 16–17). Thus this soundproofing project, the first in the nation, was also specifically of L.A., where climate is registered across atmospheric qualities of air and architecture.

LAWA's last model soundproofing home showcases a FanTech ventilation system, in which an attic fan almost noiselessly circulates coastal air through vents one turns to open and close. The house is across the street from the airport's north runway. Built in 1923, its previous owner, Mr. Trainer, participated in a 1980s soundproofing pilot program and sold his home to the airport to serve as a model house. The airport did some remodeling but kept the soundproofing as is. While we are inside, the back door is left open because the house is musty from being closed up. We listen as another plane departs. The director of LAWA's soundproofing program closes the back door so I can experience the full effect. The sealed-off-ness of the interior of the home is sense-able. Carpet dampens footsteps and words are swallowed by acoustic panels. Not an anechoic chamber, it nevertheless takes on its quality; the atmospheric pressure is palpable to me at the time and audible in a recording I make of our visit. In the front of the house, the acoustics flatten; her voice becomes close, and opening and closing the windows yields no reverberation. She points out the double windows with four operating sashes and demonstrates how they can be opened for fresh air. A FanTech ventilation system was already in the house, the fan in the basement. It draws fresh air in from outside with the turn of a dial: the words "Vari-Speed Solid State" frame a dial that can be turned from the left, "off," clockwise to "low." This was the system used in Wyle's soundproofing pilot project for houses in the climate zone closest to the beach, where outdoor air is cooler than indoor air. The house breathes with the fan, drawing in fresh air and circulating it amid the stale exhalations of its inhabitants, who, along with the house, are in suspension, becoming atmospheric with air uncoupled from sound (Choy and Zee 2015). Further inland, where HVAC systems are required, the outdoor air is warmer, there are more hot days in a year, and the wind from the west does not come right off the ocean.

The cover over the fireplace—one of the home's holes—is glass with gold trim. The carpet is greenish-gray, the walls white, and tan marble tiles surround the fireplace; nothing really matches, other than in a general tannish decorating scheme, but the gold trim stands out as an artifact from the 1980s. Back in the kitchen, toward the back of the house, her voice reverberates again. She describes the different materials of the doors, explaining that they are so heavy they need four hinges, not three. Windows required extra sealant because they are so big. The home is a time capsule. Materials have not worn with use or decayed from exposure to the elements. No one lives in this house. The hinges have not been moved every day, the windows opened and closed, the carpet walked on. Here, as in most soundproofed homes, vinyl windows were installed. Wyle engineers report that aluminum windows did not age as well (Sharp et al. 2013). Images of failing exterior walls in a report on the history of residential soundproofing suggest other histories of neighborhoods and property: the reality of the undesirability of living near an airport, decline in property values, an area that ended up housing much poorer people than previously, where landlords let things go.

I ask about vibration, as I generally do, interested in the fact that noise is limited to airborne sound. "Vibration is caused by the same sound," I'm told, and will also lessen inside due to soundproofing. Air is moved through, matter vibrated. Noise makes "materiality . . . multiple," amplifying differences between "forces and processes that exceed any one state (solid, liquid, gas), and are defined ultimately in terms of movement and process rather than stasis"; materiality is "relational insofar as these materialities/mobilities are the very sparks which ignite passages of perception and sensation, and concordances or dissonances, of bodies and things" (Anderson and Wylie 2009, 326). Vibrating air is not a model used for sound, which, as something moving through—rather than moving—air is granted a physicality in and of itself as waves or pressure. The director of the soundproofing program, who started her career in the city ethics division, explains that "sound is mechanical vibration," that it's "similar to thermal but a different philosophy." Sound is usually only described as vibration when I bring it up; otherwise it is almost always airborne. In other words, when I ask about vibration, the definition of noise or sound changes, but with an inevitability of foundationalism—sound *is* vibration—all sound, always. Vibration is matter-of-factly totalizing.

In the office, she has created an exhibit of color-printer photos tacked to a cubicle divider: "Art as Work, Food as Art, a nationally recognized perspective juxtaposing the anonymity of the workplace and the necessity of food as survival." A fold in the everyday of LAWA's Environmental Services Division, the exhibit strains against the banality of bureaucracy, making of it a creative act. Accompanying text explains that "The pictures are a provocative and unsettling depiction of the everyday working man and woman, showcasing the absurdity of the mundane as necessary, modern, and yet individualized." They create a "crescendo of normalcy," anchoring and amplifying the banality of the norms performed by postwar tract homes and aspirations toward a form that congealed into a daily practice of gendered habits, the philosophy student turned civil servant whose job perhaps makes her feel as though she has landed with a dull thud into the realm of regulation. Managing the city's soundproofing program entails recruiting potential participants, explaining process and procedure, checking off materials used, and overseeing construction. Though there are ethics and conceptual contours of this work, they must be drawn out—perhaps in terms of soundproofing as a gift, or by conceiving of the physics of sound as philosophy. A drive for philosophical conundrums finds footing elsewhere—not in whether to soundproof, or in what window treatment to use, or in whether a neighbor is in compliance, but in the office, where her impulse for intellectual prevarication or provocation turns over the ordinary objects found on desks and lunch room tables, draws them together, and amplifies their very ordinariness. The project is framed with a broader conceit, gesturing toward art movements and philosophical approaches: brutalism and nihilism punctuating—puncturing—a world of jelly beans and teddy bears. "OTTER POP AND FLAG BY MORNING LIGHT" is a view out the window, popsicle lying in the window frame, an American flag, an electric wire pole, a parking lot, a street, a fence. The L.A. light—a soft haze casting a pinkish tone on everything—is the subject of the photo. The atmosphere is one of light and sound, noise, smog, its play on buildings, entanglements of bodies and things, of work and home, of everyday objects refigured as clumsy metaphors, fabulation as fold if not worlding.

When the door of the house is open, the planes are loud; closed, the plane sound dulls, quiets. "It really does make a difference," she says, shifting from our experience to the general, the motivation for soundproofing, the difference of being "able to sleep at night." "What type of plane is that?" I ask. "The noisy kind," she laughs. Photos of the house before it was soundproofed lean against the wall. One shows a man screwing in a door frame, the gaps between wall and frame yet unsealed. The labor of soundproofing. Residents who qualify for residential soundproofing, whose homes are inside the 65 CNEL contour line, can stop by and see firsthand the windows, doors, and ventilation system their house might be equipped with if they decide to participate in the program. More than this, they can experience the sonic effect of these appurtenances, the shift in the acoustic environment when the doors are closed. Everything is dampened: voices reverberate less, and airplanes that seem to be departing nearly nonstop overhead are almost inaudible.

An owner can decline soundproofing, and in fact forty or sixty people in the neighborhood have. Mostly they do so because they dislike the vinyl windows—their houses have wood windows and Spanish tile roofs. There are no sound-rated wood windows, at least not offered by LAWA's program. And when the homeowners are offered a thick panel of glass to cover their windows, they reject it; imagine living by the beach and not being able to open the window! After declining three times, a home will be marked as "resolved," a bureaucratic checkmark counted toward the completion of the program. Sometimes there are code violations, such as garage apartments. These have to be addressed before soundproofing, and some people would rather not lose their extra living space, additional income, or family resi-

FIGURE 5.1
Noise measurement
microphone. Photo
by author.

dence. As LAWA's soundproofing program is now complete, the model house will soon be auctioned by the city. The garage is full of samples—doors and windows leaning messily against one another, plastic wrapping strewn around, making the neatly lined doors on racks difficult to access. This will have to be cleaned out before they can sell the house.

An airport noise measurement microphone is across the street from the model home, mounted high on its post on top of a telephone pole (figure 5.1). I take photos of planes flying over the house, over the noise measurement microphone. Though the interior has been turned into something of a sound studio—acoustically treated and mostly isolated—outside the sound of the planes has an immediacy. Within the innermost noise contour, one is also eligible for an avigation easement, in which the airport purchases an easement of airspace because the private outdoor area is unusable or has limited use. Noise, vibrating the matter of walls, windows, and ears, takes property into the air.

6 INDEFINITE URBANISM

Around LAX, sounds from the air shape the ground as a space of absence— rejected, abandoned, indeterminate, formless. What was once an upscale beach community, touted for its ocean views and underground utilities, is now an expanse of sandy dunes, with patches of native shrubs and grasses or still lingering ice plant, the concrete of Playa del Rey's streets and retaining walls a haunting of what once was (figure 6.1). To the north of the runways, dark green vines and shrubs explode in a wild mess within the confines of chain link fence. These are traces of an era of infrastructure, when freeways, stadiums, and airports took precedence over neighborhoods. Across the region, families took the city's money and moved, or held out and fought. At the L.A. City Archives, I search for traces of noise in the records of eminent domain around the airport. Some residents write letters requesting their homes be purchased, fearful that airport expansion will result in more noise. These letters were saved, filed with the official records. There is no mention of noise in eminent domain ordinances. With infrastructure providing legal grounds, homes to the north of LAX were acquired

FIGURE 6.1 *Airport Noise in Playa del Rey* (1967), Herald Examiner Collection, Los Angeles Public Library.

"for airport purposes," ones to the west for "public services"—a status that had recently been secured for the airport.[1] The problem of aircraft noise for residents closest to the airport was addressed in part through what cities and airports call "land recycling."[2] While this might take the form of residential soundproofing, at other times homes are purchased and demolished, replaced with shopping malls or car rental facilities. Or nothing. Demolition and conversion to infrastructural use appears as "emptiness" (McDonogh 1993). Hidden, here, in plain sight, is the invisible: a seeming void effected through noise. Noise effects are transpositions, transformations, and transductions, a proliferation of the atmospheric that takes shape in homes unmoored from their foundations at a time of social change, neighborhoods built on dunes transformed into infrastructural edge spaces now inhabited by an endangered species of butterfly.

Informed by Spanish architect Ignasi de Solà-Morales's (2014) notion of *terrain vague*, I use the term *indefinite urbanism* to attend to porous boundaries between that which is hard and that which is airy, to edge spaces of infrastructure as effects of the interplay between sounds from the sky and sensation, considering spaces shaped by atmospheric conditions and now invisible histories as a dimension of lived urbanism. Indefinite urbanism encompasses "blank space . . . ellipsis spaces, empty places, free space, liminal spaces, spaces of indeterminacy, spaces of uncertainty, vacant lands, voids" and "Dead Zones" (Doron 2007, 10). These are areas of loss and potentiality, of desire and play, of exploration and pleasure, of control and its limits, where things that may or may not be intentional happen. They do not dissipate or smooth over but remain, complicated and ambivalent, audible yet invisible, apparent yet seemingly void, formless or unformed. At the same time, indefinite urbanism extends beyond the particularity of edge spaces, affording the conceptualization of *a* city, *an* urbanism in which the openness of the indefinite does not prescribe, proscribe, or determine. Open ended, vague, undefined, or contradictory, it avoids the definitive, the definite *the*; *the* city that is modern, progressive, and growth oriented. It is city as process, in flux: emergent, ambivalent, inconclusive, vague, a "volumetric" "moving" city (Graham and Hewitt 2013; Latham and McCormack 2004).

UNDER THE CONCRETE, THE SAND

Homes in Los Angeles's postwar suburbs were built on concrete slabs as a measure of earthquake safety—there were no basements, nothing to fill in other than swimming pools, which, after the homes were removed, stood empty long enough for neighborhood youth to use them as skate ramps. In Playa del Rey, foundations laid on top of shifting sands stabilized the dunes momentarily with concrete, a metaphor for noise and its unstable bases in the subjective yet generalizable nature of human perception, stabilized, in turn, by noise metrics and zoning, or by eminent domain projects in which a generalized public good took precedent over particular peoples' property. Some of the homes were auctioned off to those who could move them, selling for little more than a thousand dollars. The former residents were not supposed to know where their homes were going, but someone reported following his as it was carried away in the night. A teenager took photos as her neighbor's homes were driven away on flatbed trailers. Years later, she was lost in El Segundo and spotted a house from her neighborhood on a residential street. She knocked on the door to ask the current owners if they knew anything about it, but they didn't. After we had coffee at the Blue Butterfly café on El Segundo's Main Street, she drove me around some of the areas affected by airport noise, but the house evaded our attempts to find it. A charity bought some and moved them to South Central Los Angeles, historic center of Black Los Angeles (see Bryant et al. 1998; Gregor 2000; Sides 2003).

A retired airport mechanic volunteering at LAX's Flight Path Museum knew someone who had flipped these houses: bought them, moved them, painted them, and resold them for a profit. And though the man who had handled the city's offers to homeowners said this was rarely done, as the process of procuring permits was cumbersome, he also told me that during this time, when airport property acquisition was one of several urban renewal and infrastructural building projects across the region, more than a dozen professional house moving companies were listed in the Yellow Pages. As I scroll through microfilm in the basement of the Central Library, their listings appear in bold white letters that struggle to emerge clearly from the black background. The Almas Brothers Star Movers ad fills the largest portion of the page, offering "experienced movers" and "leveling and shoring." Kechter House Moving Company in Compton will move everything, "from the smallest to the biggest," and also buys and sells houses. This is a business whose differences in the marketplace are emphasized by scare quotes, the unintended irony of which render an impermanence to their claims: "We move your building with care," "Our pride is satisfied customers," "For service call." Houses—perhaps equipped with hi-fi stereo systems and acoustically treated rooms prepared by engineers whose services fill adjacent pages of these same Yellow Pages—were lifted off their foundations and carried by truck along city streets, skimming wires bringing phone service and electricity to neighborhoods where the homes' attachment to the ground may have seemed a little less secure.

Yvette Kovary, who in the 1960s had spearheaded neighborhood mobilization against airport noise as chair of the citizens' committee in Playa del Rey, shows me photos that were used as evidence in her lawsuit against the airport—comparable properties, grounds that her home was worth more than the airport had offered. The yellow stickers "admitted as evidence" remain. Noise brings into focus property value and rights. Its foundation in nuisance law, concerned principally with the protection of private property, reemerges in relation to aircraft noise as values waver between affect and monetary remuneration. Lawsuits such as Kovary's draw use value into exchange value, maximizing the latter to compensate for the loss of the former. Such transduction is laden with affect, as a purportedly neutral rationality of capital absorbs—or strips bare—love and family and a sense of being settled. She said the airplane noise wasn't so bad, that what they wanted most was to stay in their home. Many of her neighbors had also re-sisted the impending loss of their homes, of a neighborhood described by a journalist as "a close-knit little Eden, set apart not just by its relative phys-ical isolation but also by the belief of its inhabitants that they lived some-where special." As a former resident told the *Daily Breeze*, "Living there was like living in paradise." Families "would often stroll two short blocks to the ocean after dinner," letting their children roam freely across the dunes and beach. "It was a delightful place to live, kind of like the French Riviera," one man said, and a retired aerospace worker and licensed pilot concurred: "'This whole area was a super neighborhood,' said Hoefler . . . . 'You couldn't beat it'" (Gregor 2000). Children who were given regular hearing tests may have screamed the first time a jet plane flew over but soon got used to it. Though Yvette Kovary also mentioned that her now middle-aged daughter's hearing loss was probably caused by the jet noise.

I listen, as photos ground memories of a neighborhood given form and dimension, her hand arcing to outline contours in the dunes—a hill, a bluff, a street running down to the beach. We are looking at an aerial pho-tograph of Playa del Rey taken from just off the coast, the date "5 4 59" printed in the upper-right-hand corner. Worn now, parts of its edges have torn or fallen off, revealing the board on which it is mounted. She tells me about her friends and neighbors, pointing to their houses and describing their personalities. Yvette's finger, pinkish and human scale against the sepia-toned miniaturization of the landscape, touches the spot where her house had stood, still visible in the image, and not, then, simply a trace on the dunes (figure 6.2). The airport runways are in the background, sur-rounded by expanses of open land. Looking at images that prompt mem-ories of a home and neighborhood, past seeps into present, emerging in the space-time fold that opens as her finger touches a map that may have been one she had brought to show to senators at 1960 congressional hear-ings—a hidden yet potent presence in transcripts that record words but not gestures, official statements but not the informal speech by those who are there to testify (see chapter 1). She says, of the photo, "I wanted to show them where we were, and what danger we were in." And she tells me, fifty-six years after the hearings, "I knew exactly what they were doing." Rather than staying in the clear zone of the runway, the planes flew directly over their homes. "I could stand in my backyard and see the nose of the plane skid across the horizon" as the pilot held the plane low instead of gaining altitude. She took what she described as an intentional, dangerous, and unnecessary act personally but left possible motivation open. Her touch

FIGURE 6.2 Touching her former home under the flight path. Photo by author.

tends to the memory manifest in a tattered aerial photograph—a photograph made with a technology afforded by flight, captured by a photographer pointing a camera out the door of a helicopter, with its own engine roar as it circled over the airport and its margins.

The aerial image is intrinsically atmospheric: coterminous with technologies of flight, it captures and is made possible by meteorological conditions of sunlight and air. Ambiguous, it "made possible new dynamic interplays between 'seen' and 'unseen' elements" (Kaplan 2018, 4). The first aerial images were made from a hot air balloon. While affording a new scopic regime, an "all-seeing viewpoint from which to observe, locate and map" (McCormack 2009, 33), balloon flight was equally impressive for its nascent sensory effects, the stillness of sky and clouds superseding the bustle of life on the ground (Castro 2013, 119).[3] Airplanes and helicopters offer another sensory regime, with engine noise drowning out speech, ears newly shielded by headphones that allow radio communication between pilot and passenger. The silence of the city below is upstaged by the roar of the engine, impressing its presence onto the photographer. Though often treated as evidence of domination, static representation, or a finalized form of documentation, the aerial image is also an opening, "a stimulant to [architects'] creative imagination" (Roseau 2013, 214).[4] Reflecting a "search for a representable whole," the aerial image casts a city in motion, a potentiality for the implementation of the vision of planners, or otherwise, through the very incompleteness of the search and its suspension as desire (Roseau 2013, 213). Thus the entanglement of flight and modern urban planning instantiated in the aerial photo amplifies the atmospheric quality of neighborhood rezoning and property acquisition as processes that render a city unstable and indefinite— the abstraction of the "city of the future" made real by "the conquest of the air" (Roseau 2013, 217).[5]

For decades the Public Relations Department of the Department of Airports commissioned aerial photographs, which are stored in file cabinets in the Flight Path Museum. I was directed to them to see firsthand what elderly volunteers meant when they talked about "mufflers"—hangars intended to dampen engine sound and curtail its propagation through air that are visible in airport photos from the 1950s. Other photos invoke noise directly, notably those filed as "aerial sound barrier Westchester 12–30–80." But otherwise noise is present only in its effects. In part this is a result of the generalizing nature of aerial photos, which here showcase the runways and airport terminal buildings, survey "land acquisition areas," and, over time, make visible neighborhood growth and the aftermath of home removals. Aerials taken in 1973 by a company based in Inglewood show scattered homes along beachfront streets in Playa del Rey and in the fanned subdivision of West Westchester abutting an airport runway. Shrubbery bereft of a home dots the edge of an expanse of grass and a street, its even spacing betraying the care with which it was planted, the domestic scene it once announced. By 1983 the streets of Playa del Rey west of the runways and of Westchester north of the runways are devoid of homes, the lighter gray of the concrete leaving rounded grids against the dark hue of the ground.

SMOG / RIOT

Though a white resident of Playa del Rey, Kovary identified with the Arechigas of Chavez Ravine, a Mexican American family that held out against their eviction until 1959, longer than other families.[6] They were vocal in their protest, their faces and names known across the region (Becerra 2012). Not so Lomie Puckett, who in 1958 stood on the porch of her Edendale rental property with a shotgun cradled in her arms, posing for the press in protest against what she decried as an offer of too little money by the city. Later, police dressed as newsmen provided a ruse to draw her from her house, as bulldozers standing by demolished it (Los Angeles Times 1992). In Playa del Rey, Mahria Decker, who a few years before had run for city council as the self-declared "people's voice" on the platform of "People controlling progress, not progress controlling people," was dragged from her home after refusing to sell until the city paid her what she claimed it was worth. When sheriff's deputies entered the home and began emptying its contents into a waiting moving van, Mahria took her eighteen-month-old grandson from her daughter, "insisting she would not be moved." A deputy grabbed the baby from her "for safekeeping," and they dragged her from the house. Her lawsuit still pending, "within an hour the house was bulldozed to the ground," making way for an airport parking lot whose contractor had set a deadline (Long Beach Press-Telegram 1975; Billings Gazette 1975).

The seeming stability of homes and neighborhoods was a recent achievement bolstered by postwar incentives for homeownership and subdivision development (Cuff 2000; Nicolaides 2002; see also Boyer 1986). Racially based restrictive covenants and redlining propped a fiction of commonality conflating epidermal signification with fortification and exclusion, establishing certain "securities" in a now internalized position of force (Crawley 2017; Harris 1993). All this required work—at minimum a discriminatory deed whose language was affirmed or overlooked, a tacit acceptance of property rights designating unequal status and crafting a segregated city. That groups mobilizing against airport noise (or for the protection of private property) were largely chaired by women can be attributed to a normative family form and gendered politics of work. Women stayed home with the children, who might scream in fear at the sound of an aircraft or race to look up in awe and excitement. Some of these women formed groups to deal with the noise of the planes and the impending encroachment of the airport on their neighborhoods, the potential loss of their dream homes built near the coast. They went door to door, knocking and asking for signatures to take to the airport noise group or the city councilperson. They rankled neighbors and were coolly included in afternoon cocktail parties. They used their husbands' names at first, though the men were at work all day and not affected by the noise. Even as they fought to maintain the lives they knew, there was a straining against the constraints of gender, of the household, of labor or the lack thereof.

As residents of neighborhoods still, though not much longer, under restrictive covenants continued their battle against airport noise, Watts, im-

FIGURE 6.3 *Smog/Riot*, by Norm Laich.

mediately east of Inglewood, burned with the fires of a riot stoked by the precarity of urban inequality, of structures of abandonment manifest in subpar housing and public services, along with the imminent threat of police violence.[7] The Black Panther Party's 1972 Ten-Point Program included housing as a human right, a rights claim yet to be realized. It was hot that summer, and the Situationist International (1965) wrote: "The Los Angeles rebellion is the first in history able to justify itself by the argument that there was no air conditioning during a heatwave." An atmosphere of change shimmered in the air, in bodies, in city infrastructure. "Sous les pavés la plage," under the paving stone the beach, a call to action both literal and symbolic: the paving stone a weapon against the police during 1968 riots in Paris manifesting the potential of liberation, of transforming the capitalist city into a space of freedom. And while not revolutionary in these terms, the return of the dunes, the seeping up of the sand in all its indeterminacy, also pushed against the stability of property.

In Norm Laich's print, the words SMOG RIOT stand one above the other, black-outlined red SMOG floating in a blue sky, black RIOT cast across the streets La Brea, Crenshaw, and Vermont, which recede into verdant hills (figure 6.3). Fire darts across the horizon, a setting sun round and yellow. The image conveys the conterminous yet vertically distinct concerns of the moment, SMOG floating in the air as fires consume the ground. The sign suggests a divide between the solidity of issues on the ground and the

ephemerality of that which is "in the air." Yet despite the apparent gulf between the political concerns of these adjacent neighborhoods—noise and
smog cast as aerial concerns that seemingly float above the heat on the
ground—they share an atmospheric orientation, an attunement toward
the quality of matter and its ephemerality: smoke from Watts wafting into
the sky, smog and airplane noise imbuing sense and breath with the atmospheric. In aerial photographs of Watts taken at the time, smoke from
burning buildings can be seen rising into the sky. Smoke signaling a burning building from blocks away. Smoke clouding the view from above even as
the photographer captured the billowing blackness from a distance. Smoke
dispersing into atmosphere. Smoke becoming smog. Smoke that made pilots
keep their planes high in the air before descending steeply to land at LAX, in
what became known as the "Watts Approach."[8] And though it may be a priv-
ilege to be concerned with the aerial when others have lost their homes to
fire, air—heavy with pollution or ash—matters; it is not "out there" above
the fray. Instead, air and ground are drawn together in shifting atmospheric
entanglements of airplane noise and desegregation, a general sense of instability and uncertainty settling into the city.

Air as a milieu of movement and freedom, as providing the possibility of
breath and flight, is unevenly distributed. Langston Hughes's poem "Restrictive Covenants" maps flight onto a freedom of whiteness: "When I move /
Into a neighborhood / Folks fly." "Why?" stands alone, punctuating the
poem, a break between the movement of those who "can move," a question
that destabilizes the normalization of racial segregation. After the break
are those who don't move and those who can't: the moon, the sun, the author, restricted by covenants, is "Hemmed in / On the South Side / Can't
breathe free." "But the wind blows there," wind that "must care" as it destabilizes the fixity of race, tearing away its grounding in that which is seemingly solid: the home on its concrete slab, the neighborhood with its hedges
and sidewalks.[9] As wind, air becomes a medium of escape from the dull certainty, the constraining, restricting pressure of racialized real estate, zones
and zoning, of being unable to breathe, a condition drawn into the present
but already invoked in a photo of the United Civil Rights Committee, whose
sign reads "Police Brutality MUST STOP" (Sides 2003, 164). In the aftermath
of the Watts rebellion, artist Noah Purifoy took the charred timbers and
signs and recast them as assemblages materializing the transformative
nature of fire, an emblem of the destructive plasticity that reverberated
across the region. Musician and artist Kim Gordon describes how in late
1960s Los Angeles, there was a pervasive sense of "disquiet . . . [a] shrugging

kind of anchorlessness" (2015, 57), a feeling also conveyed by Joan Didion in *The White Album* (1979). As schools in Inglewood, Westchester, and Playa del Rey were desegregated, a nervousness seemed to affect the lived condition of residential segregation, putting pressure on an experience shaped by the naturalization of racial differences as mapped onto cities worldwide for nearly a century (Nightingale 2012). In South Gate, to the east of Watts, residents mobilized against the threat of any change to their white working-class suburb. They stood guard over homes that were "key to their status, their history, and their very identity" (Nicolaides 2002, 1–2), protecting them from the violence of the rebellion and from Blackness itself.

Housing policy hardens race. Difference is produced, inscribed in neighborhoods intentionally segregated from one another; experienced as such, everyday life makes what one sees—epidermality as a sign of commonality or difference—seem natural. There are sedimentations of practices, many of which are inscribed as law; but these are neither explanatory frameworks nor forms of truth residing somewhere under the surface. If invisible, it is made so by means of representation, naturalization, or what Bourdieu calls "doxa." Emergent rather than explanatory, such dynamics are not eternally fixed; rather, like the "moving city" exemplified by concrete's hardening and degradation (Latham and McCormack 2004), bureaucratic categories of "land recycling," rezoning, and urban renewal are (less than natural) rhythms of urban life. Material entanglements proliferate as already existing categories. Yet race, sutured to lived experience through zoning laws and real estate practices, is less fixed, less a solidity than a set of differences into which Angelenos, like others, were—and continue to be—trained to experience bodily, visually, aurally. The tools of segregation coalesce into forms that are physical, legal, moral, and more (Rothstein 2017). In Carl H. Nightingale's global history of urban segregation, he provides a wonderfully sprawling list of the range of things used to separate people from one another—of the creation and maintenance of difference made tangible and hard, naturalized in the landscape and movement of capital:

> walls, palisades, battlements, bastions, fences, gates, guard shacks, checkpoints, booms, railroad tracks, highways, tunnels, rivers, canals, inlets, mountainsides and ridges, buffer zones, free-fire zones, demilitarized zones, *cordon sanitaires*, screens of trees, road blocks, violent mobs, terrorism, the police, armies, curfews, quarantines, pass laws, labor compounds, building clearances, forced removals, restrictive covenants, zoning ordinances, racial steering practices, race-

infused economic incentives, segregated private and public housing developments, exclusive residential compounds, gated communities, separate municipal governments and fiscal systems, discriminatory access to land ownership and credit, complementary systems of rural reservations, influx control laws, and restrictions against overseas immigration. (2012, 32)

In no apparent order, they nonetheless hang together. In Los Angeles, the Realty Board "established tough, enforceable deed restrictions as a fairly reliable method of controlling large, newly subdivided residential and commercial developments" (Weiss 1987, 80). Such covenants might address allowable colors for a house or those to whom it could not be sold.

A history of desegregation and neighborhood change in southwest Los Angeles has yet to be written. In my research, fragments emerged in archives and interviews, providing glimpses of what the experience may have been like. Sociologists Edna Bonacich and Robert F. Goodman, then researchers at System Development Corporation, initially planned on using Inglewood as the basis for a simulation game about school district policy conflict. The city was an ideal site insofar as it was "in the midst of a serious desegregation controversy" (Bonacich and Goodman 1972, vi). Finding that what was happening did not fit existing models, they also published a case study based on their encounters. What comes out of the slim volume is the time spent listening to residents, who talked openly about their attitudes about race in relation to neighborhood and school demographics. Only a few years after the formation of that city's anti–airport noise coalition, the Citizens' Health and Welfare Committee, community groups formed in response to the issue of school desegregation. Those in favor of desegregation based their argument on the grounds of community "stabilization" (Bonacich and Goodman 1972, 46–65). Yet surveys suggested that residents perceived their neighbors as conservative—segregationist and overtly racist.

In listening to memories of mobilizing against airport noise, I hear another story nestled in their folds, one that crackles and pops with affect in its telling. She recalls looking out the window at Westchester High and witnessing four "six-foot-tall" Black youth walking down the path, arms linked, two girls, two boys. A little blonde girl tried to pass them; when they didn't give way, she darted around a bush. The storyteller is the girl's mother. She does not say whether the girl acted threatened or playful. The gap of her silence is suggestive, but it is not entirely clear what is intended. She transferred her daughters to El Segundo High, gaining admittance by silently passing their photos—"smiling, apple cheeked, blonde"—across the desk to the school superintendent who, without a pause, said okay.[10] Her explanation is that the vacant lots in the area had brought people who hung out along the fence in their cars, doing who knows what. Another silence, another gap. Stories percolate in the gaps, spilling out from the space created when disparate things are drawn together. These are moments of parataxis, in which something emerges in the drawing together, in relationships created through juxtaposition, that present themselves without necessarily making sense. Some things appear to add up, as situations in flux dot the terrain around the airport; skittering across fragments of memory and geography, any suturing reads as overdetermination, a desire for something not yet achieved, or an achievement resting on (un)stable grounds of difference and discrimination.

Such uncertainty is palpable in the faces of Black children bused to Westchester's Loyola Village School. The images of Playa del Rey in the Los Angeles Public Library photo archive mostly depict young people sunbathing on the beach and oil wells dotting the coast. Among these are three documenting 1964 school integration. In one, a young girl sits in the front row, her arms crossed, a look of trepidation if not suspicion on her face, as "Mike Shane, 11, standing at left, student council president at Loyola Village School in Playa del Rey, welcomes some of 82 pupils from Manchester Avenue School who were transferred to Loyola." The photo caption hints at the turmoil around desegregation: "A total of 151 students from two predominantly 'Negro' schools were transported to two all-white schools without an incident." The children, almost all of whom are Black, sit in wooden seats held together by shared armrests reminiscent of Eames's airport seating. Almost all of them look at the boy in the front of the room, who stands at the edge of the photo, a patch on his shirt sleeve the most visually compelling feature, parted blonde hair held firmly in place with a thick coat of gel, a hint of a wave at the front. The direction of the children's gaze suggests they are listening, though to what, we do not know. Two girls look directly at the camera, their gaze meeting ours.

Twelve years later, when congresswoman Yvonne Brathwaite Burke testified before the Aviation Subcommittee of the U.S. Senate Committee on Public Works and Administration, she described Inglewood as "a city in racial transition, which," she said, "causes another set of problems."[11] She explained that noise had caused businesses on Arbor Vitae to close, a street that fifty years later is the site of car rental companies. A photo she provided as evidence shows the empty buildings of Airport Junior High School, only

FIGURE 6.4 *Airport Junior High School, January 17, 1976.* Yvonne Brathwaite Burke Papers. Courtesy of University of Southern California, on behalf of the USC Libraries Special Collections.

a decade old, lurking behind a looming For Sale sign (figure 6.4). Ground and air—where seemingly different kinds of things are happening—are drawn together in the *terrain vague* of now-vacant lots across the street from LAX's rental car facilities. I walked past them once, along a wide road not meant to be traversed by pedestrians. A sign on a chain link fence warns passersby not to feed the birds, as they are a hazard to aircraft. A fallen tree lies on the ground, its branches dry and bare, small yellow flowers at its base standing witness.

De/territorializing

Residents in Playa del Rey mobilized against rezoning, not noise. Then, as now, the airport was the threat, the enemy against which their rage and resentment was directed. "'It's insidious,'" one "said of the airport's appetite for land." The violence they felt materialized in an accident, an eleven-year-old boy "crushed to death by rubble from a demolished home while playing on a vacant lot" (Gregor 2000). A violence resides in the project and practice of zoning: zoning that is also police power and zoning that authorizes infrastructure; zoning as urban soundproofing and zoning as protecting the value of private property and neighborhoods of single-family homes; zoning "as a tool for social segregation," enacted through things such as restrictive covenants and urban renewal; zoning as a tool for urban transformation (Fischel 2015; Hirt 2014; Thomas and Ritzdorf 1997). Rezoning plans for areas west of the airport were already in place as early as 1945. California Assembly Bill No. 807 (1945) allowed airports to acquire land and airspace necessary for airport uses. A hand-drawn map of airport rezoning included in developer Fritz Burns's papers next to a copy of this bill shows airport expansion, with most of the area west of the runways hand colored with a yellow pencil marking its status as an "area to be rezoned," noted, in the area, as "R-1 to M-2."[12]

After they had been purchased by the airport but had not yet been demolished, some of the empty homes were used for soundproofing tests; vacant, they became experiments in matter. "Inside there are piles of discarded soundproofing material. The project's personnel install various types of material—such as fiberboard, gypsum board, fiberglass, thin sheets of lead, a seven-inch thickness of foam—alone and in combinations in the walls, floors, and ceilings, then take careful sound level readings to determine the effectiveness. Then the material is ripped out and another kind installed" (Chicago Tribune 1968, 16). And while by 1968 "the land around these houses, which once were surrounded by green lawns, has reverted to sand dunes" (Chicago Tribune 1968, 16), a few houses remained until 1975. Yvette Kovary's was one of these; on Valentine's Day 1973, she wrote that "Sand has blown from airport-owned lots during recent storms, inundating our iceplant and driveway."[13]

Residents who remained in Playa del Rey planted ice plant in an effort to halt the sand that, freed from its containment under concrete, drifted here and there, blowing into streets, driveways, and still cultivated yards when the wind was strong. Ice plant, *Carpobrotus edulis*, also known as Hottentot fig, with its shallow roots and creeping, rhizomatic form, takes hold quickly and spreads. Native to South Africa, it flourishes in Mediterranean climates. Needing little water, it blooms a brilliant lavender or pink flower, a burst of color against the olive green field. Its thick clusters cover the ground around beachfront homes, providing greenery that stands out against the more subdued hues of dune ecosystems. A succulent, it can grow when just one of its three-sided segments meets ground, developing roots, taking hold, and generating fingers and branches that spread across the sand. It crowds out native species and makes the sandy soil of coastal dunes hospitable to other nonnative plants. Host to the El Segundo blue butterfly's predators, "Once established, the exotic plants tend to overtake coastal buckwheat, the butterfly's sole food source" (Kowsky 1995). Ice plant gives root to a desire for fixity and control. It made the development of Manhattan Beach possible, keeping "the shifting sands" of dunes "in place," dunes that "ignored artificial constructions of the landscape, reappearing in alleyways and athwart thoroughfares" (Masters 2012). Later those dunes were leveled, the sand shipped to Hawaii to create Waikiki Beach. First introduced to Southern California in the early 1900s to stabilize soil along railway lines, ice plant continues to be planted extensively along freeways. A rhizome that territorializes rather than deterritorializes, it spreads quickly, taking over areas that might be otherwise populated, especially if sparsely, as dune habitats tend to be (Marder 2016). To remove it, as I learned during a dunes restoration volunteer event, you start from the outside in, digging in with your fingers to feel beneath the shallow roots, pulling up each of its "arms" until they clump around their starting point, which, more deeply anchored, requires the use of a knife to dig around and into the cluster and free the thicker roots from the sand. We were warned to not leave a single segment lying on the ground. Its status as invasive species is marked by this warning, though the word isn't used. Instead I only hear "native/nonnative," perhaps a more benign designation, which nonetheless still evokes a human parallel (Hartigan 2014; Mastnak, Elyacher, and Boellstorff 2014).

Ice plant stabilized the known, fixing the surface against otherwise unstoppable changes.[14] Yvette Kovary wrote to then mayor Tom Bradley, explaining that she had planted ice plant in the vacant lots across the street from her house "to keep some of the sand in place and from drifting across to fill our driveway," but that much of the area looked terrible, like "the aftermath of a war—a war declared by the City of Los Angeles against its own residents and taxpayers."[15] Her anger seeps onto the page, her outrage framed with a biting cordiality: "Dear Sir, . . . Respectfully Yours." "Unbelievable in this day of environmental concern," the "once-lovely community" now has "rubble-strewn vacant lots" with "weeds up to eight feet in height, . . . smashed and unrepaired sidewalks, . . . sidewalks covered with sand (often to the roadway), . . . damaged or missing street signs, and . . . boarded-up houses." A glimpse of an anthropogenic future, the neighborhood stands as a culmination of Smithson's "ruins in reverse," the "memory-traces of an abandoned set of futures" ([1967] 1979, 54, 55) once more returned to rubble (figure 6.5; Gordillo 2014).

NOISY SILENCE

Departing planes now fly over the Pacific before turning back for easterly flights. The flight path is directly above the dunes, which, as was discovered in the early 1970s, are habitat for the El Segundo blue, an endangered species of butterfly. Visually, the ground above which planes from LAX depart prompts designations of "ghost town" by bloggers, eager to explore but thwarted by the chain link fence, through which one can see the pavement of streets that once formed a neighborhood. The ground rolls across the dunes, its hue the gray-brown of sand and gray-green of coastal flora. It is an indefinite place, indeterminate and ambiguous (Königstein 2014). Infrastructural edges are not the "abandoned" space of capitalist speculation, left under- or unutilized until their value makes them worth putting the land back into circulation as commodity. It is unlikely that this terrain—like traffic islands or hillsides flanking freeways or dirt-floored caverns under bridges and overpasses—will be commodified, sold or rented, privatized, capitalized on. But that does not mean it is outside capital, or that it is available for creative use or critique (Mariani and Barron 2014). Instead, capital subsists in urban growth and its twin of security, a capitalist city shaped by and through its public infrastructure. Once a cruising space, after 9/11 the thoroughfares that had provided cover of darkness beyond the scrutiny of "eyes on the street" were also fenced off. Enclosure is justified on the grounds of property: that of the airport, overseen by an autonomous city agency. Shaped by our use of the skies, the area is devoid of human habitation as much for safety and security as noise mitigation. And to protect the butterflies.

Tracing noise, I arrive at butterflies—delicate, winged, darting about in flight, coasting on wind currents or perching on coastal buckwheat, gently opening and closing their wings, they are atmospheric. Dwelling with them becomes a stilled moment in a final eddy of the proliferation of atmospheric phenomenon. In the dunes to the west of the runways noise is present even as it falls away, palpable in its effects. Encounters with the butterfly strain toward a more than human orientation that nonetheless continues to pull back into the sensible, into regulation and rationality. Yet, in attuning toward this small, delicate, and threatened species, the question of what we

FIGURE 6.5 Dunes. Photos by author.

can know of another's experience resonates. Atmospheric in its relationship to the air, for most of its life cycle the butterfly withdraws from view, echoing the history of the place in which it lives. At once living being and metaphor, this very uncertainty seems to inspire wonder and care. With most of the homes no longer standing, entomologists from the Natural History Museum returned to the dunes, whose wildlife had been cataloged in the decades prior to residential development. I find only two references from this time. In 1970 the El Segundo blue butterfly made an appearance in an unpublished manuscript by a former Natural History Museum entomologist (Laufer 2009, 140). In 1973, the year the Endangered Species Act was passed, it was included in *The Butterflies of Southern California*, published in the Natural History Museum of Los Angeles County Science series (Emmel and Emmel 1973).

My copy of *The Butterflies of Southern California* arrives well worn and tattered, its cover once held together with Scotch tape now encased in a plastic sleeve, also crumpled and taped. Notes fill the pages; photocopies of hand-typed inserts with keys to the image plates are carefully taped onto facing

pages. The book is inscribed by the authors, "With best regards, John F. Emmel [and] Thomas C. Emmel," each signing his name in elegant, antiquated script. An address stamp on the title page tells me the book once belonged to Olga Clarke of Glendale, California. Olga Clarke, a lover of butterflies, a butterfly expert, a collector of butterflies and all things butterfly; also in the book are strips of thirteen-cent butterfly postage stamps and, in the middle, between pages describing the California hairstreak, the sylvan hairstreak, the desert hairstreak, the dryope hairstreak, a butterfly, pressed and wrapped with care in plastic wrap. I gasp when I discover it—the thing itself, a material presence, a mattering of the book in and as practice. Its burnt orange and yellow wings are still nearly intact, though its body has decayed and flaked apart inside the plastic. The touch of Olga Clarke, already present in the dog-eared pages and penciled notes of the book intensifies here in the butterfly, the care of its capture and killing exuding a violent love—a love of typology and classificatory systems, a love of the fluttering movements of multihued wings, a love of the exploration of the coast and its flora, or of her own Glendale yard. The El Segundo blue entry reads:

MARTIN'S PHILOTES, *Philotes battoides martini Mattoni, Philotes battoides* **subspecies, Plate 8, figures 1–3.**

> On the immediate coast of Los Angeles County, an undescribed sub-species of *battoides* flies in July and August. It uses *Eriogonum parvifolium* Sm. in Rees (Polygonaceae) as a host. Populations will exist on the El Segundo sand dunes at the western end of the runways of the Los Angeles International Airport, and in a few limited localities along the coast in the Palos Verdes area. The butterfly will probably become extinct unless some sort of action is taken to preserve the habitat area. (Emmel and Emmel 1973, 70)

The entry is unique in its lack of description of the butterfly, iterating, instead, a hard specificity of infrastructure, an airport whose runways abutted dunes, where, in 1973, homes still stood, but already a politics of nature was being asserted. Butterflies now in need of protection, an unspoken human in the call to action, the call for preservation. Lepidopterists as political subjects. In 1976 the El Segundo blue butterfly was the first insect to be granted endangered status by the federal government.

The interspecies encounter of butterfly and human takes form within and beyond a physical encounter. A sighting of a butterfly by human eyes is a sensory encounter that proliferates into forms that are both physical and abstract, the touch of butterfly capture imbricated in regulatory regimes. Yet, following Malabou, "the materialism of the encounter" is at once immanent and uncertain, and "doesn't presuppose any telos, reason, or cause" (2015, 49). There is something in the encounter between human and butterfly of what Yusoff calls the "insensible," meaning that which "alerts us to the work of sense in securing the *bringing into* relation, its configurations, and its a priori orientations," even as it "highlights the conditions under which we make knowledge and the way in which these conditions are directed towards certain resolutions of entities, of arrangements, of matter that are already *towards* the coherency of an event, as phenomenon, as writing, as sense work" (2013, 224). The insensible is Bataille's *l'informe*, or "nonknowledge," a force between sense and nonsense, "between material and virtual, inhuman and human, organic and nonorganic, time and the untimely" (Bataille 1985; Yusoff 2013, 213). And though the butterfly-human encounter almost immediately moves into the sensible—law, science, notions of ecology, humanistic modes of planetary care, metaphor, the biopolitical subject of environmentality—something remains of the "strange, nonintuitive, insensible[,] remote from human comprehension or intelligibility" (Yusoff 2013, 225; see also Asdal, Druglitrø, and Hinchliffe 2017). The butterfly exceeds human knowledge of it, even as it is potentially at risk of extinction at human hands.

An orientation of care that privileges human over butterfly draws the two together in a series of encounters; yet even "the specific materiality and multiplicity of the subject" does not quite undo the preeminence of the human, does not quite yield to a sense that "the 'human' . . . is not now, and never was, itself" (Wolfe 2003, 9). Rather, what is formed in these encounters is butterfly as object of human desire and care—of silence, fragility, precarity, posed against the roar of the jet. Anthropogenic charity embodied by the butterfly and manifest in bodily encounters with plants and soil. A nonteleological form of the encounter between butterfly and human is shaped but not determined by other forms, encounters that, though not structuring per se, do not come out of nowhere. Something of history, of long-conditioned modes of thought, endures and inscribes meaning in form. Metaphor and physicality draw together around the human-butterfly encounter. Care, enacted through the physicality of sight and touch, is iterated as such, hand meeting soil as volunteers plant coastal buckwheat in the dunes to provide a habitat for the El Segundo blue butterfly. "Using a spade, she got on her hands and knees and dug a generous hole in the ground. Patting the earth with her hands, she created a cradle of freshly tilled soil for the little seedling" (Kowsky 1995). Care does not extend to the nonnative, the invasive, the ice plant. Instead, "The volunteers . . . offered to pull up some ice plant—non-native vegetation introduced to the area by developers in the early '50s—on the sand dunes overlooking the ocean" (Kowsky 1995; see also U.S. Fish and Wildlife Service 1998, 7).

During the 1980s, the butterflies were at the center of a political drama over the use of the dunes, with the finality of federal legislation in the form of the Endangered Species Act superseding a desire to golf under planes rising loudly into the air as they depart over the Pacific. If the Dunes Press clippings filed in LAWA's Flight Path Museum library are indicative, it was highly contentious, a battle pitched as butterflies versus humans: the city councilperson representing the butterflies, men writing letters to the editor making rights claims as humans. A proposal for a golf course and recreation area was first denied by the California Coastal Commission, which insisted on the preservation not only of the butterfly but of the coastal sand dune ecosystem, itself an endangered formation that once stretched down the coast to Mexico. Rudi Mattoni argued for wholesale dunes restoration, his role in "discovering" the El Segundo blue at the dunes as a teenager and overseeing its habitat during its first decade of protection inscribed in the butterfly's Latin name. He gushed, "'What's remarkable about this coastal prairie is that it was the only one like it in the area. . . . It is a very important part of our natural heritage. It's as great a value as any work of art'" (Kowsky 1995). Kovary finds satisfaction in the fact that the butterflies were found, and the area could not be developed, and Mattoni describes the airport "as a blessing in disguise. 'If LAX wasn't there,' he says, 'this plot of land would have been a shopping center a long time ago'" (Moloney 1992). The golf course continued to have advocates, but a compromise that designated two hundred acres as El Segundo blue habitat and one hundred acres for a golf course never yielded the latter. The entire dunes area west of the airport is enclosed in chain link fence, inside of which is a large blue sign announcing in white letters that the area is the "El Segundo Blue Butterfly Habitat Restoration Area," and that "This effort to preserve an endangered species is sponsored by the City of Los Angeles," signed by the Board of Airport Commissioners.

Inhabiting a place deemed unfit for human habitation, the butterfly undergoes complete metamorphosis on, and under, coastal buckwheat plants, plants with "a profound relationship with the soil and shifting sand" (Russell 2004, 168). Though the El Segundo blue is one of several pollinators of coastal buckwheat, it is the only one that relies on the plant for its entire life cycle. This is, importantly, not the common buckwheat, which, planted by the airport as landscaping, attracts a moth that preys on the El Segundo blue. With a life cycle spanning a year, they become butterflies between mid-June and early September, their ability to fly coinciding with the flowering of the buckwheat. Weather or climate or other forces might disrupt this temporal confluence. One rainy year the buckwheat bloomed early, and there was concern that the butterflies would suffer and their population decline. Butterfly metamorphosis is Malabou's plasticity: one form destroyed, another form emerging from the destruction. Plasticity, Renisa Mawani writes, "is most visually apparent in the process of metamorphosis. . . . Throughout this process, form is simultaneously emergent and eradicated. A . . . larva reconstructs itself at the pupal stage and has little resemblance to an adult" (2015, 165). Plasticity is thus a worlding, an emergent, transformative mode of existence, "a possible line of flight" (Mawani 2015, 167). Staying close to the crown of the plant, the butterflies mate (Arnold 1983, 82; U.S. Fish and Wildlife Service 1998, 11). The females eat and lay eggs on the flower head—a cluster of small white and pink flowers. The eggs hatch in three to five days if not consumed by a parasitic wasp, who protects the buckwheat (Raffles 2011). After eating two or three flower heads over the course of a little over three weeks, the caterpillars burrow under the sand among the roots of the buckwheat, where they pupate, lying still and quiet for the next eleven months, inaccessible, then, to humans.

A flurry of interspecies entanglements take place during the month in which the butterfly lives on the flowers of the buckwheat plant. Plants sense insects, responding chemically to caterpillars munching their leaves (Karban 2015, 22). Such sensing is also sonic; in a lab it was found that "*Arabidopsis* plants that were played recordings of vibrations caused by feeding caterpillars"—though not wind or insect singing—"primed their defenses against virtual attack" (Karban 2015, 29). Ants protect the larvae from the parasitic wasp that protects the plant. Rudi Mattoni relayed the process, explaining that the larvae are "attended by ants, which protect them from parasitoids."[16] These ants drink a "sweet secretion," exuded from glands that emerge as the ant strokes the larva's back—a seeming symbiosis of pleasure and protection in which the biopolitical subject of an endangered species is entangled in an interspecies assemblage of transformation and becoming. Ant pleasure and pupae secretion sparks the imagination of biologists and butterfly aficionados. Mattoni described the nectar as a "delicious honey solution. They get high, they love it." And as the larvae secrete, they sing, communicating via very quiet sounds at very high frequencies, inaudible to humans, but within the realm of transducible sound (DeVries 1990).[17]

Some scientists, however, shift from the titillation of ant pleasure, of peaceable communication between species, to suggest such ant-caterpillar relationships may be less equanimable (Hojo, Pierce, and Tsuji 2015; Maestripieri 2012).[18] Their framework of biological market does a different kind of work: larvae compete for the attention of fewer ants by producing more nectar but produce less when there are many ants present. The ants, who do not need the sugary secretion, may also eat a larva that is not producing nectar, thus eliminating "the free riders from the population" (Maestripieri 2012, 214). A *Science* headline puts it bluntly: "Butterflies Drug Ants, Turn Them into Bodyguards" (Asher 2015). In this account, because the caterpillars need the ants but not vice versa, the caterpillars manipulate the ants with chemicals in their sweet secretion, or, in other words, they "use nectar to drug unsuspecting ants with mind-altering chemicals." Yet the nectar imparts a caterpillar's version of cruel optimism, as the ants who drink it run aggressively around the caterpillars rather than defending them from wasps and spiders.

Extortion, psychological manipulation, and death tinge the desire for sweet secretion with malevolence and violence, another kind of metaphor for the transformation of dunes into neighborhoods, neighborhoods into rubble, across which "invasive" species flourished, only to be removed slowly by human hands pushing sharp spades into the sand, cutting branches and roots with little knives, "restoring" an earlier ecosystem as an emblem of planetary care. Such an account of insect interaction complicates *metamorphosis* as a metaphor for the emergence of a more beautiful self, with iridescent wings and the possibility of flight, an ephemeral, atmospheric being cleansed of the troubles of the Earth. This is a metaphor more readily applied to the ATV riders who cut the chain link fence and drove their vehicles over the dunes, destroying native species already planted and waiting to be planted as part of habitat restoration. A local journalist interpreted their actions as intentionally cruel, intentionally destructive, with implications on a broader scale, a "new kind of hate crime" directed against nature rather than people (Daily Breeze 1994). Though this is nature that was rather obviously cultivated, a logical intentionality across objects of destruction—fence, plant, greenhouse, PVC pipe—is not obvious.

Nor is there a logical intentionality to ant-butterfly relations, whether cast in terms of a rationality of market relations or the physical pleasure of interspecies touch and intoxication. The latter, which suggests an "*affective ecology* shaped by pleasure, play, and experimental propositions" (Hustak and Myers 2012, 78), is nonetheless as much an anthropocentric projection as the former. And, while extortion and manipulation more readily serve a neo-Darwinian model of evolution, both accounts of the butterfly-ant dynamic draw together a physicality of sensation with an interpretation of its meaning, folding a relationship between insects into one between insects and humans. Missing are the ways in which the relationship between butterfly and ant, however it is cast and whatever its motivations might be, is "a reciprocal capture," an "'intra-active' phenomenon" of "creative involution," Deleuze and Guattari's formulation that "amplifies relations constituted through affinity" (Hustak and Myers 2012, 97). There is a possibility of formlessness presented by the butterfly-ant encounter, an insensibility that has the potential to undermine an anthropocentric stance by pulling "these relations into a strange territory" (Yusoff 2013, 225) of pleasurable pain, of purposeless consumption of an other, of drunken ants wobbling around an oozing larva. Ant stroking caterpillar secreting sweet nectar drunk by ant protecting caterpillar is a becoming "'in which the discernability of points disappears'" (Deleuze and Guattari, quoted in Hustak and Myers 2012,

97)—albeit one of interested parties, with "asymmetries of power between partners" (106).

Despite the (al)lure of a zone of nonhuman agency, butterfly-ant becomings yield to butterfly-human entanglements both immediate and metaphoric. Following Mawani, "The vivid materialization of plasticity in insects is partly what has rendered them enigmatic and compelling figures, sources of wonderment that mark the limits of the human in Western philosophy and literature" (2015, 165). The butterfly is sign and metaphor. It travels with transplanted buckwheat and appears as coffee shop logo, street name (Mariposa), the environmental stamp of an oil company. A former gang member's story is intertwined with the butterfly's preservation; a longtime volunteer at the dunes whom Mattoni hired as his assistant, he told the *Los Angeles Times*, "I'm saving them from extinction and they're saving me from the street" (Slater 1996). Or, as ecologist Travis Longcore told *People* magazine, "he treats the butterflies as equals . . . he understands how hard it is to be a butterfly" (Lipton 1998). The "suffering and trauma" experienced by the butterfly, or the fact that, as Mattoni told the *Daily Breeze*, "Nature is very hard; nature is very tragic," bolsters the need for human care, drawing the human into an interspecies entanglement as protector, whether in an immediate, physical sense, or through law or metaphor (Robak 1988).

The airport offers an annual butterfly tour to employees. We drive down the now cracked pavement of the streets that once defined a neighborhood, through the rolling hills of the dunes with their spectacular view of the ocean and the Santa Monica Mountains in the distance, down boulevards lined with palm trees, stopping at a street that would have continued west were it not now blocked from its route by sand and a chain link fence. The fence creates a barrier between the perpendicular intersection of this now unnamed street and the busy thoroughfare of Vista del Mar, on the other side of which lies Dockweiler State Beach. The biologist leading the tour sets up a small amplifier in the sand atop a ruin of a retaining wall, still standing though the house whose foundation it protected from the sand's slow seep is gone. Dick Arnold uses the amplifier to broadcast his voice to the small group of women gathered around the coastal buckwheat plants, looking with great intensity as we try to spot a butterfly. We see one, but it is not the El Segundo blue. Wind touches the microphone, a plane whine passes over, becoming the white noise of engine sound, feedback from the small amplifier, "hooaaa," laughter, "that's a Metalmark right there," he says. At last one is spotted, a male, "flittin' around." We talk to each other about the difficulty of capturing a butterfly with a camera, listening to our

FIGURE 6.6 Attuning. Photos by author.

guide with half an ear. The flier we received when we boarded the bus has an enormous, clear, and distinct image of a male El Segundo blue butterfly, blue wings with an orange border at the back of its rear wings. We are trying to spot something that is about one inch across, blue (male) or orange and brown wings with white spots (female), against the scrubby gray and gray-green drought-afflicted coastal buckwheat plant. "There's a female. See how it's darker?" A male and female dart around each other, and those gathered express "awwws" at the arthropod romance (figure 6.6).

Our attunement toward a small, winged insect that flits in air, airborne until it lands, gently opening and closing its wings as it finds nourishment in a tiny flower emerges from an entanglement of management and care. The biologist giving the tour is also responsible for conducting a butterfly count that fulfills the regulatory regime of the law of species protection, potentially shifting its status from endangered to protected. Visuality and touch conjoin in an account of a count that is also an encounter. He describes how he walks across the preserve to conduct transect and block counts, the former a line established for the sake of the count, the latter or-

ganized around the still visible geography of human habitation. Looking, and counting, as he moves, he traverses a mile-and-a-half-long historical transect route once a week during the flight season. A block count uses the still present streets of the former neighborhood, and he counts butterflies on all the buckwheat plants in every residential block "as well as the areas that didn't have residents." These numbers are combined to calculate a population estimate of the total number of butterflies in a season. "We've had numbers as high as 100,000 in a good year but this year"—a departing plane drowns out his voice, and when it is once again audible, he's talking about how he counts the butterflies on a buckwheat plant—"slowly walk around it, and every time I see a butterfly, I'm making a mental tally of that." He uses a data dictionary in his GPS device that allows him to note the number of butterflies by male and female, including their behavior, and tie it to "this particular geographic location."

Calibrating his bodily movement to the sensibility of the butterfly, he explains that "If you move around the plant slowly and don't disturb them, they tend to do what they normally do without being bothered." This year the block counts yield around fifteen hundred butterflies; in previous years it was more like five or six thousand. He also does a marking study, using GPS and a Sharpie. Catching the butterflies with a net, he holds each one with forceps and marks its wings quickly, using a dot code to designate its number. "You have positions on the wings that represent, it's 1 2 4 7, 10 20 40 70, so if you want to do number 65, you put a dot at the 20 and 40 position and 1 and 4 position on the wings. It's quick so you don't have to hold the butterfly very long." At the end "you just put them back on the flowerhead and make sure they"—another plane flies overhead, obscuring his voice. Imagining him holding a butterfly makes me pause, surprised. The butterfly is not as delicate as it is sometimes made out to be; it withstands the metal of the forceps and the touch of an indelible marker.

Though described as "sedentary," "perching" on the buckwheat plant on which they metamorphosed into a butterfly (Arnold 1983, 82), on which they learned to fly, the butterflies are not confined to the dunes; they have been found along the coast, indicating that they can, in fact, fly. There is a level of surprise or incredulity in statements about their having crossed the highway to feed on buckwheat plants at Dockweiler State Beach. Their need for care and protection as endangered species turns on their small size, their delicate, tenuous existence. An entomologist told *National Geographic*, "'Imagine a little butterfly the size of your thumbnail trying to cross this road,' Arnold marvels. 'It's not impossible, but it's still pretty remarkable'" (Watson 2016). At Ballona Wetlands, they say, "we planted the buckwheats, and the butterflies showed up." Rudi Mattoni says they must have come with the buckwheat they transplanted, hitched a ride rather than flying that distance. El Segundo blue butterflies map new air-ground geographies that seem incomprehensible to humans. They are, after all, butterflies, whose mode of movement is flight. They know something about flying—their wings hold them aloft as they flit from flower head to flower head, nibbling then seeking out another, or one another. For longer distance the wind helps, carrying the butterflies aloft on unpredictable eddies and gusts that may deposit them somewhere near a coastal buckwheat plant or not. Theirs is what Yusoff calls "an insensible alterity," as "the sudden wind that brushes my cheek is but a graze of the sensational possibilities that are offered the insect on the wing" (2013, 216). Though I am told "there is no auditory structure in butterflies comparable to humans," I am not told about, and cannot fully know, the butterfly's sensory abilities—how it knows how to find the flower on which it feeds, or another of its kind.[19]

I can only imagine how the butterfly must feel, its wings spread as it coasts on the wind, held high in the air as it moves over a field and across a freeway. Sensing the scent of pollen of other plants, inhabiting a world of "'propositions' waiting to be registered by *interested* bodies," attuning "themselves to others" and discriminating "increasingly subtle differences in" an other's "utterances" (Hustak and Myers 2012, 105). As another sensing species, with antennae and legs and wings that experience differences in atmospheric conditions, it must also be moved by the aerial vibration of the sound of a departing plane. The butterflies do not know about the chain link fence, or about needing to stay in one place to be caught, marked, and counted. In its movement, the El Segundo blue begins to restitch a now patchworked dune ecosystem, its presence entangled with a newfound emphasis on restoration that reimagines and remakes a natural past in an urban present. The dunes were formed from sand deposited by the Los Angeles River, which, before it was concretized, flowed into the Pacific Ocean through what is now Playa del Rey. Their contours are shaped by "a combination of *littoral* drift and wind" (U.S. Fish and Wildlife Service 1998, 6). As the coastal area where water meets the shoreline, the littoral is a zone of circulation. Characterized by water lapping onto beaches or waves crashing onto rocks, its indeterminacy marks a fluidity of territorial boundaries that is also part of the indefinite urbanism of Los Angeles.

In an encounter of insect and city, noise effects shape a space of "noisy silence," literally and metaphorically, materially and conceptually—airplanes making their loudest, most "annoying" sound while a caterpillar sings softly to an ant (Königstein 2014). Ambiguous and ambivalent, this is a space of metamorphosis, transduction, plasticity, and becoming, with species transformation shifting human aspirations, federal protection of endangered species superseding municipal laws, butterflies trumping a golf course, an anthropocentric environmentalism at odds with itself settling into an uneasy truce about land use that, despite its seeming "emptiness," is anything but. The butterflies are a cul-de-sac, an eddy, a gust of wind, opening to and composing the atmospheric. The airport looms large. Though the butterfly may not "hear" the planes, people who spent years working on dunes restoration attribute their own hearing loss to jet noise. News features on the butterfly invariably use an image of a plane flying over the dunes, drawing out the incommensurability of modes of flight, their differential size, the silence of the butterfly overshadowed by the roar of the jet. Encountered via noise, El Segundo blue butterflies both echo and exceed noise. Like noise, they evade and escape immediacy, control, management. At the same time, they expose "a whole new frontier of inhuman endeavor, . . . the construction of new matterings" (Thrift 2007, 22). The butterflies compose a volumetric city of another scale. Not a miniature representation of human flight, theirs is a worldmaking venture that, like noise, draws things together and to which humans sensorially attune, turning away from the planes whose "noise" interrupts speech but not butterfly flight. Noise, thus, brings into focus a sense of an atmospheric city, a city of atmospheric sensibilities.

Introduction

1. All images in the series can be found on John Divola's website, accessed May 5, 2020, http://www.faculty.ucr.edu/~divola/.

2. The literature on air and atmosphere is proliferating, spanning discussions of chemospheres and clouds, "anticipatory objects" and "affective atmospheres," and aerial images and volumetric urbanism. Some pieces I have found especially useful to think with include Adey 2010a; B. Anderson 2009; Böhme 1998, 2000; Choy 2012; Connor 2010; Howe 2015; Hu 2016; Ingold 2007; Lewis 2012; Lowe 2010; Martin 2011; McCormack 2014, 2018; Murphy 2013; Parks 2018; Peters 2016; Shapiro 2015; Sloterdijk 2009; and K. Stewart 2011.

3. In general I use *airport noise* rather than *aircraft noise*, though at times it is necessary to use the specificity of *aircraft noise*.

4. Bateson [1972] 2000; Cage 1961; Halpern 2015; Hu 2016; Lippard 1997; Peters 2016; Tsing 2017; Turner 1966.

5. Lefebvre's (1992) spatial trialectic is useful for understanding noise as at once phenomenal and semiotic, as practice, representational, and representation.

6. While sound is often objectified in its models (especially waves) or artifacts (recorded sound), approaching sound as energy makes it necessarily intrinsic to matter in motion, whether air, ground, water, or human. Douglas Kahn's *Earth Sound, Earth Signal* offers a model for attuning to the phenomenal properties of sound as energy, especially as emergent in and through perception. Concerned with addressing "a materiality often assumed to be immaterial," Kahn (2013, 17) engages the specificity of the physicality of energy in its transductions into audible sound. A deobjectified approach to sound is thematized most explicitly in chapter 3. See also Chow and Steintrager 2011; Cox 2011; Deleuze 2005; Eidsheim 2015; Goodman 2010; Ingold 2007; Kahn 2013; Peterson 2016a; and Trower 2012.

7. On noise, see Attali 1985; Bijsterveld 2008; Dyson 2014; Goddard, Halligan, and Hegarty 2012; Goodman 2010; Hainge 2013; Hegarty 2007; Hendy 2014; Keizer 2012; Novak 2013; Schwartz 2011; and M. Thompson 2017.

8. This is by now a robust literature. See note 2 for a list of texts that I have found influential.

9. In this way my project differs from McCormack's, who, in his discussion of the balloon as "envelopment," posits a distinction between an entity and the at-

mospheric, the latter withdrawn, sensed as variation but not fully accessible in and of itself (2018, 50–51). Rather than using atmosphere as differentiated from the durable object of object-oriented studies (which also understands the object, or what McCormack would call entity, as partially withdrawn), I use the atmospheric as a means of putting pressure on durability or solidity, moving toward entanglements between different forms of matter. Instead, this project is more closely aligned with Craig Martin's discussion of fog "as a gathering-force, intensifying the discussion of immanent entanglements of body *with* world" (2011, 454).

10. For affect in relation to atmosphere and sensation, see B. Anderson 2016; Heller, forthcoming; Massumi 2002; and D. McCormack 2010.

11. Work in sensory studies that I have found most helpful for thinking through perception as phenomenal and the body as entangled with its milieu includes that of Classen 2005; Connor 2003; Howes 2009; Laplantine 2015; Manning 2006; Paterson 2007; and Seremetakis 1996.

12. See especially Chen 2012; Hartigan 2014; Karban 2015; Kirksey 2014, 2015; Kohn 2013; Marder 2016; Marder and Irigaray 2016; Raffles 2011; Song 2013; Tsing 2017; and Wohlleben 2016.

13. Sonic weaponry generally relies on this capacity of noise, while using frequencies beyond the range of human audibility and hence shifting from airborne sound to vibration (Daughtry 2015; Goodman 2010; Volcler 2013).

14. See especially Alaimo 2010; Nash 2007; Roberts 2017; Shapiro 2015; Shapiro and Kirksey 2017; and Tousignant 2018.

15. For ways of thinking through and using glitch as method, see Berlant 2016; M. Chavez 2012; Kelly 2009; Krapp 2011; and Larkin 2008.

16. I find Barad's formulation especially compelling: "Theories are not mere metaphysical pronouncements on the world from some presumed position of exteriority. Theories are living and breathing reconfigurings of the world. The world theorizes as well as experiments with itself. Figuring, reconfiguring. Animate and (so-called) inanimate creatures do not merely embody mathematical theories; they *do* mathematics. But life, whether organic or inorganic, animate or inanimate, is not an unfolding algorithm. Electrons, molecules, brittlestars, jellyfish, coral reefs, dogs, rocks, icebergs, plants, asteroids, snowflakes, and bees stray from all calculable paths, making leaps here and there, or rather, making here and there from leaps, shifting familiarly patterned practices, testing the waters of what might yet be/have been/could still have been, doing thought experiments with their very being" (2012, 207–8).

CHAPTER 1. Aerial Attunements

1. The first commercial transatlantic flight, from New York to London, had occurred the previous year.

2. Los Angeles Airport became known as Los Angeles International Airport in 1949, with the designation LAX. Los Angeles World Airports (LAWA), established as the Los Angeles Department of Airports, is the airport authority that owns

and operates LAX and Van Nuys Airport (VNY) for the City of Los Angeles. It previously owned and operated Ontario International Airport (ONT) and Palmdale Regional Airport (PMD). LAWA's offices are on LAX grounds.

3. Key texts on airports as infrastructure are Adey 2010b; Cwerner, Kesselring, and Urry 2009; A. Gordon 2008; Hirsh 2016; Kasarda and Lindsay 2011; Launius and Bednarek 2003; Law 2002; Le Corbusier 1947; Pascoe 2001; Salter 2007; Schaberg 2016; and Westwick 2012.

4. Little work addresses the exterior of the airport; some sources that do are Friedman 1978; Hailey 1968; Manaugh 2017; and Smith 2004. For coverage of 2017 protests of a presidential travel ban, held strategically at airports, see "Protests against Executive Order 13769," Wikipedia, last updated October 11, 2018, https://en.wikipedia.org/w/index.php?title=Protests_against_Executive_Order_13769&oldid=863492116.2018.

5. Duke, a retired aircraft mechanic in his eighties who volunteers at the Flight Path Museum, told me they were required to wear earplugs beginning in the late 1950s. It was a "rule for your hearing, for your own good. You would go deaf if you didn't. It's part of the reason I wear hearing aids now." The engine would be running, making a lot of noise, and he wasn't aware of it damaging his hearing. First, they were given a rubber plug (perhaps the one designed by Veneklasen for the air force); later they had earmuffs. The plug wasn't as good as regular muffs, which strapped over the top of your head and had an earpiece inside. Foam rubber, with a cushioned seal around the muff, cut the noise way down. But it was hard to hear people talking; they had to yell or use sign language. "A jet airplane, it makes a lot of noise," he says. The older planes were even noisier though. Referred to as "burners," extra fuel in the tail pipe gave the engine more thrust but also made fire and smoke as the airplane took off.

6. Torgerson's news article was posted on the Playa del Rey Facebook group, the crash still a palpable memory for some.

7. Residents around LAX were not alone in protesting airport noise; citizen groups also formed on Long Island and in Queens, Newark, Boston, and Chicago.

8. The term *airport noise* emphasizes its infrastructural dimension along with the embeddedness of the airport in the city. The airport provides the possibility for movement from air to ground and is the interface between the range of actors concerned with its noise.

9. Kenneth Hahn Collection, Huntington Library, San Marino, California.

10. Office of the County Counsel to Kenneth Hahn, 1959, folder 6.4.5.8.2, box 10024, Kenneth Hahn Collection, Huntington Library, San Marino, California.

11. Causby's business consisted of selling eggs to hatcheries. They owned a few roosters and hundreds of hens, whose work was to lay fertile eggs that would be sent to hatcheries where the chicks would be raised into hens, *their* eggs sold to stores where people would buy them to eat: scrambled for breakfast; mixed into a cake; separated and whipped for a soufflé; whites used to insulate ice cream that magically stays cool in a hot oven, presented after dinner as baked Alaska; or, more likely, processed, dried, and powdered and sent to American troops fighting

in World War II, the demand for eggs keeping prices high. Even for the era, it was a small operation, affording an intimacy not offered in larger settings. Thomas and Tinie were fifty years old in 1941, the year that military planes first frightened their chickens. They did not tell the court how long they had had chickens, but perhaps they were among those who had been drawn into it during the Depression, when "an increasing number of the jobless, or those with modest savings" became small-scale chicken farmers (Smith and Daniel 1975, 260). Smith and Daniel emphasize the rural pastoral life offered by chicken farming, which allowed married couples to work together, sharing "responsibilities and . . . pleasures of a rural economy" and "the cheerful cooperation between man and bird" (Smith and Daniel 1975, 241, 240). Though as the 1946 bestseller *The Egg and I* attested to, it may not have been as pleasant an experience for all involved (Becker 2016; MacDonald 1945).

12. In *Causby* the Supreme Court held, "The common law doctrine that ownership of land extends to the periphery of the universe has no place in the modern world," and that "the air above the minimum safe altitude of flight prescribed by the Civil Aeronautics Authority is a public highway and part of the public domain, as declared by Congress in the Air Commerce Act of 1926, as amended by the Civil Aeronautics Act of 1938." At the same time, it placed limits on the public use of airspace, maintaining that "Flights of aircraft over private land which are so low and frequent as to be a direct and immediate interference with the enjoyment and use of the land are as much an appropriation of the use of the land as a more conventional entry upon it" and hence that there was "a taking of private property for public use." This, the Court ruled, was supported by the Fifth Amendment, which ends with the clause "nor shall private property be taken for public use, without just compensation." If, then, flights render property uninhabitable, making it such that "respondents could not use this land for any purpose, their loss would be complete." The justices agreed that, though it would constitute a taking, "it would only be an easement of flight." The Court remanded the case to the court of claims to outline the specific "nature and duration" of the easement (*U.S. v. Causby* [1946]). For *Causby*, the height of the easement was set at eighty-three feet. This was not intended to be a generalizable height.

Noise from the sky experienced half a century ago continues to organize airspace territoriality, as the experience of Thomas and Tinie Causby—and of their chickens—is reinscribed in the context of new technologies of unmanned flight. Today, discussions of drone flight height regulation invariably invoke *Causby*, an indeterminate foundation appropriate to its status in shaping atmospheric sensibilities. The vagueness of the ruling affords its circulation into diverse interpretive frames. In an episode of the TV series *The Good Wife*, "Unmanned" (season 7, episode 18, 30:25–32:33), lawyers battle over a community group leader's right to fly a drone over her neighborhood as surveillance and a resident's right to shoot it down as it flies at two hundred feet over his house. The defense introduces *Causby* and lays out the heights delineated by the case. The judge asks, "Exactly eighty-three feet?" "That was the height at which the Supreme Court found an airplane flying over Mr. Causby's land would frighten his chickens." "Of course," the judge responds, with a slight smile. A lawyer for the FAA confirms this: "As far as the FAA is concerned, if a drone is flying at eighty-three or below, Dr. Nochman would be within his rights to take it down. Above five hundred feet it would be illegal." "And at two hundred feet?" "Well, it's not clearly his property, at that point, but it's not clearly not," the lawyer replies, shaking his head as he speaks, a puzzled look on his face. The judge's brow furrows slightly. "As a representative of the FAA's legal department, would you like to clear that up?" "No," he says, shaking his head. "Between eighty-three and five hundred feet, it's Wild Wild West." The seeming confusion over heights reflects the FAA's lack of clarity around regulating drones in general.

Despite the unregulated status of drone flight, the *Wall Street Journal* published a graphic of the heights above ground that various modes of flight use; an image of a drone nudges at the four-hundred-foot mark, noted as being the area in which the FAA recommends drones remain. Below is a mark for eighty-three feet, where "aircraft . . . are subject to a 1946 Supreme Court" ruling that "landowners have 'exclusive control of the immediate reaches' above their land" (Nicas 2015; see also Rule 2015). Airspace used for takeoff and landing, addressed though not resolved by *Causby*, remains a contested space, emergent in relation to noise that is generated in the air and experienced on the ground.

13. The airport was also exempt from nuisance claims based on its status as public infrastructure, with its "conduct" that might "constitute a private nuisance" authorized by legislature (Committee on Interstate and Foreign Commerce 1963, 644; see also Banner 2008; and Whitehead 2009).

14. L. E. Timberlake, memorandum on motion to control aircraft noise, Noise Abatement Committee, 1960, Los Angeles City Archives.

15. Lee L. Sopher to Kenneth Hahn, 1965, folder 10, box 296, Kenneth Hahn Collection, Huntington Library, San Marino, California.

16. The rest of the hearings were held in Washington, DC, and dealt mostly with procedure and regulation; one set of hearings in Washington was dedicated to the then strange case of Chicago, where Midway had become the only "ghost" airport in the country, and O'Hare, built on a former Douglas airfield, was already causing noise problems for nearby neighbors. There were other hearings on noise in 1960, notably hearings before the Special Investigating Subcommittee of the Committee on Science and Astronautics of the U.S. House of Representatives. Published under the title *Noise: Its Effect on Man and Machine*, their report emphasized testimony by experts: NASA, two engineers from BBN, psychoacoustician Karl Kryter, the coordinator of noise and vibration control at Wright-Patterson Air Force Base, the head of the FAA, an engineer from Pratt and Whitney, and U.S. Navy researchers. Leo Beranek was unable to attend these hearings but sent a detailed statement. He had declined to represent a community group in the other noise hearings because of what he said was a conflict of interest (U.S. House 1960).

17. As Manning asks, "What if the skin were a porous, topological surfacing of myriad potential strata that field the relation between different milieus, each of them a multiplicity of insides and outsides?" (2009, 34).

18. I am not trying to provide definitions of terms here but simply drawing out some of the gradation between what is called perception, sense, feeling, and experience. I use the terms descriptively, amplifying something of the ethnographic as it adheres to academic discussions. Of these, *perception* affords the most work in a materialist approach to noise and atmospheric.

19. "Veterans Day 2015—WWII Pilot Yvette Hyatt Kovary," video, 3:19 min., uploaded by TorranceCitiCABLE, November 10, 2015, https://www.youtube.com /watch?v=nPmsS8I5hWc.

20. Wesley Marx, "No Place to Hide: Our Modern Way of Life Has Become a Noisy Madhouse," *Frontier*, February 1961, 13.

21. Arthur Burke to Yvette Kovary, April 26, 1960, in possession of Yvette Kovary.

22. Documents in possession of Yvette Kovary.

23. *Airport Noise*, 1967, acetate, Kenneth Hahn Collection, Huntington Library, San Marino, California.

24. "Berlant Concertone Reel to Reel Tape Recorders," Museum of Magnetic Sound Recording, accessed May 3, 2020, http://museumofmagneticsoundrecording .org/RecordersBerlantConcertone.html.

CHAPTER 2. Noise Annoys

1. ThinkGeek Annoy-a-Tron Prankster Pack 3.0, 2018, https://www.prankcrazy .com/product/thinkgeek-annoy-a-tron-prankster-pack-3-0-includes-3-thinkgeek -prank-products-annoy-a-tron-ringtone-annoy-a-tron-and-eviltron/.

2. Only one word in the song changes in its repetition; amplifying noise as grafting a generational divide, its intensity increases and then subsides: "Have you heard your mommy say . . . ? Have you heard your mommy shout . . . ? Have you heard your mommy scream . . . ? Have you heard your mommy say . . . ?" As oft reflected on during public hearings on noise in the United States in the preceding decade, the "subjective" nature of noise pivots on differing desires of old and young, for which the electric guitar is exemplary.

3. The depth, perhaps, of the "annoyance fringe around an airport" that a 1930 tome on *Airports: Their Location, Administration and Legal Basis* determined to be between a quarter mile and an indefinite distance, a fringe that might be "temporary" or might not exist. And though this fringe might be indexed through complaints, its substance—annoyance—though distinguished from noise, remained undefined (Hubbard, McClintock, and Williams 1930, 162, 163).

4. Department of City Planning, Los Angeles, California, "Noise Element," 1975, 1, City of Los Angeles Archives, City Council File 74-4204, B529.

5. Department of City Planning, Los Angeles, California, "Noise Element," 6.

6. Noise Regulation, 1969, 11, City of Inglewood, file 10, box 296, Kenneth Hahn Collection, Huntington Library, San Marino, California. According to Brag-

don, elements of Inglewood's ordinance provided a precedent followed by other municipalities, which adopted its designation of "specific acoustical provisions" (Bragdon 1973, 2a; see also Ordinance 2018, An Ordinance of the City of Inglewood, California, Prohibiting Emission or Creation of Noise Beyond Certain Levels and Adding Chapter 6 to Article IV of the Inglewood Municipal Code Accordingly, 1969, folder 10, box 296, Kenneth Hahn Collection, Huntington Library, San Marino, California).

7. Many anchor a discussion of urban noise in race, with the warranted assumption that noise maps onto Blackness and that the regulation of noise is unevenly applied across demographic groups. It is hard to know whether what is happening here is a "conflation of darkness/blackness with noise," in which "fuscous color coalesces with loud sound"; nonetheless, the coterminous history of noise abatement with racial change resonates across a longer history of such doubling, in which "noise, in general, became racialized as the other of Europe, as the other of rationality, as the other of the proper" (Crawley 2017, 140). Though noise is not explicitly mapped onto race in the city's noise ordinance, a poll of Inglewood residents found that aircraft noise (61 percent) was second only to crime control (73 percent) as the most important issue facing the city (U.S. Senate 1972, 250; see Cardoso 2018; for a discussion of changing demographics in the area, see chapter 6).

8. Alan Untereiner, Reply Brief of Petitioner, *Adrian D. Horien v. City of Rockford*, S. Ct., no. 03-18 (August 2003).

9. I met Blomberg on a small island off the coast of Vermont where he stays for a week every summer. Off the grid and accessible only by boat, the island has no mechanical noise other than that from a loudly humming generator used by the snack and sandwich shop and jeeps made available for park rangers. When we missed the ferry, Blomberg came to fetch us in his canoe. We helped paddle back from the mainland, water sloshing into the boat from our inexpert gestures and off-balance bodies. Vicki, a friend and fellow anthropologist of sound, taught my son, Cassius, then three, how to skip rocks—the thin, black slate disks filling the beach were perfect for skimming across the surface of the lake. I sat with Blomberg at a weathered picnic table and talked about noise. He recalled how he was invited to found and direct the NPC by Harriet Barlow, who had $50,000 in funding from writer Adam Hochschild, heir to a fortune built on copper mining. Barlow's motivation was simply that she "didn't like noise." The organization serves as a resource on noise pollution, a lobbying group, and a hub for those concerned about noise and wanting to do something about it. Among other material, the NPC holds the bulk of the EPA's Office of Noise Abatement and Control (ONAC) records.

10. Another example of a more capacious metric is the effective perceived noise level (EPNL), which is "an outgrowth of the Perceived Noise Level (PNL) and differs from the latter in two respects: first, it takes into account the duration of the aircraft noise. This is accomplished by adding a correction to the PNL value based upon the length of time the aircraft flyover noise level is within 10 PNdB of its

maximum PNL value. The second difference is that the EPNL considers the pure tone components that are characteristic of jet aircraft noise, particularly those aircraft employing turbofan engines. The EPNL hence is the latest step in the state of the art regarding methods of subjectively rating aircraft noise. Unfortunately, there exist no widespread studies as yet which could be used to test the improvement of EPNL over the earlier PNL" (Veneklasen and Associates 1968, 41).

11. The development of the decibel, along with competing noise measurement metrics, is discussed across the literature (Bijsterveld 2008; Thompson 2004). Bijsterveld (2008) in particular outlines the development of different European noise perception scales for aircraft noise and their basis in field experiments. Rather than addressing how aspirations for fixity were achieved, I am more interested in drawing out some of the vagaries of the process and logics of metricization, dwelling in the stories that underscore the indeterminacy of metrics, which are otherwise deemed objective.

12. Kryter went on to serve as director of the Sensory Sciences Research Center at the Stanford Research Institute, a "consortium of oil companies" that some say intentionally took ten years to figure out what smog was in L.A., and that now takes credit for solving the problem (Jacobs and Kelly 2008).

13. Vern O. Knudsen, "Noise," 1949, 1, Vern Oliver Knudsen Papers, UCLA Library Special Collections.

14. BBN's involvement with all sides of airport noise management is conveyed by Beranek's account of secret noise measurement tests they conducted with Boeing that confirmed the difference in dB levels between propeller and jet planes, the results of which they "agreed not to disclose . . . until the PNdB was broadly accepted" (2007, 97).

15. Metrics themselves may provide the basis for mobilization against noise. In *Handbook for Acoustic Ecology*, Barry Truax, a founding member of the World Soundscape Project with R. Murray Schafer, provides a comprehensive list of "terms and systems for noise measurement" (1999). Concerned, like Schafer, with noise pollution as a pressing issue, he is nonetheless critical of systems of measurement, which, he argues, are "premised on the assumption that more elaborate statistical procedures will bring us closer to measuring what is happening and its effects." Moreover, "All of these systems treat the sonic environment as an object on which increasingly complex measurements may be carried out. They all isolate sound from the way in which human beings understand it." Truax proposes the term "sound pollution" to address "an imbalance of a soundscape"; this puts less emphasis on loudness than on whether "a sound is understood by someone to be annoying or out-of-place, or to be crowding out other sounds." The *Handbook* is intended to provide readers with tools to create or advocate for a balanced soundscape. Systems of measurement are provided to critique them. "If you are to act within a society committed to talking about sound as opposed to understanding it, you will need the benefit of the technical terminology in order to challenge it when it is used misleadingly. . . . Our intention, then, of exhaustively including all such terms is to bring their number and attitude to the reader's attention,

with some detail on how they operate so that they may be defeated on their own ground."

16. Kryter co-authored a 1944 report titled *The Relative Annoyance Produced by Various Bands of Noise*, published by the Harvard Psycho-Acoustic Lab (Reese and Kryter 1944). Walter Spieth describes the study, concluding that "It just seems that annoyance as a function of frequency or intensity is an elusive phenomenon very susceptible to the effects of variations in experimental procedure" (1955, 877).

17. Arthur de Vany, "Benefits of Noise Abatement," n.d., Records of the Environmental Protection Agency Office of Noise Abatement and Control, National Archives and Records Administration II, College Park, Maryland (hereafter Archives II).

18. De Vany, "Benefits of Noise Abatement."

19. Los Angeles World Airports, "LAX Internet Flight Tracking System," LAWA website, accessed November 29, 2018, https://www.lawa.org/en/lawa-environment /noise-management/lawa-noise-management-lax/lax-internet-flight-tracking -system.

20. Los Angeles World Airports, "LAX Internet Flight Tracking System."

21. Delft Institute of Positive Design, "Annoyance," Negative Emotion Typology, accessed May 4, 2020, https://emotiontypology.com/typology/list /annoyance.

22. In amplifying noise as annoying, *misophonia*—literally the "hatred of sound"—draws out emotion as bodily, a sensory-affective register of something (sound) sensed and made sense of through the "irrationality" of emotion, emotion felt as a bodily sense as much as a feeling that can be labeled and parceled as *annoyance* or *rage* or *joy*. Misophonia is a condition in which sounds, maybe specific sounds, possibly soft sound, or perhaps all sounds, are especially annoying. The *mis* is that of *misanthropy*, which Shane Greene conjures through the figure of G. G. Allin, someone who made a lot of audible noise, accompanied by various activities that might also be described as "noise" (Greene 2018). For someone with misophonia, sounds are said to cause anger and rage. There are support groups and studies, but it is not, as of yet, officially inscribed as a mental disorder in *DSM-5*, the fifth edition of the *Diagnostic and Statistical Manual of Mental Disorders*. The documentary *Quiet Please* insists on its neurological status, a medicalization of a negative affective entanglement with everyday atmospheric conditions, in which the senses balk at present modes of existence, pushing away from sociality, pushing people away from one another, misophonia merging with misanthropy when one cannot stand the sound of a person chewing. Annoyance of noise on overdrive, the website for the film explains that "your senses backfire and they elicit rage, anxiety, and a life of isolation." Said to be related to the central auditory system in the brain and not the ears, it anchors hearing as a bodily sense, an aspect of balance that allows a certain level of stabilization in an unstable world (Gould 2016; "Misophonia" 2011).

1. *Noise Control Magazine*, published from 1955 to 1961, and the National Noise Abatement Council are examples of this.

2. See Diederichsen and Franke's (2013) catalog for their exhibit on the Whole Earth Catalog, titled *The Whole Earth: California and the Disappearance of the Outside*. Caldwell (1970) captures the environmental ethos of the time, and Rome provides a reading of the environmental movement as an iteration of the era (2003).

3. *Oxford English Dictionary*, s.v. "environment," noun, 2nd, "frequently with '*the*,'" quotations from 1948 and 1967 emphasize "man's impact": "The most obvious way in which man has contaminated his environment is by polluting the air with smoke." Only later does "man" recede, to be supplanted by a manufactured (or "man"-made) product, the agent of its use silenced: "The greater the energy use, the greater the carbon footprint, and the worse for the environment a product is."

4. Aircraft noise differs from that of supersonic transport (SST) in the formulation of noise pollution. Rather than emitting noise from its engine, SST creates a sonic boom by moving faster than the speed of sound. Here noise is produced as an effect of motion, the movement of air sounding. Yet the EPA defines noise pollution as airborne sound, or "Sound that reaches the point of interest by propagation through air" (U.S. Senate 1972, 363). At the same time, a sonic boom is an incredible example of atmospheric noise. Not generated by an engine, it is a noise produced by the air itself: as the aircraft flies faster than the speed of sound, it compresses the air, creating a shock wave that spreads behind it in a cone-shaped formation that is experienced—heard and felt—by anyone within its area.

Nonetheless, SST plays an intriguing role in the formulation of noise as pollution. Supersonic transport had been in operation since the late 1940s and became a crucial form of technological competition during the Cold War. People who experienced sonic booms may have been bothered, but they tended to not complain on the grounds of their being part of military operations. To determine whether increased use of SST for both military and civilian purposes would be possible, in 1964 the U.S. government flew test flights over Oklahoma City eight times a day for six months. The National Opinion Research Council (NORC) surveyed residents about their experience, and they reported property damage and decreasing tolerance for sonic booms. In March 1970 the Coalition Against the SST was formed, composed of members of environmental groups and congressional staffers who lobbied elected officials to vote against a bill authorizing SST development. The bill (in the Department of Transportation) was voted down a year later, and the SST as a project of the U.S. government ended. While SST served as a rallying point for environmental activists during the 1960s, in legislative documents on noise pollution, the SST is addressed as deferred, a future possibility; it was not constitutive of the nature and substance of noise pollution and its regulation (Suisman 2015).

5. A letter from John V. Tunney to Edmund Muskie reads: "Of all the major sources of noise pollution aircraft noise is by far the most noxious. Using the standard unit of measurement of sound, the decibel, conversational speech will typically be at the level of sixty dB, heavy city traffic at ninety-two dB, and a jet airliner 500 feet overhead at 115 dB. Because the decibel scale is a logarithmic scale, a difference of ten units is actually 100 times as intense. If a factor for the irritation of high frequency sounds is taken into account, aircraft noise measures even higher" (U.S. Senate 1974b, 114).

6. The Noise Abatement Office was an agency that oversaw work that had been done by the Noise Abatement staff over the preceding year. On March 22, 1967, President Lyndon Johnson issued a memo directing "Heads of the Departments, Agencies and Establishments of the Executive Branch of Government" to take airport noise into consideration whenever it is relevant for a given case. Further, they should coordinate with the Department of Transportation for the "prevention, control and abatement of aircraft noise," and with HUD regarding land use around airports. Balancing the "growth of aviation" and "the welfare of our people," he maintained that "we must do all in our power to assure that the environment in which we live is not overburdened with any form of pollutant, including excessive noise" to support the "pursuit of other desirable activities and the quiet enjoyment of property" (Johnson 1967).

7. In 1972 there was renewed effort for the EPA to have authority over the FAA around issues of noise, as "making the FAA responsible for [noise pollution] is like putting the fox in charge of the chicken coop" (U.S. Senate 1972, 187). Senator Tunney, along with others, including Randall Hurlburt, environmental standards supervisor for the City of Inglewood, pushed for the EPA to oversee noise issues, including those currently under the jurisdiction of the FAA (U.S. Senate 1972, 186). A bill for the EPA to have authority over the FAA was voted against in Congress, the issue of safety and the specific expertise needed for flight and aircraft taking precedence.

8. This pertains to the use of the term in English, according to a Google ngram, which might reflect a general tendency though falter in the details (Pechenick, Danforth, and Dodds 2015). Many thanks to Keith Murphy for suggesting I create an ngram of "noise pollution," and to Logan Cull for tracking down the early sources.

9. As Emily Thompson writes, Smilor's work "suggests concerns more contemporary than historical" (2004, 360n32). Moreover, the term "*noise pollution* appears in none of the sources" she examined from the period 1900–1933 (2004, 361n33).

10. The shift of noise from a category unto itself into that of pollution comes out in presidential speeches. In 1963 JFK talked of an "area of congestion and pollution, man-made noise, and dirt" (Kennedy 1963). In 1968, in Lyndon Johnson's "Special Message to the Congress on Conservation: 'To Renew a Nation,'" he addressed air, water, and oil pollution in great depth. Noise control was treated separately and briefly, with an emphasis on aircraft noise, followed by a lengthier discussion of surface mining (Johnson 1968). Two years later, Richard Nix-

on's "Statement About the Council on Environmental Quality" pledged to "look into new problems for which little government policy now exists, matters such as noise pollution, the growth of debris and solid wastes, and other unanticipated byproducts of our advancing technology" (Nixon 1970). Nevertheless, noise slides around, slipping out from the umbrella of pollution. In Nixon's statement on the formation of the Environmental Protection Agency and the National Oceanic and Atmospheric Administration (NOAA) in July 1970, Nixon addresses "air, water, and land pollution."

11. 112 Cong. Rec. 8745 (1966).

12. McCormack's career as a journalist spanned more than fifty years; when her papers were acquired by the Columbia University Library, its archivist described her work as offering "insights into the minor fascinations and nagging fears of a generation, while largely avoiding the existential threats that shadowed Cold War society" (Columbia University Libraries 2014).

13. Farr's publications included "Medical Consequences of Environmental Home Noises" (1967), *Treatment of the Nephrotic Symptom* (1951), "Relation of Medicine to the Problem of Radioactive Fallout" (1968), "The Impact of Nuclear Science on Medicine" (1953), "Atomic Medicine by Charles F. Behrens" (1950), and "Smoking and Children: A Pediatric Viewpoint" (1969), as well as a patent on "Double Window Having Improved Weather Sealed Ventilation," US4129964A, filed November 25, 1977, and issued December 19, 1978, https://patents.google.com/patent/US4129964.

14. Women who chaired many of the civic groups mobilizing against airport noise did not tend to complain of appliances, or of a general right to quiet. Their work was targeted toward the airport, based in a specificity of experience that made them experts in airlines, aircraft, flight paths, and aerial heights. And, at least initially, they did not link their work with a nascent environmental movement.

15. Ryan was a liberal senator from New York who spoke up against the Vietnam War and was active in the civil rights movement. He died in 1972 at age fifty (Black et al. 2003). On January 20, the date Ryan first introduced the Noise Control Act, he also spoke out against the closure of Job Corps centers, in favor of publicizing U.S. diplomacy regarding the Middle East, and against funding for the Vietnam War.

16. 116 Cong. Rec. 332 (1970).

17. 116 Cong. Rec. 485, 486 (1970).

18. 116 Cong. Rec. 38605 (1970).

19. Public health was folded into the environment from the outset, with the EPA's mandate that of protecting public health and welfare.

20. Hatfield was a Republican senator from Oregon who held office for thirty years, from 1967 to 1997. Deemed too liberal to be Nixon's running mate, his numerous publications focus on how to resolve the contradictions between one's Christian faith and public service, with titles like *Between a Rock and a Hard Place* (1976) and *Conflict and Conscience* (1971).

21. Public Law 92-574, or the Noise Control Act of 1972, authorized the formation of the Office of Noise Abatement and Control (ONAC). Closed in 1981 by Ronald Reagan, its records have been dispersed; some can be found in Archives II in College Park, Maryland, while others are held privately, having been given by a former ONAC staff member to the director of the Noise Pollution Clearinghouse.

22. Ingold (2011), conversely, draws an analogy between sound and wind.

23. On July 9, 1970, Nixon introduced plans to establish both the EPA and the NOAA (Nixon 1970). The EPA would address air, water, and land, with an emphasis on forms of pollution that cross the three. NOAA would be responsible for oceans and atmosphere. Dividing the Earth in a such a way had consequences for what noise pollution would be. Acousticians had been developing hydrophones coterminously with studies on airborne environmental noise. Vern Knudsen, along with others who were closely involved in legislation about noise control and noise pollution, developed hydrophone technology for the navy during World War II. The 1965 meeting of the Acoustical Society of America featured papers on both. And *Songs of the Humpback Whale* (R. Payne 1970) was a crucial moment in shaping environmental imaginaries; in particular, it drew the nonhuman into the "environment" through sound at a time when the concept of the environment was decidedly anthropocentric, as underscored by the EPA's mandate of public health. Under the EPA, noise pollution became solely airborne noise, an emphasis that is now shifting, with new work on the effects of shipping noise on marine life. NOAA has only recently begun to address underwater noise in a systematic way (NOAA 2018).

24. In then governor of California Ronald Reagan's 1971 State of the State address, included in 1972 hearings on noise pollution, he described noise as a condition of "debauchment," a term that evokes drunken revelry and its aftermath. As a verb, *to debauch* is to "destroy or debase the moral purity" of something, to corrupt—a word that moves closer to an understanding of noise as corrupting a signal, making a legible message illegible, either through interference or masking. The repetition of "debauch" and its grammatical modifications sutures noise to environment and ecology, unstated aspects of which have been "debauched," even as "acoustical environment" is set apart from environment in general. "In the area of environment and ecology, it is and must be our continuing goal to refurbish and reclaim what has been debauched and to protect that which is still clean, fresh and open. . . . The situation, with respect to noise, could not be more succinctly stated. Our acoustical environment is debauched and the degree of debauchment is increasing. Steps should be taken to halt this trend and to reclaim that which can be reclaimed and both should be done in a responsible way" (U.S. Senate 1972, 301).

Not just an additive or overlay, Reagan's word choice rends a transformation of a state (of, perhaps, a natural resource) that may not be recuperable. The suggestion of violation, seduction, and even deflowering in the dictionary definition of *debauch* draws gendered, sexualized violence into environmental politics, casting the relationship between human and planet as one of antagonism and unidirectional aggression. While drawing out noise as a condition polluting a sonic atmosphere, his statement shifts from a concern for human health to the "cleanliness" of the "environment."

25. Noise remains an environmental pollutant insofar as it is part of the environmental impact report process at the state level, mandated in California by the California Environmental Quality Act; modeled on NEPA, it was enacted in 1970.

26. A note at the beginning of the section on Acid Deposition Control, or acid rain, explains, "The 1990 Clean Air Act Amendments added a new title IV, relating to acid deposition control, without repealing the existing title IV, relating to noise pollution" (U.S. EPA 2017).

27. At every hearing someone from the acoustics engineering firm of BBN was either on a panel or giving expert testimony, a culmination, it appears, of the professional coordination of sound engineers to contribute expertise to pending legislation, and perhaps provide requisite services under newly enacted regulation (Lang 1991; U.S. EPA Office of Noise Abatement and Control 1971h, 6, 8–9).

28. National Noise Abatement Council Collection, Niels Bohr Library and Archives, American Institute of Physics, College Park, Maryland.

29. The proliferation of publications on noise and noise pollution in 1970 conveys a sense of discovery and of urgency. Many of these address noise pollution as a new crisis that must be addressed swiftly (Baron 1970; Berland 1970). Public relations pieces, they urge readers to lobby their elected leaders to enact legislation. Some were written by founders of prominent antinoise citizen groups, including Citizens against Noise and Upper Sixth Avenue Noise Abatement Association/Citizens for a Quieter City. Noise is situated as one among other planetary concerns; Henry Still, author of *In Quest of Quiet* (1970), wrote a number of other books around that time on subjects that included the future of the human race, space travel, and aviation, with a final publication in 1977 on the male midlife crisis. Even children's books take up the subject; advocating quiet behavior, they mark a shift from the message of books like *The Little Woman Wanted Noise* (Teal [1943] 1972), which described a world of happily noisy children and a woman who sought them out.

30. Macro Synetic Systems, "California San Pedro Bay Intercontinental Airport" (Canoga Park, CA: Macro Synetic Systems, 1970), Alphonzo Bell Papers 142:27, University of Southern California Special Collections.

31. John Tunney is the basis for Robert Redford's character in the movie *The Candidate*. An active environmentalist, in 1975 he published *The Changing Dream*, arguing for government intervention into environmental issues.

32. Though with water the metaphor for sound, a notion of immersion maintains a differentiation between human body and environment: sound is still outside the person, who floats in, rather than vibrates with, noise.

33. Thus Carson's (2002) permeable body goes beyond that of Sloterdijk (2009), who locates the emergence of atmospheric concepts in the gas warfare of World War I, the body's relationship to air manifest in the gas mask, which emphasized breath as the site of exchange.

34. Nash describes the difficulty industrial hygienists, or occupational health officials, had pinning down the effects of pesticides on farmworkers, who moved from farm to farm, and whose exposure to different pesticides affected their overall response to any given one. "The human body, like the natural environment, was unpredictable and resistant to quantification. It exhibited an agency of its own that escaped both control and scientific description. As biomedical and environmental knowledge increased so did uncertainty" (2007, 211).

35. In L. K. Smith's "Noise as a Pollutant," published in the *Canadian Journal of Public Health* in 1970, he writes, "Already some authorities state that urban noise levels are increasing at a rate of one decibel each year. Now one decibel a year may not seem much but the catch is that the decibel is a logarithmic unit such that there is now generated ten times as much acoustic power on our city streets as there was in 1960 and by 1980 it will be 100 times" (475).

36. In a cruel twist of fate, Bernie Krause's home and archive were destroyed in the 2017 fires in Santa Rosa, California, generally understood to have been a consequence of climate change.

CHAPTER 4. Murmurs: Experiments in Glitching

1. Vagueness is a philosophical paradox. Pushing at existing theories of vagueness, Delia Graff Fara's work delved into the vagueness of vagueness, the "shifting sands" (as one of her articles was titled; 2000) of determinations and designations—the mutable and changing interests affecting the point at which one thing becomes another. This might be the perspective of the person making the designation, or a person's own changing interests. There is a poetics to her work, as someone who could introduce children as subjects of philosophy, writing with and against "logic."

2. "Complaint: Low Flying—Noise," LAWA Flight Path Museum Archive, Los Angeles, CA.

3. Vern O. Knudsen, "Proposed Standards for the Measurement of Noise," 1933, Vern Knudsen Collection, UCLA Special Collections.

4. *Transcript of Record*, 10.

5. *Transcript of Record*, 54.

6. *Transcript of Record*, 76.

7. *Transcript of Record*, 198.

8. "Lee Causby," Ancestry.com, accessed May 4, 2020, https://www.ancestry.com /search/?name=Lee_Causby&death=_NC; "Thomas Lee Causby (1891–1971)," Memorial, Find A Grave, accessed December 10, 2018, https://www.findagrave.com /memorial/33933833.

1. Hillel Schwartz writes that "'Proofing' a space for sound was a hit or miss proposition before 1900. . . . People suffocated in telephone booths that were rather airtight than soundproof; when engineers added ventilating fans, these could be so loud that the booths were noisier than music halls. . . . Of the 1,364 pages in a major encyclopedia of architecture, three short paragraphs were devoted to the topic, under the rubric of 'pugging,' or plastering the boards beneath floors and behind walls, an approach that turned sound-deadening air pockets into sound-transmitting solids"; as architect James Colling suggested in 1882, "this word 'solid' is simply a deception; for it is a fact that the more solid a building is made, the more sonorous it becomes. . . . A fireproof house, which is built with concrete floors or brick arches, rings like a bell" (Schwartz 2011, 337).

2. Bartholomew Spano is brilliant at animating material in his account of sound. He tells a panel of senators: "A high frequency sound pulses at an extremely rapid pace," that of the frequency of jet engines. "This very high pulsing as it strikes a wall tends to set the wall into motion but the wall having mass simply refuses to pulse at the rate of 4,000 frequencies per second. So that high frequencies when they hit a wall or even the simplest type of construction, like a plain glass window, cannot set it in motion because it is going too fast; instead it bounces off and is deflected backward" (U.S. House 1963, 109–10). This is different from how noise travels "through the atmosphere." Low frequencies "travel through the atmosphere with relatively little reduction." But "high frequencies . . . are lost through the atmosphere. The low frequencies to transmit through the atmosphere pulse through the air, first compresses it and rarefies it, and these pulses go out in the spherical pattern. The air doesn't mind being pulsed at low frequencies but at high frequencies, say of 2,000 cycles per second, air actually has mass and when the pressure or pulsing gets up too high, let's say 2,000, this high frequency runs into trouble when it hits the air because the air being of some weight tends to refuse to be pulsed too rapidly. As the frequency increases, say, at 10,000 cycles per second, the pulsing is so rapid that the air simply refuses to pulse with it and the sound is very rapidly absorbed and only gets a very short distance away" (U.S. House 1963, 110).

3. Simplifying materials to mass affords uniform comparison of their capacity for sound absorption. Wyle lists the parts of the home in order of sound transmission level, lowest to highest: windows, exterior doors, roof-ceiling systems, floor systems, walls. Culprits that allow sound inside are louvered windows and wood hollow-core doors with a window; plaster ceilings with wood shingles; asphalt shingle or gravel roofs; wood floors with a vented air space; wood frame walls with plaster inside and stucco outside. Better are "fixed glass windows" and "sliding glass doors," unable to open or have many dreaded cracks. "Concrete slab foundations" draw the house into the ground through which vibration, but not high-pitched sound, might travel. Of the various inexpensive building materials used,

"wood frame walls with wood paneling inside and stucco outside" were best at drawing sound into them, not letting it pass through.

4. D. J. Waldie describes the construction of Southern California postwar suburban homes, the kind of house found in neighborhoods across L.A. County, from the area around the airport to now gentrifying neighborhoods north of downtown, where they will likely be demolished to make room for larger, though not necessarily more solid, buildings. The economy of his prose echoes that of the building materials:

> The outside walls are stucco, a mixture of sand and Portland cement.
>
> The exterior coat is about an eighth-inch thick, with a ratio of four parts of sand to one part of cement.
>
> The middle coat is three-eighths of an inch. The ratio of sand to cement is five to one.
>
> The first layer of stucco—three-eighths of an inch of four parts of sand to one part cement—was quickly troweled over chicken wire. The wire was furred a quarter-inch from tarpaper sheets nailed to the outside of the studs.
>
> The surface of a stucco house clings to this network of light wire and not to the wood frame. The wire intersections support the stucco over the empty span of the walls.
>
> The brittle exterior of these houses is a little more than an inch thick.
>
> (2005, 43)

5. Ingold (2011) advocates for the notion of "medium" to describe sound's phenomenal properties, with humans "immersed" in sound. This formulation differentiates between sound and perception, as if sound is anything in and of itself.

6. Veneklasen and Associates's 1968 community noise survey provided noise contours that could be laid over a map of Inglewood. These were contours of the effective perceived noise level (EPNL) for discrete aircraft, four engine turbofan, four engine turbojet, three engine turbofan, all landing with a three-degree glide slope (1968, 57–59). Maps are marked with measurement locations and flight paths. Today's noise contour maps follow the 1979 Aviation Safety and Noise Abatement Act, which mandated uniform noise standards: "a single system of measuring noise . . . a single system for determining the impact of noise upon individuals . . . which includes . . . intensity, duration, frequency, and time of occurrence" as well as the identification of "land uses which are normally compatible with various impacts of noise on individuals" (U.S. House 1979, 4–5). The metrics ultimately used were those presented in the EPA standards document of 1974, notably DNL (then L_{dn}), with a 65 DNL cutoff selected as the outer limit.

7. That the EPA levels document suggests 55 DNL as the outdoor limit continues to be a source of contestation (Albee 2002). Cost was at stake, and it seems there was a study that showed a peak at 65 DNL, suggesting the majority of people bothered—or complaining—would be included in a 65 DNL contour. California airports use CNEL, which provides greater weight to nighttime hours. The CNEL is

produced by FAA's Integrated Noise Model software. DNL and CNEL are temporal averages of dbA measurements.

8. On hi-fi and stereo sound, see Adinolfi 2008; Borgerson, Schroeder, and Miller 2017; Keightley 2008; Taylor 2001; and Theberge, Devine, and Everett 2015.

9. The word *stereophonic* was coined in 1927 by Western Electric, the company responsible for much of the materialization of sound as electric, as signal that required the suppression or diversion of noise. Stereo recording, to be developed in the following decade, was a technological achievement; presented to captivated audiences as an event unto itself, it first transformed the cinematic experience.

10. Office of Noise Abatement, *First Federal Aircraft Noise Abatement Plan: FY 1969–70* (Washington, DC: U.S. Government Printing Office, 1969), Alphonzo Bell Papers 174:16, University of Southern California Special Collections.

11. Beranek developed the anechoic chamber for the U.S. Army to test loud-speakers that were to be used for its Ghost Army, a platoon of inflated tanks and recorded sounds of a camp being set up intended to keep the German army at bay, an incredible project of camouflage writ large (Beyer and Sayles 2015; Cox 2004; Goodman 2010; Heller, forthcoming; Samuel, n.d.).

12. The episode can be viewed on YouTube: "John Cage—Water Walk," video, 9:22 min., uploaded by holotone, May 4, 2007, https://www.youtube.com/watch ?time_continue=1&v=SSulycqZH-U.

CHAPTER 6. Indefinite Urbanism

1. Resolution No. 8204, file 74-5050, Los Angeles City Archives and Records Center.

2. Taking "transduction beyond the realm of the auditory," land recycling is another "process of constituting, structuring, and modifying spatial and logical relations" (Helmreich 2007, 662). Or, as the airport puts it, land recycling is the "acquisition of incompatible property and conversion of that property to compatible land use" (Los Angeles International Airport 2012).

3. Thomas Baldwin's balloon flight of 1785 is credited with giving "birth to the aerial view as a record of the direct experience of flight" (Thébaud-Sorger 2013, 47). For Baldwin, the experience of making aerial images in the form of engravings was one of new, almost indescribable sensation in which atmospheric conditions imbued photographic technologies and their subject matter. As a consequence of attending to the particularities of sensorial experience, atmospheric phenomena—weather, clouds, light—were drawn into cartography, providing "a new way of looking at the earth, an atmospherically based approach" (Thébaud-Sorger 2013, 59).

4. Nadar perhaps best conveys "the aerial . . . [a]s central to the modern imagination" (Dorrian and Pousin 2013, 1). Most famous for his portraits of performers, writers, and artists such as Sarah Bernhardt, George Sand, Proust, Delacroix,

and Baudelaire, Nadar drew together nascent technologies of flight, light, and image as part of a project of pushing photographic potential. Marking its status as a new and singular technological development with possible market value, in 1858 he filed a patent for the aerial photograph (McCormack 2009, 32). Yet "the materiality of interaction between photographic equipment, environmental conditions and the object to be represented" was not only in service of technological progress (Robic 2013, 169). The previous year his attempt to photograph the Earth from a balloon was unsuccessful because "the gas escaping from the balloon reacted with the emulsion of photographic plates, and the result was a blackened image" (Bann 2013, 86). Exploiting the limits of the volumetric city, Nadar also went underground to take photographs without natural light. These projects reflected the two sides of the modern city: the bird's-eye view of a rationalizing city and its counter, the underworld of that city, which was already transformed from Victor Hugo's imagined terror into a sanitized space newly accessible to the Parisian bourgeoisie via pleasure tours. Using artificial lighting and long exposures, Nadar made images of these previously unseen spaces, complete with mannequins—which could be still for the long exposure times—to stand in for workers. As Benjamin writes, "This is the first time that the lens is given the task of making discoveries" (1978, 150).

5. As captured by the mid-nineteenth-century aerial images made by Alfred Guesdon, the modern European city was literally a city in motion, an atmospheric city of smoke, steam, smog, and mobility beyond its borders (Besse 2013).

6. In East Los Angeles, a nascent Chicano movement asserted emergent identifications and membership claims. Hippies hanging out on the Sunset Strip prompted the passage of Municipal Code 41.18d, more recently used to remove homeless from Skid Row sidewalks (Peterson 2012). That these "events" remain separate isolated histories—and are largely narrated as such—manifests, in part, the entrenchment of segregation in a city where a multiculturalism laid out across a sprawling urban landscape is touted as definitive of its postmodern character (E. Chavéz 2002; Dear 2000; Hunt and Ramón 2010; James 2003; Jones 2017; Kun and Pulido 2014; Soja 1996).

7. See Cohen and Murphy 1966; Horne 1997; Hunt and Ramone 2010; Revoyr 2008; Schleuss 2015; and Schulberg 1967.

8. Echoing the Black Panthers' 1967 Ten-Point Program, in 1970 the City of Inglewood prepared a "10-Point Action Program for the Alleviation of Noise Pollution." Point 8 provides an aerial response to events on the ground by calling for a "Glide Slope Increase" of "at least 4 degrees." Staying high in the air before descending at an angle almost twice that of the normal 2 or 2.5 degrees, "Such approaches were done for a long period during the 1965 Watts riots, and have become known locally as 'a Watts approach'" (U.S. Senate 1972, 200). And while used to avoid perceived danger from the ground, such a steep approach—which relieves those on the ground from the noise of the arriving plane—was otherwise deemed too dangerous in and of itself.

9.

"Restrictive Covenants"

Langston Hughes

When I move
Into a neighborhood
Folks fly.

Even every foreigner
That can move, moves

Why?

The moon doesn't run.
Neither does the sun.

In Chicago
They've got covenants
Restricting me—
Hemmed in
On the South Side,
Can't breathe free.

But the wind blows there.
I reckon the wind
Must care.

10. As this story suggests, the area around LAX is not uniform. Westchester, El Segundo, and Playa del Rey remained predominantly white. Lennox and Hawthorne are now communities with a majority of Latin American immigrants.

11. Testimony of Hon. Yvonne Burke (Calif.) Before the Aviation Subcommittee of the Committee on Public Works and Transportation, 1976, Yvonne Brathwaite Burke Papers, 339:9, USC Libraries Special Collections.

12. Fritz Burns Papers, CSLA-4, series 1, boxes 87 and 88, Department of Archives and Special Collections, William H. Hannon Library, Loyola Marymount University, Los Angeles.

13. Yvette Kovary to Mr. Baker, February 14, 1973, in possession of Yvette Kovary.

14. A patchwork of property lies below the surface, portioned out between the heirs of those who left and the gas company. At one point during the property acquisition process, a resident asked the airport for mineral rights and set a precedent. Deeds suggest that owners who had held out generally secured higher prices for their homes and 100 percent of mineral rights, rather than the 0 or 50 percent earlier sellers were awarded. These were granted without "the right to enter, drill or penetrate in or upon the surface of said real property or within 500 feet thereof for the purpose of removing said crude oil, petroleum, gas, brea, asphaltum and all kind of kindred substances and other minerals" (uncataloged box, Los Ange-

les City Archives and Records Center). Today some say there is nothing more to extract, that it has already been pumped dry; but others raise the possibility of horizontal drilling, a technological feat those writing the deeds had probably not imagined.

15. Yvette H. Kovary to Honorable Thomas Bradley, Mayor (September 1, 1973), in possession of Yvette Kovary.

16. As Schoch reports in the *Los Angeles Times*, "Mattoni found his first blue butterfly 50 years ago mounted in a cardboard box at the Los Angeles County Museum of Natural History. At the time, he was a schoolboy fascinated by butterflies, collecting them, puzzling over the colors of caterpillars that clung to the bush outside his bedroom window in Beverly Hills. Then, as a teen-ager during World War II, he visited the dunes for the first time and witnessed the butterfly alive. The airport was tiny then, and only a few houses perched on the dunes. He remembered flocks of butterflies and huge expanses of coastal buckwheat" (1994, 10).

17. In *An Obsession with Butterflies: Our Long Love Affair with a Singular Insect*, Sharman Russell describes how, with metalmarks, a common butterfly similar to the El Segundo blue, "ants are so eager for this honeydew they will stroke the caterpillar over and over again. . . . When it grows weary of the attention, the caterpillar audibly taps the ground" (Russell 2004, 32).

18. Many thanks to Rebecca Lewis for directing me to this literature.

19. Plants are, however, affected by the vibration of sound waves, growing thicker stalks to withstand the movement. And though they might not have a favorite genre of music (Tompkins and Bird 1989; Weinberger and Graefe 1973), they are "keenly attuned sensors" with the capacity to *"articulate difference"*—"to discern subtle differences in their worlds" (Hustak and Myers 2012, 105). And, as entomologist Richard Karban writes, "There is no doubt that plants can produce sound, as for example when tension in a plant's water transport system is abruptly released" (2015, 28). What, then, of the entanglement of plant and insects, in which the plant is not only mute ground to the ant-caterpillar play but a sensory body articulating with ant, caterpillar, butterfly, wasp?

Acoustical Society of America. 1965. *Program of the Sixty-Ninth Meeting of Acoustical Society of America*. Washington, DC: Acoustical Society of America.

Adey, Peter. 2010a. *Aerial Life: Spaces, Mobilities, Affects*. Chichester: Wiley-Blackwell.

Adey, Peter. 2010b. "Airports: Terminal/Vector." In *Geographies of Mobilities: Practices, Spaces, Subjects*, edited by Tim Cresswell and Peter Merriman, 137–50. Surrey: Ashgate.

Adey, Peter. 2013. "Securing the Volume/Volumen: Comments on Stuart Elden's Plenary Paper 'Secure the Volume.'" *Political Geography* 34:52–54. https://doi.org/10.1016/j.polgeo.2013.01.003.

Adinolfi, Francesco. 2008. *Mondo Exotica: Sounds, Visions, Obsessions of the Cocktail Generation*. Translated by Karen Pinkus. Durham, NC: Duke University Press.

"Aid Underwater Hearing." 1965. *Science News-Letter* 87 (25): 389.

Alaimo, Stacy. 2010. *Bodily Natures: Science, Environment, and the Material Self*. Bloomington: Indiana University Press.

Alaimo, Stacy. 2016. *Exposed: Environmental Politics and Pleasures in Posthuman Times*. Minneapolis: University of Minnesota Press.

Albee, William. 2002. "Why We Must Supplement DHL Noise Analysis." Wyle Laboratories Acoustics Group, May 2002. https://www.marchjpa.com/documents/docs_forms/airport_docs/articles/dhlnoiseanalysis.pdf.

Alekshun, Joseph J., Jr. 1969. "Aircraft Noise Law: A Technical Perspective." *American Bar Association Journal* 55 (8): 740–45.

Anand, Nikhil, Akhil Gupta, and Hannah Appel, eds. 2018. *The Promise of Infrastructure*. Durham, NC: Duke University Press.

Anderson, Ben. 2009. "Affective Atmospheres." *Emotion, Space and Society* 2 (2): 77–81. https://doi.org/10.1016/j.emospa.2009.08.005.

Anderson, Ben. 2016. *Encountering Affect*. New York: Routledge.

Anderson, Ben, and Paul Harrison, eds. 2010. *Taking-Place: Non-Representational Theories and Geography*. Farnham, Surrey: Routledge.

Anderson, Ben, and John Wylie. 2009. "On Geography and Materiality." *Environment and Planning A: Economy and Space* 41 (2): 318–35. https://doi.org/10.1068/a3940.

Anderson, Tim. 2006. *Making Easy Listening: Material Culture and Postwar American Recording*. Minneapolis: University of Minnesota Press.

Arnold, Richard A. 1983. *Ecological Studies of Six Endangered Butterflies (Lepidoptera, Lycaenidae): Island Biogeography, Patch Dynamics, and the Design of Habitat Preserves*. Berkeley: University of California Press.

Asdal, Kristin, Tone Druglitrø, and Steve Hinchliffe, eds. 2016. *Humans, Animals and Biopolitics*. London: Routledge.

Asher, Claire. 2015. "Butterflies Drug Ants, Turn Them into Bodyguards." *Science*, August 7, 2015. https://www.sciencemag.org/news/2015/08/butterflies-drug -ants-turn-them-bodyguards.

Attali, Jacques. 1985. *Noise: The Political Economy of Music*. Translated by Brian Massumi. Minneapolis: University of Minnesota Press.

Augé, Marc. 1995. *Non-Places: An Introduction to Supermodernity*. Translated by John Howe. London: Verso.

Banham, Reyner. 1984. *The Architecture of the Well-Tempered Environment*. Chicago: University of Chicago Press.

Bann, Stephen. 2013. "Nadar's Aerial View." In *Seeing from Above: The Aerial View in Visual Culture*, edited by Mark Dorrian and Frédéric Pousin, 83–95. London: Tauris.

Banner, Stuart. 2008. *Who Owns the Sky? The Struggle to Control Airspace from the Wright Brothers On*. Cambridge, MA: Harvard University Press.

Barad, Karen. 2007. *Meeting the Universe Halfway: Quantum Physics and the Entanglement of Matter and Meaning*. Durham, NC: Duke University Press.

Barad, Karen. 2012. "On Touching—The Inhuman That Therefore I Am." *differences* 23 (5): 206–23.

Baron, Robert Alex. 1970. *The Tyranny of Noise*. New York: Harper and Row.

Bataille, Georges. 1985. "Formless." In *Visions of Excess: Selected Writings, 1927–1939*, edited by Allan Stoekl, 31. Minneapolis: University of Minnesota Press.

Bateson, Gregory. [1972] 2000. *Steps to an Ecology of Mind: Collected Essays in Anthropology, Psychiatry, Evolution, and Epistemology*. Chicago: University of Chicago Press.

Becerra, Hector. 2012. "Decades Later, Bitter Memories of Chavez Ravine." *Los Angeles Times*, April 5, 2012.

Becker, Paula. 2016. *Looking for Betty MacDonald: The Egg, the Plague, Mrs. Piggle-Wiggle, and I*. Seattle: University of Washington Press.

Bednarek, Janet R. 2001. *America's Airports: Airfield Development, 1918–1947*. College Station: Texas A&M University Press.

Benjamin, Walter. 1978. *Reflections*. Edited by Peter Demez. Translated by Edmund Jephcott. New York: Harcourt Brace Jovanovich.

Bennett, Jane. 2010. *Vibrant Matter: A Political Ecology of Things*. Durham, NC: Duke University Press.

Benthien, Claudia. 2002. *Skin*. Translated by Thomas Dunlap. New York: Columbia University Press.

Beranek, Leo. 2007. "The Noisy Dawn of the Jet Age." *Sound and Vibration* 41 (1): 94–99.

Beranek, Leo. 2008. *Riding the Waves: A Life in Sound, Science, and Industry*. Cambridge, MA: MIT Press.

Berglund, Birgitta, Ulf Berglund, and Thomas Lindvall. 1975. "Scaling Loudness, Noisiness, and Annoyance of Aircraft Noise." *Journal of the Acoustical Society of America* 57 (4): 930–34. https://doi.org/10.1121/1.380535.

Berland, Theodore. 1970. *Noise—The Third Pollution*. Public Affairs Pamphlet No. 449. New York: Public Affairs Committee.

Berlant, Lauren. 2016. "The Commons: Infrastructures for Troubling Times." *Environment and Planning D: Society and Space* 34 (3): 393–419. https://doi.org /10.1177/0263775816645989.

Besse, Jean-Marc. 2013. "Thomas Baldwin's 'Airopaidia,' or the Aerial View in Color." In *Seeing from Above: The Aerial View in Visual Culture*, edited by Mark Dorrian and Frédéric Pousin, 66–83. London: Tauris.

Beyer, Rick, and Elizabeth Sayles. 2015. *The Ghost Army of World War II: How One Top-Secret Unit Deceived the Enemy with Inflatable Tanks, Sound Effects, and Other Audacious Fakery*. New York: Princeton Architectural Press.

Beyer, Robert T. 1999. *Sounds of Our Times: Two Hundred Years of Acoustics*. New York: Springer.

Bijsterveld, Karin. 2008. *Mechanical Sound: Technology, Culture, and Public Problems of Noise in the Twentieth Century*. Cambridge, MA: MIT Press.

Billings Gazette. 1975. "Woman Refuses Offers, Her House Is Flattened." *Billings (MT) Gazette*, July 13, 1975.

Black, Allida, June Hopkins, John Sears, Christopher Alhambra, Mary Jo Binker, Christopher Brick, John S. Emrich, Eugenia Gusev, Kristen E. Gwinn, and Bryan D. Peery, eds. 2003. "William Fitts Ryan (1922–1972)." In *Eleanor Roosevelt, John Kennedy, and the Election of 1960: A Project of the Eleanor Roosevelt Papers*. Columbia, SC: Model Editions Partnership. https://www2.gwu.edu /~erpapers/mep/displaydoc.cfm?docid=erpn-wfitts.

Böhme, Gernot. 1998. "The Atmosphere of a City." *Issues in Contemporary Culture and Aesthetics*, no. 7: 5–13.

Böhme, Gernot. 2000. "Acoustic Atmospheres." *Soundscape Journal* 1 (1): 14–18.

Bonacich, Edna, and Robert F. Goodman. 1972. *Deadlock in School Desegregation: A Case Study of Inglewood, California*. Westport, CT: Praeger.

Borgerson, Janet, Jonathan Schroeder, and Daniel Miller. 2017. *Designed for Hi-Fi Living: The Vinyl LP in Midcentury America*. Cambridge, MA: MIT Press.

Botteldooren, Dick, Andy Verkeyn, and Peter Lercher. 2003. "A Fuzzy Rule-Based Framework for Noise Annoyance Modeling." *Journal of the Acoustical Society of America* 114 (3): 1487–98. https://doi.org/10.1121/1.1604125.

Bowker, Geoffrey C., and Susan Leigh Star. 1999. *Sorting Things Out: Classification and Its Consequences*. Cambridge, MA: MIT Press.

Boyer, M. Christine. 1986. *Dreaming the Rational City: The Myth of American City Planning*. Cambridge, MA: MIT Press.

Bragdon, Clifford R. 1971. *Noise Pollution: The Unquiet Crisis*. Philadelphia: University of Pennsylvania.

Bragdon, Clifford R. 1973. "Community Noise Ordinances: Their Evolution, Purpose and Impact." Paper presented at the 74th National Meeting of the American Institute of Chemical Engineers, New Orleans, Louisiana, March 13, 1973.

Brennan, Teresa. 2004. *The Transmission of Affect*. Ithaca, NY: Cornell University Press.

Bridge, Gavin. 2013. "Territory, Now in 3D!" *Political Geography* 34:55–57. https://doi.org/10.1016/j.polgeo.2013.01.005.

Brown, Bill. 2003. *A Sense of Things: The Object Matter of American Literature*. Chicago: University of Chicago Press.

Brush, Stephen G. 1986. *The Kind of Motion We Call Heat: A History of the Kinetic Theory of Gases in the Nineteenth Century*. Vol. 1, *Physics and the Atomists*. Amsterdam: North Holland.

Bryant, Clora, Buddy Collette, William Green, Steven Isoardi, Jack Kelson, Horace Tapscott, Gerald Wilson, and Marl Young, eds. 1998. *Central Avenue Sounds: Jazz in Los Angeles*. Berkeley: University of California Press.

Butler, Octavia E. 2000. *Parable of the Sower*. New York: Grand Central.

Cage, John. 1961. *Silence: Lectures and Writing*. Middletown: Wesleyan University Press.

Cage, John. 1967. *A Year from Monday: New Lectures and Writings*. Middletown, CT: Wesleyan University Press.

Cage, John, and David Tudor. [1959] 1992. *Indeterminacy: New Aspect of Form in Instrumental and Electronic Music*. Washington, DC: Smithsonian Folkways Recordings. CD.

Caldwell, Lynn Keith. 1970. *Environment: A Challenge to Modern Society*. Garden City, NY: Doubleday.

California Energy Commission. 2017. "Building Climate Zones." https://energyarchive.ca.gov/maps/renewable/BuildingClimateZonesMap.pdf.

Campt, Tina M. 2017. *Listening to Images*. Durham, NC: Duke University Press.

Cardoso, Leonardo. 2018. "Sound-Politics in São Paulo: Noise Control and Administrative Flows." *Current Anthropology* 59 (2): 192–208. https://doi.org/10.1086/697062.

Carson, Rachel. 2002. *Silent Spring*. Boston: Houghton Mifflin Harcourt.

Carson, Rachel, and Charles Pratt. 1965. *The Sense of Wonder*. New York: Harper and Row.

Castro, Teresa. 2013. "Aerial Views and Cinematism, 1898–1939." In *Seeing from Above: The Aerial View in Visual Culture*, edited by Mark Dorrian and Frédéric Pousin, 118–33. London: Taurus.

Chávez, Ernesto. 2002. *"¡Mi Raza Primero!" (My People First!): Nationalism, Identity, and Insurgency in the Chicano Movement in Los Angeles, 1966–1978*. Berkeley: University of California Press.

Chavez, Maria. 2012. *Of Technique: Chance Procedures on Turntable*. Brooklyn, NY: Rolling Press.

Chen, Mel Y. 2012. *Animacies: Biopolitics, Racial Mattering, and Queer Affect*. Durham, NC: Duke University Press.

Chicago Tribune. 1968. "Soundproofing Experiment Tests Materials and Costs." *Chicago Tribune*, November 2, 1968.

Chion, Michel. 2016. *Sound: An Acoulogical Treatise*. Translated by James A. Steintrager. Durham, NC: Duke University Press.

Chow, R., and J. A. Steintrager. 2011. "In Pursuit of the Object of Sound: An Introduction." *differences* 22 (2–3): 1–9. https://doi.org/10.1215/10407391 -1428816.

Choy, Timothy. 2012. "Air's Substantiations." In *Lively Capital: Biotechnologies, Ethics, and Governance in Global Markets*, edited by Kaushik Sunder Rajan, 121–54. Durham, NC: Duke University Press.

Choy, Timothy, and Jerry Zee. 2015. "Condition—Suspension." *Cultural Anthropology* 30 (2): 210–23. https://doi.org/10.14506/ca30.2.04.

Chua, Charmaine. 2018. "'Sunny Island Set in the Sea': Singapore's Land Reclamation as a Colonial Project." *Funambulist* 17 (May–June): 20–25.

Classen, Constance. 2005. *The Deepest Sense: A Cultural History of Touch*. Oxford: Berg.

Clough, Patricia Ticineto. 2018. *The User Unconscious: On Affect, Media, and Measure*. Minneapolis: University of Minnesota Press.

CNRS. 2008. "Amorphous Materials: How Some Solids Flow Like Liquids." *ScienceDaily*, July 7, 2008. https://www.sciencedaily.com/releases/2008/07 /080704153507.htm.

Coates, Peter A. 2005. "The Strange Stillness of the Past: Toward an Environmental History of Sound and Noise." *Environmental History* 10 (4): 636–65.

Cockayne, Emily. 2008. *Hubbub: Filth, Noise, and Stench in England, 1600–1770*. New Haven, CT: Yale University Press.

Coffin, Harold. 1966. "The Needle." *Elyria (OH) Chronicle Telegram*, October 28, 1966.

Cohen, Jerry, and William Murphy. 1966. *Burn, Baby, Burn! The Los Angeles Race Riot, August 1965*. New York: Dutton.

Colomina, Beatriz. 2007. *Domesticity at War*. Cambridge, MA: MIT Press.

Columbia University Libraries. 2014. "Rare Book & Manuscript Library Acquires Papers of Patricia S. McCormack." https://library.columbia.edu/about/news /libraries/2014/2014-9-26_RBML_Acquires_McCormack_Papers.html.

Comaroff, John L., and Jean Comaroff. 1997. *Of Revelation and Revolution*. Vol. 2, *The Dialectics of Modernity on a South African Frontier*. Chicago: University of Chicago Press.

Comaroff, Joshua. 2014. "Built on Sand: Singapore and the New State of Risk." *Harvard Design Magazine*, no. 39. http://www.harvarddesignmagazine.org /issues/39/built-on-sand-singapore-and-the-new-state-of-risk.

Connor, Steven. 2003. *The Book of Skin*. Ithaca, NY: Cornell University Press.

Connor, Steven. 2010. *The Matter of Air: Science and the Art of the Ethereal*. London: Reaktion Books.

Coole, Diana, and Samantha Frost, eds. 2010. *New Materialisms: Ontology, Agency, and Politics*. Durham, NC: Duke University Press.

Cox, Christoph. 2004. "Edison's Warriors: Deceive to Defeat." *Cabinet* 13. http://cabinetmagazine.org/issues/13/cox.php.

Cox, Christoph. 2011. "Beyond Representation and Signification: Toward a Sonic Materialism." *Journal of Visual Culture* 10 (2): 145–61.

Crawley, Ashon T. 2016. *Blackpentecostal Breath: The Aesthetics of Possibility*. New York: Fordham University Press.

Cuff, Dana. 2000. *The Provisional City: Los Angeles Stories of Architecture and Urbanism*. Cambridge, MA: MIT Press.

Cvetkovich, Ann. 2012. *Depression: A Public Feeling*. Durham, NC: Duke University Press.

Cwerner, Saulo, Sven Kesselring, and John Urry. 2009. *Aeromobilities*. London: Routledge.

Daily Breeze. 1994. "Vandalism of Dunes an Ecological Blow." *Daily Breeze*, El Segundo, CA, July 27, 1994.

Damerow, Gail. 2019. "26 Sounds that Chickens Make and What They Mean." *Flip Flop Ranch* (blog), March 18, 2019. http://flipflopranch.com/chicken-talk/.

Daughtry, J. Martin. 2015. *Listening to War: Sound, Music, Trauma, and Survival in Wartime Iraq*. Oxford: Oxford University Press.

Dear, Michael J. 2000. *The Postmodern Urban Condition*. Oxford: Blackwell.

de la Cadena, Marisol. 2018. "Uncommons." *Fieldsights*, March 29. https://culanth.org/fieldsights/uncommons.

Deleuze, Gilles. 2005. *Francis Bacon: The Logic of Sensation*. Minneapolis: University of Minnesota Press.

Deleuze, Gilles, and Félix Guattari. 1987. *A Thousand Plateaus: Capitalism and Schizophrenia*. Translated by Brian Massumi. Minneapolis: University of Minnesota Press.

Deleuze, Gilles, and Félix Guattari. 1996. *What Is Philosophy*? Translated by Hugh Tomlinson and Graham Burchell. New York: Columbia University Press.

DeLillo, Don. 1985. *White Noise*. New York: Viking Adult.

Delta Democrat-Times. 1966. "'Noise Pollution' Is Newest Phrase." *Delta Democrat-Times*, Greenville, MS, April 28, 1966.

DeVries, P. J. 1990. "Enhancement of Symbioses between Butterfly Caterpillars and Ants by Vibrational Communication." *Science* 248 (4959): 1104–6.

Dewey, Scott Hamilton. 2000. *Don't Breathe the Air: Air Pollution and U.S. Environmental Politics, 1945–1970*. College Station: Texas A&M Press.

Dictionary.com. s.v. "amorphous." accessed May 6, 2020. https://www.dictionary.com/browse/amorphous?s=t.

Didion, Joan. 1979. *The White Album*. New York: Simon and Schuster.

Diederichsen, Diedrich, and Anselm Franke, eds. 2013. *The Whole Earth: California and the Disappearance of the Outside*. Berlin: Sternberg Press.

Dix, Virginia. 1963. "Mrs. John Kovary: Varied Careers Bring Adventure." *Culver City (CA) Star News*, March 28, 1963.

Doolittle, James H. 1952. *The Airport and Its Neighbors: The Report of the President's Airport Commission*. Washington, DC: U.S. Government Printing Office.

Doron, Gil. 2007. "Badlands, Blank Space, Border Vacuums, Brown Fields, Conceptual Nevada, Dead Zones." *Field: A Free Journal for Architecture* 1 (1): 10–23.

Dorrian, Mark, and Frédéric Pousin, eds. 2013. *Seeing from Above: The Aerial View in Visual Culture*. London: Tauris.

Douglas, Mary. 1994. "The Genuine Article." In *The Socialness of Things: Essays on the Socio-Semiotics of Objects*, edited by Stephen Harold Riggins, 9–22. Berlin: Mouton de Gruyter.

Douglas, Mary. [1966] 2002. *Purity and Danger: An Analysis of Concepts of Pollution and Taboo*. New York: Routledge.

Dyson, Frances. 2014. *The Tone of Our Times: Sound, Sense, Economy, and Ecology*. Cambridge, MA: MIT Press.

Eidsheim, Nina Sun. 2015. *Sensing Sound: Singing and Listening as Vibrational Practice*. Durham, NC: Duke University Press.

Elden, Stuart. 2013. "Secure the Volume: Vertical Geopolitics and the Depth of Power." *Political Geography* 34:35–51. https://doi.org/10.1016/j.polgeo.2012.12.009.

Elliott, Dean. 1962. *Zounds! What Sounds!* Los Angeles: Capitol. LP.

Emmel, Thomas C., and John F. Emmel. 1973. *The Butterflies of Southern California*. Los Angeles: Natural History Museum of Los Angeles County.

Eno, Brian. 1978. *Ambient 1: Music for Airports*. Polydor Records AMB 001. LP.

Erie, Steven. 2004. *Globalizing L.A.: Trade, Infrastructure, and Regional Development*. Stanford, CA: Stanford University Press.

Erlmann, Veit. 2010. *Reason and Resonance: A History of Modern Aurality*. Brooklyn, NY: Zone Books.

Eureka Times Standard. 1972. "A Silent Pollution Affecting Us All." *Eureka (CA) Times Standard*, February 7, 1972.

Ewing, Ann. 1965. "Ultrasound 'Sees' Tumors." *Science News-Letter* 87 (25): 389.

Fara, Delia Graff. 2000. "Shifting Sands: An Interest-Relative Theory of Vagueness." *Philosophical Topics* 28 (1): 45–81.

Farr, Lee E. 1950. "Atomic Medicine by Charles F. Behrens." *Science* 111 (2882): 313.

Farr, Lee E. 1951. *Treatment of the Nephrotic Syndrome*. Springfield, IL: Thomas.

Farr, Lee E. 1953. "The Impact of Nuclear Science on Medicine." *American Scientist* 41 (4): 556–71.

Farr, Lee E. 1967. "Medical Consequences of Environmental Home Noises." *Journal of the American Medical Association* 202 (3): 171–74. https://doi.org/10.1001/jama.1967.03130160045006.

Farr, Lee E. 1968. "Relation of Medicine to the Problem of Radioactive Fallout." *Pediatrics* 41 (1): 373–77.

Feld, Steven. 1982. *Sound and Sentiment: Birds, Weeping, Poetics, and Song in Kaluli Expression*. Philadelphia: University of Pennsylvania Press.

Feld, Steven. 1996. "Waterfalls of Song: An Acoustemology of Place Resounding in Bosavi, Papua New Guinea." In *Senses of Place*, edited by Keith H. Basso, 91–135. Seattle: University of Washington Press.

Fidell, Sanford. 2003. "The Schultz Curve 25 Years Later: A Research Perspective." *Journal of the Acoustical Society of America* 114 (6): 3007–15.

Fidell, Sanford. 2014. "Psychoacoustics and Community Noise Impact Assessment." *Acoustics Today*, Fall, 40–47.

Fidell, Sanford, Vincent Mestre, Paul Schomer, Bernard Berry, Truls Gjestland, Michel Vallet, and Timothy Reid. 2011. "A First-Principles Model for Estimating the Prevalence of Annoyance with Aircraft Noise Exposure." *Journal of the Acoustical Society of America* 130 (2): 791–806. https://doi.org/10.1121/1.3605673.

Fischel, William A. 2015. *Zoning Rules! The Economics of Land Use Regulation.* Cambridge, MA: Lincoln Institute of Land Policy.

Foucault, Michel. [1970] 1994. *The Order of Things: An Archaeology of the Human Sciences.* New York: Vintage Books.

Friedman, Paul David. 1978. "Fear of Flying: The Development of Los Angeles International Airport and the Rise of Public Protest over Jet Aircraft Noise." Master's thesis, UC Santa Barbara.

Froesch, Charles, and Walter Prokosch. 1946. *Airport Planning.* London: Chapman and Hall.

Goddard, Michael, Benjamin Halligan, and Paul Hegarty, eds. 2012. *Reverberations: The Philosophy, Aesthetics, and Politics of Noise.* New York: Bloomsbury Academic.

Goodie, Jo. 2001. "The Invention of the Environment as a Subject of Legal Governance." In *Rethinking Law, Society and Governance: Foucault's Bequest*, 79–92. Portland, OR: Hart.

Goodman, Steve. 2010. *Sonic Warfare: Sound, Affect, and the Ecology of Fear.* Cambridge, MA: MIT Press.

Gordillo, Gastón R. 2014. *Rubble: The Afterlife of Destruction.* Durham, NC: Duke University Press.

Gordon, Alastair. 2008. *Naked Airport: A Cultural History of the World's Most Revolutionary Structure.* Chicago: University of Chicago Press.

Gordon, Kim. 2015. *Girl in a Band: A Memoir.* New York: HarperCollins.

Gould, Jeffrey Scott, dir. 2016. *Quiet Please . . .* Branch, NJ: Action Media Productions. http://www.quietpleasefilm.com.

Graham, Stephen, and Lucy Hewitt. 2013. "Getting off the Ground: On the Politics of Urban Verticality." *Progress in Human Geography* 37 (1): 72–92. https://doi.org/10.1177/0309132512443147.

Greene, Shane. 2018. "On Misanthropology (Punk, Art, Species-Hate)." In *Between Matter and Method: Encounters in Anthropology and Art*, edited by Gretchen Bakke and Marina Peterson, 35–50. London: Bloomsbury.

Greenhouse, Carol J. 1994. *Law and Community in Three American Towns.* Ithaca, NY: Cornell University Press.

Greenwald, Alvin G. 1970. *Law of Noise Pollution.* Environment Reporter Monograph No. 2. Washington, DC: Bureau of National Affairs.

Gregg, Melissa, and Gregory J. Seigworth, eds. 2010. *The Affect Theory Reader.* Durham, NC: Duke University Press.

Gregor, Ian. 2000. "LAX Takeover Still Rankles Ex-Neighbors." *Daily Breeze*, El Segundo, CA, August 27, 2000.

Grubbs, David. 2018. *Now That the Audience Is Assembled*. Durham, NC: Duke University Press.

Hailey, Arthur. 1968. *Airport*. New York: Bantam.

Hainge, Greg. 2013. *Noise Matters: Towards an Ontology of Noise*. New York: Bloomsbury.

Halpern, Orit. 2015. *Beautiful Data: A History of Vision and Reason since 1945*. Durham, NC: Duke University Press.

Hamilton Daily News Journal. 1965. "New Insulation Product Helps Cut Home Noises." *Hamilton (OH) Daily News Journal*, April 6, 1965.

Haraway, Donna J. 1992. "The Promises of Monsters: A Regenerative Politics for Inappropriate/d Others." In *Cultural Studies*, edited by Lawrence Grossberg, Cary Nelson, and Paula A. Treichler, 295–337. New York: Routledge.

Harman, Graham. 2018. *Object-Oriented Ontology: A New Theory of Everything*. London: Penguin.

Harnetty, Brian. n.d. "Forest Listening Rooms." Brian Harnetty website. Accessed February 19, 2019. http://www.brianharnetty.com/forest-listening-rooms.

Harris, Cheryl I. 1993. "Whiteness as Property." *Harvard Law Review* 106 (8): 1707–91. https://doi.org/10.2307/1341787.

Hartigan, John, Jr. 2014. *Aesop's Anthropology: A Multispecies Approach*. Minneapolis: University of Minnesota Press.

Hatfield, Mark O. 1971. *Conflict and Conscience*. Waco, TX: Word Books.

Hatfield, Mark O. 1976. *Between a Rock and a Hard Place*. Waco, TX: Word Books.

Hays, Stuart Randolph. 1961. "United States v. Causby: An Extension Thereof." *William and Mary Law Review* 3 (1): 36–64.

Hegarty, Paul. 2007. *Noise/Music: A History*. New York: Continuum.

Heller, Michael C. Forthcoming. *Just Beyond Listening: Sound and Affect Outside of the Ear*. Berkeley: University of California Press.

Helmreich, Stefan. 2007. "An Anthropologist Underwater: Immersive Soundscapes, Submarine Cyborgs, and Transductive Ethnography." *American Ethnologist* 34 (4): 621–41.

Henderson, Malcolm C. 1963. "Sound in Air: Absorption and Dispersal." *Sound* 2 (6): 28–36.

Hendy, David. 2014. *Noise: A Human History of Sound and Listening*. New York: Ecco.

Hirsh, Max. 2016. *Airport Urbanism: Infrastructure and Mobility in Asia*. Minneapolis: University of Minnesota Press.

Hirt, Sonia A. 2014. *Zoned in the USA: The Origins and Implications of American Land-Use Regulation*. Ithaca, NY: Cornell University Press.

Hise, Greg. 1997. *Magnetic Los Angeles: Planning the Twentieth-Century Metropolis*. Baltimore: Johns Hopkins University Press.

Hojo, Masaru K., Naomi E. Pierce, and Kazuki Tsuji. 2015. "Lycaenid Caterpillar Secretions Manipulate Attendant Ant Behavior." *Current Biology: CB* 25 (17): 2260–64. https://doi.org/10.1016/j.cub.2015.07.016.

Holland, Sharon P., Marcia Ochoa, and Kyla Wazana Tompkins. 2014. "On the Visceral." *GLQ: A Journal of Lesbian and Gay Studies* 20 (4): 391–406. https://doi.org/10.1215/10642684-2721339.

Horne, Gerald. 1997. *Fire This Time: The Watts Uprising and the 1960s.* New York: Da Capo.

Howe, Cymene. 2015. "Life above Earth: An Introduction." *Cultural Anthropology* 30 (2): 203–9. https://doi.org/10.14506/ca30.2.03.

Howes, David, ed. 2009. *The Sixth Sense Reader.* New York: Berg.

Hu, Tung-Hui. 2016. *A Prehistory of the Cloud.* Cambridge, MA: MIT Press.

Hubbard, Henry Vincent, Miller McClintock, and Frank Backus Williams. 1930. *Airports: Their Location, Administration and Legal Basis.* Cambridge, MA: Harvard University Press.

Hunt, Darnell, and Ana-Christina Ramón, eds. 2010. *Black Los Angeles: American Dreams and Racial Realities.* New York: NYU Press.

Hustak, Carla, and Natasha Myers. 2012. "Involutionary Momentum: Affective Ecologies and the Sciences of Plant/Insect Encounters." *differences* 23 (5): 74–118.

Ihde, Don. 1973. *Sense and Significance.* Pittsburgh, PA: Duquesne University Press.

Ingold, Tim. 2005. "The Eye of the Storm: Visual Perception and the Weather." *Visual Studies* 20 (2): 97–104. https://doi.org/10.1080/14725860500243953.

Ingold, Tim. 2007. "Earth, Sky, Wind, and Weather." *Journal of the Royal Anthropological Institute* 13 (S1): S19–38. https://doi.org/10.1111/j.1467-9655.2007.00401.x.

Ingold, Tim. 2010. "Footprints through the Weather-World: Walking, Breathing, Knowing." *Journal of the Royal Anthropological Institute* 16 (S1): S121–39. https://doi.org/10.1111/j.1467-9655.2010.01613.x.

Ingold, Tim. 2011. "Four Objections to the Concept of Soundscape." In *Being Alive: Essays on Movement, Knowledge, and Description,* 136–39. London: Routledge.

Irigaray, Luce. 1999. *The Forgetting of Air in Martin Heidegger.* Translated by Mary Beth Mader. Austin: University of Texas Press.

Isenstadt, Sandy. 2006. *The Modern American House: Spaciousness and Middle Class Identity.* Cambridge: Cambridge University Press.

Jackson, John L. 2013. *Thin Description: Ethnography and the African Hebrew Israelites of Jerusalem.* Cambridge, MA: Harvard University Press.

Jacobs, Chip, and William J. Kelly. 2008. *Smogtown: The Lung-Burning History of Pollution in Los Angeles.* Woodstock, NY: Overlook Press.

James, David. 2003. *Sons and Daughters of Los: Culture and Community in L.A.* Philadelphia: Temple University Press.

Johnson, Lyndon B. 1967. "Memorandum on Aircraft Noise and Land Use in the Vicinity of Airports." March 22, 1967. The American Presidency Project. https://www.presidency.ucsb.edu/documents/memorandum-aircraft-noise-and-land-use-the-vicinity-airports.

Johnson, Lyndon B. 1968. "Special Message to the Congress on Conservation: 'To Renew a Nation.'" March 8, 1968. The American Presidency Project. https://

www.presidency.ucsb.edu/documents/special-message-the-congress
-conservation-renew-nation.

Jones, Kellie. 2017. *South of Pico: African American Artists in Los Angeles in the 1960s and 1970s*. Durham, NC: Duke University Press.

Kahn, Douglas. 1999. *Noise, Water, Meat: A History of Sound in the Arts*. Cambridge, MA: MIT Press.

Kahn, Douglas. 2013. *Earth Sound, Earth Signal: Energies and Earth Magnitude in the Arts*. Berkeley: University of California Press.

Kalas, Rayna. 2007. *Frame, Glass, Verse: The Technology of Poetic Invention in the English Renaissance*. Ithaca, NY: Cornell University Press.

Kapchan, Deborah. 2015. "Body." In *Keywords in Sound*, edited by David Novak and Matt Sakakeeny, 33–44. Durham, NC: Duke University Press.

Kaplan, Caren. 2018. *Aerial Aftermaths: Wartime from Above*. Durham, NC: Duke University Press.

Karban, Richard. 2015. *Plant Sensing and Communication*. Chicago: University of Chicago Press.

Kasarda, John D., and Greg Lindsay. 2011. *Aerotropolis: The Way We'll Live Next*. New York: Farrar, Straus and Giroux.

Keightley, Keir. 1996. "'Turn It Down!' She Shrieked: Gender, Domestic Space, and High Fidelity, 1948–59." *Popular Music* 15 (2): 149–77.

Keightley, Keir. 2008. "Music for Middlebrows: Defining the Easy Listening Era, 1946–1966." *American Music* 26 (3): 309–35.

Keizer, Garret. 2012. *The Unwanted Sound of Everything We Want*. New York: Public Affairs.

Kelly, Caleb. 2009. *Cracked Media: The Sound of Malfunction*. Cambridge, MA: MIT Press.

Kennedy, John F. 1963. "Remarks upon Arrival at the Airport, Ashland, Wisconsin." September 24, 1963. The American Presidency Project. https://www.presidency.ucsb.edu/documents/remarks-upon-arrival-the-airport -ashland-wisconsin.

King, Richard L. 1973. *Airport Noise Pollution: A Bibliography of Its Effects on People and Property*. Metuchen, NJ: Scarecrow Press.

Kirksey, Eben, ed. 2014. *The Multispecies Salon*. Durham, NC: Duke University Press.

Kirksey, Eben. 2015. *Emergent Ecologies*. Durham, NC: Duke University Press.

Klein, Norman M. 1997. *The History of Forgetting: Los Angeles and the Erasure of Memory*. London: Verso.

Knudsen, Vern O. 1928. "'Hearing' with the Sense of Touch." *Journal of General Psychology* 1:320–52.

Knudsen, Vern O. 1931. "The Effect of Humidity upon the Absorption of Sound in a Room, and a Determination of the Coefficients of Absorption of Sound in Air. *Journal of the Acoustical Society of America* 3 (1): 126–38.

Knudsen, Vern O. 1955. "Noise, the Bane of Hearing." *Noise Control* 1 (3): 11–13.

Kohn, Eduardo. 2013. *How Forests Think: Toward an Anthropology beyond the Human*. Berkeley: University of California Press.

Königstein, Guy. 2014. "Paradoxical Spaces." In *Terrain Vague: Interstices at the Edge of the Pale*, edited by Manuela Mariani and Patrick Barron, 130–37. New York: Routledge.

Kowsky, Kim. 1995. "Plant-Life Dispute Blooms at Airport : Environmentalist Sees Exotic Plants at LAX as Threat to Survival of Endangered Butterfly." *Los Angeles Times*, April 24, 1995.

Krapp, Peter. 2011. *Noise Channels: Glitch and Error in Digital Culture*. Minneapolis: University of Minnesota Press.

Krause, Bernie. 2015. *Voices of the Wild: Animal Songs, Human Din, and the Call to Save Natural Soundscapes*. New Haven, CT: Yale University Press.

Kryter, Karl D. 1950. *The Effects of Noise on Man*. Urbana, IL: American Speech and Hearing Association.

Kryter, Karl D. 1959. "Scaling Human Reactions to the Sound from Aircraft." *Journal of the Acoustical Society of America* 31 (11): 1415–29.

Kryter, Karl D. 1970. "Annoyance (Perceived Noisiness)." In *Transportation Noises: A Symposium on Acceptability Criteria*, edited by James D. Chalupnik, 69–84. Seattle: University of Washington Press.

Kun, Josh, and Laura Pulido, eds. 2014. *Black and Brown in Los Angeles: Beyond Conflict and Coalition*. Berkeley: University of California Press.

Kushner, S. Steven. 1958. *A Review of Nuisance and Hazardous Noise*. IP-263. Industry Program of the College of Engineering, University of Michigan, Ann Arbor.

Lacan, Jacques. 2006. *Écrits*. Translated by Bruce Fink. New York: Norton.

Laird, Donald A., and Kenneth Coye. 1929. "Psychological Measurements of Annoyance as Related to Pitch and Loudness." *Journal of the Acoustical Society of America* 1 (38): 158–63.

Lally, Sean. 2014. *The Air from Other Planets: A Brief History of Architecture to Come*. Zurich: Lars Müller.

Lampland, Martha, and Susan Leigh Star. 2009. *Standards and Their Stories: How Quantifying, Classifying, and Formalizing Practices Shape Everyday Life*. Ithaca, NY: Cornell University Press.

Lang, William W. 1991. "An Informal Account of the Early Years of the Institute of Noise Control Engineering." In *Noise Control—Twenty Years of Progress and Future Trends: NOISE-CON 91 Proceedings*, edited by Daniel A. Quinlan and Marehalli G. Prasad, 701–54. New York: Noise Control Foundation.

Laplantine, François. 2015. *The Life of the Senses: Introduction to a Modal Anthropology*. Translated by Jamie Furniss. New York: Bloomsbury Academic.

Larkin, Brian. 2008. *Signal and Noise: Media, Infrastructure, and Urban Culture in Nigeria*. Durham, NC: Duke University Press.

Larkin, Brian. 2013. "The Politics and Poetics of Infrastructure." *Annual Review of Anthropology* 42 (1): 327–43. https://doi.org/10.1146/annurev-anthro -092412-155522.

Latham, Alan, and Derek P. McCormack. 2004. "Moving Cities: Rethinking the Materialities of Urban Geographies." *Progress in Human Geography* 28 (6): 701–24. https://doi.org/10.1191/0309132504ph515oa.

Latour, Bruno. 1993. *We Have Never Been Modern*. Cambridge, MA: Harvard University Press.

Latour, Bruno. 2004. "Why Has Critique Run out of Steam? From Matters of Fact to Matters of Concern." *Critical Inquiry* 30:225–48.

Latour, Bruno. 2007. *Reassembling the Social: An Introduction to Actor-Network-Theory*. Oxford: Oxford University Press.

Latour, Bruno. 2009. *The Making of Law: An Ethnography of the Conseil d'Etat*. Malden, MA: Polity.

Latour, Bruno. 2012. "Visualisation and Cognition: Drawing Things Together." *Avant: Trends in Interdisciplinary Studies* 3 (T): 207–60.

Latour, Bruno, Steve Woolgar, and Jonas Salk. 1986. *Laboratory Life: The Construction of Scientific Facts*. 2nd ed. Princeton, NJ: Princeton University Press.

Laufer, Peter. 2009. *The Dangerous World of Butterflies: The Startling Subculture of Criminals, Collectors, and Conservationists*. Guilford, CT: Lyons Press.

Launius, Roger D., and Janet R. Bednarek, eds. 2003. *Reconsidering a Century of Flight*. Chapel Hill: University of North Carolina Press.

Law, John. 2002. *Aircraft Stories: Decentering the Object in Technoscience*. Durham, NC: Duke University Press.

Le Corbusier. 1947. *The Four Routes*. London: Dobson.

Lefebvre, Henri. 1991. *The Production of Space*. Oxford: Wiley-Blackwell.

Lewis, Jayne Elizabeth. 2012. *Air's Appearance: Literary Atmosphere in British Fiction, 1660–1794*. Chicago: University of Chicago Press.

Lien, Marianne Elisabeth. 2015. *Becoming Salmon: Aquaculture and the Domestication of a Fish*. Berkeley: University of California Press.

Lippard, Lucy R. 1997. *Six Years: The Dematerialization of the Art Object from 1966 to 1972*. Berkeley: University of California Press.

Lipton, Michael A. 1998. "Butterfly Man." *People*, January 26, 1998. https://people.com/archive/butterfly-man-vol-49-no-3/.

Lispector, Clarice. 2018. *Complete Stories*. Edited by Benjamin Moser. Translated by Katrina Dodson. Cambridge, MA: New Directions.

Long Beach Press-Telegram. 1966. "Noisy Bandwagon." *Long Beach (CA) Press-Telegram*, May 13, 1966.

Long Beach Press-Telegram. 1975. "Dispute Finished—City Evicts Woman." *Long Beach (CA) Independent, Press-Telegram*, July 13, 1975.

Los Angeles International Airport. 2012. "LAX Specific Plan Amendment Study Draft EIR." Los Angeles: Los Angeles International Airport.

Los Angeles Sound Abatement Coordinating Committee. 1971. *Final Report: Aircraft Sound Attenuation of Classrooms for Joint Powers' Project*. Los Angeles: Los Angeles World Airports Public Relations Archive.

Los Angeles Times. 1992. "Lomie Puckett: Stood Ground for 5 Days in Effort to Save Rental Home." *Los Angeles Times*, February 25, 1992.

Love, Heather. 2013. "Close Reading and Thin Description." *Public Culture* 25 (3): 401–34. https://doi.org/10.1215/08992363-2144688.

Lowe, Celia. 2010. "Viral Clouds: Becoming H5N1 in Indonesia." *Cultural Anthropology* 25 (4): 625–49. https://doi.org/10.1111/j.1548-1360.2010.01072.x.

Lutz, Catherine A. 1988. *Unnatural Emotions: Everyday Sentiments on a Micronesian Atoll and Their Challenge to Western Theory*. Chicago: University of Chicago Press.

Lyon, Richard. 2009. "Leo Beranek." Interview transcript, August 10, 2009. American Institute of Physics. https://www.aip.org/history-programs/niels -bohr-library/oral-histories/34719.

MacDonald, Betty. 1945. *The Egg and I*. Philadelphia: Lippincott.

Maestripieri, Dario. 2012. *Games Primates Play: An Undercover Investigation of the Evolution and Economics of Human Relationships*. New York: Basic Books.

Makowski, R. 1950. "Torts: The Nature of Nuisance." *Marquette Law Review* 33 (4): 240–46.

Malabou, Catherine. 2015. "Whither Materialism? Althusser/Darwin." In *Plastic Materialities: Politics, Legality, and Metamorphosis in the Work of Catherine Malabou*, edited by Brenna Bhandar and Jonathan Goldberg-Hiller, 47–72. Durham, NC: Duke University Press.

Manaugh, Geoff. 2017. "Inside LAX's New Anti-Terrorism Intelligence Unit." *Atlantic*, January 9, 2017. https://www.theatlantic.com/technology/archive/2017/01 /threat-center/510644/.

Manning, Erin. 2006. *Politics of Touch: Sense, Movement, Sovereignty*. Minneapolis: University of Minnesota Press.

Manning, Erin. 2009. "What If It Didn't All Begin and End with Containment? Toward a Leaky Sense of Self." *Body and Society* 15 (3): 33–45.

Manning, Erin. 2016. *The Minor Gesture*. Durham, NC: Duke University Press.

Marder, Michael. 2016. *Grafts*. Minneapolis: Univocal.

Marder, Michael, and Luce Irigaray. 2016. *Through Vegetal Being: Two Philosophical Perspectives*. New York: Columbia University Press.

Mariani, Manuela, and Patrick Barron, eds. 2014. *Terrain Vague: Interstices at the Edge of the Pale*. New York: Routledge.

Martin, Craig. 2011. "Fog-Bound: Aerial Space and the Elemental Entanglements of Body-with-World." *Environment and Planning D: Society and Space* 29 (3): 454–68. https://doi.org/10.1068/d10609.

Massumi, Brian. 2002. *Parables for the Virtual: Movement, Affect, Sensation*. Durham, NC: Duke University Press.

Masters, Nathan. 2012. "Manhattan Beach: The City Built on Sand Dunes Celebrates Its Centennial." KCET, December 13, 2012. https://www.kcet.org/shows /lost-la/manhattan-beach-the-city-built-on-sand-dunes-celebrates-its-centennial.

Mastnak, Tomaz, Julia Elyachar, and Tom Boellstorff. 2014. "Botanical Decolonization: Rethinking Native Plants." *Environment and Planning D: Society and Space* 32 (2): 363–80. https://doi.org/10.1068/d13006p.

Mawani, Renisa. 2015. "Insects, War, Plastic Life." In *Plastic Materialities: Politics, Legality, and Metamorphosis in the Work of Catherine Malabou*, edited by Brenna Bhandar and Jonathan Goldberg-Hiller, 159–88. Durham, NC: Duke University Press.

McCormack, Derek P. 2009. "Aerostatic Spacing: On Things Becoming Lighter than Air." *Transactions of the Institute of British Geographers* 34 (1): 25–41.

McCormack, Derek P. 2010. "Remotely Sensing Affective Afterlives: The Spectral Geographies of Material Remains." *Annals of the Association of American Geographers* 100 (3): 640–54. https://doi.org/10.1080/00045601003795004.

McCormack, Derek P. 2013. *Refrains for Moving Bodies: Experience and Experiment in Affective Spaces.* Durham, NC: Duke University Press.

McCormack, Derek. 2014. "Atmospheric Things and Circumstantial Attunements." *Cultural Geographies* 21 (4): 605–25.

McCormack, Derek P. 2018. *Atmospheric Things: On the Allure of Elemental Envelopment.* Durham, NC: Duke University Press.

McCormack, Patricia. 1964a. "Need for Do-Nothing Quietude Stressed." *Lubbock (TX) Avalanche Journal*, November 18, 1964.

McCormack, Patricia. 1964b. "Save Your Nerves With a Daily 'Quiet Break.'" *Logan (UT) Herald Journal*, April 21, 1964.

McDonogh, Gary W. 1993. "The Geography of Emptiness." In *The Cultural Meaning of Urban Space*, edited by Robert Rotenberg and Gary W. McDonogh, 3–16. Westport, CT: Bergin and Garvey.

McLean, Stuart J. 2017. *Fictionalizing Anthropology: Encounters and Fabulations at the Edges of the Human.* Minneapolis: University of Minnesota Press.

Merleau-Ponty, Maurice. 2002. *Phenomenology of Perception.* New York: Routledge.

Miller, Matt. 1975. *Los Angeles International Airport Airline CNEL Study.* WCR 75-11. El Segundo, CA: Wyle Labs.

"Misophonia: When Annoying Noises Send You into a Rage." 2011. *HuffPost*, September 8, 2011. https://www.huffpost.com/entry/misophonia-annoying-noises-disorder_n_953892.

Mitman, Gregg, Michelle Murphy, and Christopher Sellers. 2004. "Introduction: A Cloud over History." *Osiris* 19:1–17.

Moloney, Kathleen. 1992. "Dune." *Los Angeles Times Magazine*, November 22, 1992.

Morton, David. 2004. *Sound Recording: The Life Story of a Technology.* Westport, CT: Greenwood.

Morton, Timothy. 2013. *Hyperobjects: Philosophy and Ecology after the End of the World.* Minneapolis: University of Minnesota Press.

Murata, Junichi. 1999. "The Indeterminacy of Images: An Approach to a Phenomenology of the Imagination." In *Phenomenology: Japanese and American Perspectives*, edited by B. C. Hopkins, 169–83. Dordrecht: Kluwer Academic.

Murphy, Michelle. 2013. "Studying Unformed Objects: Deviation." *Fieldsights*, July 15. https://culanth.org/fieldsights/studying-unformed-objects-deviation.

Nancy, Jean-Luc. 2007. *Listening.* Translated by Charlotte Mandell. New York: Fordham University Press.

Nash, Linda. 2007. *Inescapable Ecologies: A History of Environment, Disease, and Knowledge.* Berkeley: University of California Press.

New York State Unified Court System. 2014. "Theodore R. Kupferman." Appellate Division, First Judicial Department, Supreme Court of the State of New York.

2014. https://www.nycourts.gov/courts/AD1/centennial/Bios/trkupferman2
.shtml.

New York Times Service. 1965. "Noise Pollution: Engineers Find U.S. Gets Louder."
Arizona Republic, June 6, 1965.

Newman, E. B. 1955. "Psycho-Physical Effects of Noise." *Noise Control* 1 (4): 16–21.

Ngai, Sianne. 2007. *Ugly Feelings*. Cambridge, MA: Harvard University Press.

Nicas, Jack. 2015. "Drones Boom Raises New Question: Who Owns Your Airspace?" *Wall Street Journal*, May 13, 2015.

Nicolaides, Becky M. 2002. *My Blue Heaven: Life and Politics in the Working-Class
Suburbs of Los Angeles, 1920–1965*. Chicago: University of Chicago Press.

Nightingale, Carl H. 2012. *Segregation: A Global History of Divided Cities*. Chicago:
University of Chicago Press.

Nixon, Richard. 1970. "Statement About the Council on Environmental Quality."
January 29, 1970. American Presidency Project. https://www.presidency
.ucsb.edu/documents/statement-about-the-council-environmental-quality.

NOAA. 2018. "What Is Ocean Noise?" National Ocean Service, NOAA. Last updated
June 25, 2018. https://oceanservice.noaa.gov/facts/ocean-noise.html.

N.O.I.S.E. 2019. "2019 Legislative Priorities." N.O.I.S.E. website. Accessed August
6, 2020. http://www.aviation-noise.org/legadvocacy.

"Noise Pollutes Air." 1965. *Science News-Letter* 87 (25): 389.

NORC. 1954. *Community Aspects of Aircraft Annoyance*. Report 54. Chicago: University of Chicago, National Opinion Research Center.

Novak, David. 2013. *Japanoise: Music at the Edge of Circulation*. Durham, NC: Duke
University Press.

Novak, David. 2015. "Noise." In *Keywords in Sound*, edited by David Novak and
Matt Sakakeeny, 125–38. Durham, NC: Duke University Press.

Ochoa Gautier, Ana María. 2015. "Silence." In *Keywords in Sound*, edited by David
Novak and Matt Sakakeeny, 183–92. Durham, NC: Duke University Press.

Oliver, Myrna. 1975. "Inglewood Residents' Suit on Airport Noise Dismissed." *Los
Angeles Times*, January 17, 1975.

Oliver, Myrna. 2006. "Ellen Stern Harris, 76; Activist Who Helped Establish
State's Coastal Conservation Act." *Los Angeles Times,* January 3, 2006.

Owusu, Ilona. 2011–12. "Design for Pride." Delft Institute of Positive Design, November 2011–December 2012. http://studiolab.ide.tudelft.nl/diopd/projects
/design-for-pride/.

Oxford English Dictionary. Online ed. https://www.oed.com/.

Palca, Joe, and Flora Lichtman. 2011. *Annoying: The Science of What Bugs Us*. Hobo-
ken, NJ: Wiley.

Pallasmaa, Juhani. 2012. *The Eyes of the Skin: Architecture and the Senses*. Chichester: Wiley.

Panagia, Davide. 2009. *The Political Life of Sensation*. Durham, NC: Duke University Press.

Parks, Lisa. 2018. *Rethinking Media Coverage*. New York: Routledge.

Pascoe, David. 2001. *Airspaces*. London: Reaktion Books.

Paterson, Mark. 2007. *The Senses of Touch: Haptics, Affects, and Technologies*. New York: Berg.

Payne, Michael. 2001. "Exterior Soundproofing that Works." *JLC: The Journal of Light Construction*, April 1, 2001. https://www.jlconline.com/how-to/exteriors/exterior-soundproofing-that-works_0.

Payne, Roger S. 1970. *Songs of the Humpback Whale*. Del Mar, CA: CRM Records. LP.

Pechenick, Eitan Adam, Christopher M. Danforth, and Peter Sheridan Dodds. 2015. "Characterizing the Google Books Corpus: Strong Limits to Inferences of Socio-Cultural and Linguistic Evolution." *PLOS One* 10 (10): e0137041. https://doi.org/10.1371/journal.pone.0137041.

Peters, John Durham. 2016. *The Marvelous Clouds: Toward a Philosophy of Elemental Media*. Chicago: University of Chicago Press.

Peterson, Marina. 2012. "Utopia/Dystopia: The Arts and Downtown Development in Los Angeles." In *Global Downtowns*, edited by Marina Peterson and Gary W. McDonogh, 209–33. Philadelphia: University of Pennsylvania Press.

Peterson, Marina. 2016a. "Emergent Sound: Labor, Materiality, and Nonrepresentational Music." *Popular Music and Society* 39 (3): 317–31. https://doi.org/10.1080/03007766.2016.1141520.

Peterson, Marina. 2016b. "Sensory Attunements: Working with the Past in the Little Cities of Black Diamonds." *South Atlantic Quarterly* 115 (1): 89–111. https://doi.org/10.1215/00382876-3424764.

Pinney, Christopher. 2004. *"Photos of the Gods": The Printed Image and Political Struggle in India*. Oxford: Oxford University Press.

Radovac, Lilian. 2011. "The 'War on Noise': Sound and Space in La Guardia's New York." *American Quarterly* 63 (3): 733–60.

Raffles, Hugh. 2011. *Insectopedia*. New York: Vintage.

Reese, T. W., and Karl D. Kryter. 1944. *The Relative Annoyance Produced by Various Bands of Noise*. Cambridge, MA: Harvard Psycho-Acoustic Lab and U.S. National Defense Research Committee.

Revoyr, Nina. 2008. *Southland*. New York: Akashic Books.

Reynolds, Ann. 2003. *Robert Smithson: Learning from New Jersey and Elsewhere*. Cambridge, MA: MIT Press.

Robak, Warren. 1988. "Butterfly Blues: El Segundo's Coastal Dunes Habitat at Risk." *Daily Breeze*, El Segundo, CA, September 4, 1988.

Roberts, Elizabeth F. S. 2017. "What Gets Inside: Violent Entanglements and Toxic Boundaries in Mexico City." *Cultural Anthropology* 32 (4): 592–619. https://doi.org/10.14506/ca32.4.07.

Robic, Marie-Claire. 2013. "From the Sky to the Ground: The Aerial View and the Ideal of the Vue Raissonneé in Geography during the 1920s." In *Seeing from Above: The Aerial View in Visual Culture*, edited by Mark Dorrian and Frédéric Pousin, 163–87. London: Tauris.

Rome, Adam. 1996. "Coming to Terms with Pollution: The Language of Environmental Reform, 1865–1915." *Environmental History* 1 (3): 6–28.

Rome, Adam. 2003. "'Give Earth a Chance': The Environmental Movement and the Sixties." *Journal of American History* 90 (2): 525–54.

Roseau, Nathalie. 2013. "The City Seen from the Aeroplane: Distorted Reflections and Urban Futures." In *Seeing from Above: The Aerial View in Visual Culture*, edited by Mark Dorrian and Frédéric Pousin, 210–26. London: Taurus.

Rosen, George. 1974. "Public Health Then and Now: A Backward Glance at Noise Pollution." *American Journal of Public Health* 64 (5): 514–17.

Rosen, Samuel, Moe Bergman, Dietrich Plester, Aly El-Mofty, and Mohamed Hamad Satti. 1962. "Presbycusis Study of a Relatively Noise-Free Population in the Sudan." *Annals of Otology, Rhinology, and Laryngology* 71 (September): 727–43. https://doi.org/10.1177/000348946207100313.

Rothstein, Richard. 2017. *The Color of Law: A Forgotten History of How Our Government Segregated America*. New York: Liveright.

Rule, Troy A. 2015. "Airspace in an Age of Drones." BUL *Review* 95:155–208.

Russell, Sharman Apt. 2004. *An Obsession with Butterflies: Our Long Love Affair with a Singular Insect*. New York: Basic Books.

Salter, Mark B., ed. 2008. *Politics at the Airport*. Minneapolis: University of Minnesota Press.

Samuel, Dana. n.d. "Beranek's Box—Sensory Studies." Accessed June 12, 2019. http://www.sensorystudies.org/picture-gallery/untitled/.

San Rafael Daily Independent Journal. 1966. "Is Noise Pollution?" *San Rafael (CA) Daily Independent Journal*, June 1, 1966.

Schaberg, Christopher. 2015. *The End of Airports*. London: Bloomsbury.

Schaeffer, Pierre. 2004. "Acousmatics." In *Audio Culture*, edited by Christoph Cox and Daniel Warner, 76–81. London: Continuum.

Schaeffer, Pierre. 2012. *In Search of a Concrete Music*. Translated by John Dack and Christine North. Berkeley: University of California Press.

Schafer, R. Murray. 1970. *The Book of Noise*. New Zealand: Price Milburn.

Schafer, R. Murray. 1994. *The Soundscape: Our Sonic Environment and the Tuning of the World*. Rochester, NY: Destiny Books.

Schafer, R. Murray. 2004. "The Music of the Environment." In *Audio Culture*, edited by Christoph Cox and Daniel Warner, 29–39. London: Continuum.

Scheppele, Kim Lane. 1990. "Facing Facts in Legal Interpretation." *Representations* 30:42–77.

Schleuss, Jon. 2015. "Inside the Watts Curfew Zone." *Los Angeles Times*, August 11, 2015.

Schoch, Deborah. 1994. "Butterfly Safety Net." *Los Angeles Times*, October 13, 1994.

Schomer, Paul. 2005. "Biases Introduced by the Fitting of Functions to Attitudinal Survey Data." Paper presented at ASA/NOISE-Con 2005, Minneapolis, Minnesota, October 17, 2005. https://acoustics.org/pressroom/httpdocs/150th/Schomer.html.

Schulberg, Budd, ed. 1967. *From the Ashes: Voices of Watts*. New York: New American Library.

Schultz, Theodore J. 1978. "Synthesis of Social Surveys on Noise Annoyance." *Journal of the Acoustical Society of America* 64 (2): 377–405.

Schwartz, Hillel. 2011. *Making Noise: From Babel to the Big Bang and Beyond.* Brooklyn, NY: Zone Books.

Seaver, Nick. 2011. "'This Is Not a Copy': Mechanical Fidelity and the Re-Enacting Piano." *differences* 22 (2–3): 54–73. https://doi.org/10.1215/10407391-1428843.

Sekula, Allan. 1986. "The Body and the Archive." *October* 39:3–64. https://doi.org/10.2307/778312.

Seremetakis, C. Nadia. 1996. *The Senses Still.* Chicago: University of Chicago Press.

Serres, Michel. 1997. *Genesis.* Translated by Genevieve James and James Nielson. Ann Arbor: University of Michigan Press.

Serres, Michel. 2009. *The Five Senses: A Philosophy of Mingled Bodies.* Translated by Margaret Sankey and Peter Cowley. New York: Continuum.

Serres, Michel. 2010. *Malfeasance: Appropriation through Pollution?* Translated by Anne-Marie Feenberg-Dibon. Stanford, CA: Stanford University Press.

Shapiro, Nicholas. 2015. "Attuning to the Chemosphere: Domestic Formaldehyde, Bodily Reasoning, and the Chemical Sublime." *Cultural Anthropology* 30 (3): 368–93. https://doi.org/10.14506/ca30.3.02.

Shapiro, Nicholas, and Eben Kirksey. 2017. "Chemo-Ethnography: An Introduction." *Cultural Anthropology* 32 (4): 481–93. https://doi.org/10.14506/ca32.4.01.

Sharp, Ben H., Yuriy A. Gurovich, Ferdows K. Fazeli, and Eric Miller. 2013. "Assessment of Sound Insulation Treatments: Final Report Prepared for ACRP Transportation Research Board of The National Academies." Arlington, VA: Wyle.

Shaviro, Steven. 2014. *The Universe of Things: On Speculative Realism.* Minneapolis: University of Minnesota Press.

Shipley, Jesse Weaver, and Marina Peterson. 2012. "Introduction—Audio Work: Labor, Value, and the Making of Musical Aesthetics." *Journal of Popular Music Studies* 24 (4): 399–410. https://doi.org/10.1111/jpms.12000.

Sides, Josh. 2003. *L.A. City Limits: African American Los Angeles from the Great Depression to the Present.* Berkeley: University of California Press.

Situationist International. 1965. *The Decline and the Fall of the "Spectacular" Commodity-Economy.* New York: Frontier Press.

Slater, Eric. 1996. "Repaying a Debt to Butterflies: Former Gang Member Restores Habitat and Breeds the Insects He Says Saved Him from Street." *Los Angeles Times*, May 13, 1996.

Sloterdijk, Peter. 2009. *Terror from the Air.* Los Angeles: Semiotext(e).

Sloterdijk, Peter. 2011. *Bubbles: Microspherology.* Vol. 1 of *Sphères.* Los Angeles: Semiotext(e).

Smilor, Raymond W. 1977. "Cacophony at 34th and 6th: The Noise Problem in America, 1900–1930." *American Studies* 18 (1): 23–38.

Smilor, Raymond W. 1980. "Toward an Environmental Perspective: The Anti-Noise Campaign, 1893–1932." In *Pollution and Reform in American Cities, 1870–1930*, 135–51. Austin: University of Texas Press.

Smith, L. K. 1970. "Noise as a Pollutant." *Canadian Journal of Public Health* 6:475–80.

Smith, Michael J. T. 2004. *Aircraft Noise*. New York: Cambridge University Press.

Smith, Page, and Charles Daniel. 1975. *The Chicken Book*. Boston: Little, Brown.

Smithson, Robert. [1967] 1979. *The Writings of Robert Smithson: Essays with Illustrations*. Edited by Nancy Holt. New York: NYU Press.

Soja, Edward W. 1996. *Thirdspace: Journeys to Los Angeles and Other Real-and-Imagined Places*. Cambridge, MA: Blackwell.

Solà-Morales, Ignasi de. 2014. "Terrain Vague." In *Terrain Vague: Interstices at the Edge of the Pale*, edited by Manuela Mariani and Patrick Barron, 24–30. New York: Routledge.

Song, Hoon. 2013. *Pigeon Trouble: Bestiary Biopolitics in a Deindustrialized America*. Philadelphia: University of Pennsylvania Press.

Soundproofing Company. 2019. "Understanding the Triple Leaf Effect and Air Cavity Depth." Soundproofing Company website. https://www.soundproofing company.com/soundproofing101/triple-leaf-effect/.

Spieth, Walter. 1956. "Annoyance Threshold Judgments of Bands of Noise." *Journal of the Acoustical Society of America* 28 (5): 872–77.

Spigel, Lynn. 1992. *Make Room for TV: Television and the Family Ideal in Postwar America*. Chicago: University of Chicago Press.

Starosielski, Nicole. 2019. "Thermal Vision." *Journal of Visual Culture* 18 (2): 147–68.

Stauffer, Jill. 2018. *Ethical Loneliness: The Injustice of Not Being Heard*. New York: Columbia University Press.

Stauffer, Reto, Georg J. Mayr, Markus Dabernig, and Achim Zeileis. 2015. "Somewhere over the Rainbow: How to Make Effective Use of Colors in Meteorological Visualizations." *Bulletin of the American Meteorological Society* 96 (2): 203–16. https://doi.org/10.1175/BAMS-D-13-00155.1.

Sterne, Jonathan. 2003. *The Audible Past: Cultural Origins of Sound Reproduction*. Durham, NC: Duke University Press.

Sterne, Jonathan. 2012. *MP3: The Meaning of a Format*. Durham, NC: Duke University Press.

Stevens, Stanley S., ed. 1965. *Sound and Hearing*. Life Science Library. New York: Time.

Stevenson, Gordon McKay, Jr. 1972. *The Politics of Airport Noise*. Belmont, CA: Duxbury Press.

Stewart, Kathleen. 2007. *Ordinary Affects*. Durham, NC: Duke University Press.

Stewart, Kathleen. 2011. "Atmospheric Attunements." *Environment and Planning D: Society and Space* 29 (3): 445–53. https://doi.org/10.1068/d9109.

Stewart, Kathleen. 2013. "Studying Unformed Objects: The Provocation of a Compositional Mode." *Fieldsights*, June 30. https://culanth.org/fieldsights /studying-unformed-objects-the-provocation-of-a-compositional-mode.

Stewart, Susan. 1992. *On Longing: Narratives of the Miniature, the Gigantic, the Souvenir, the Collection*. Durham, NC: Duke University Press.

Still, Henry. 1970. *In Quest of Quiet*. Harrisburg, PA: Stackpole Books.

Sturken, Marita. 2014. "Seeing the Temperature in Weather Media." *International Journal of Communication* 8:2525–27.

Suisman, David. 2015. "The Oklahoma City Sonic Boom Experiment and the Politics of Supersonic Aviation." *Radical History Review* 2015 (121): 169–95. https://doi.org/10.1215/01636545-2800022.

Swensen, Cole. 2011. *Noise that Stays Noise: Essays*. Ann Arbor: University of Michigan Press.

Taylor, Timothy D. 2001. *Strange Sounds: Music, Technology, and Culture*. New York: Routledge.

Teal, Val. [1943] 1972. *The Little Woman Wanted Noise*. New York: Rand McNally.

Thébaud-Sorger, Marie, and F. Pousin. 2013. "Thomas Baldwin's Airopaidia, or the Aerial View in Color." In *Seeing from Above: The Aerial View in Visual Culture*, edited by Mark Dorrian and Frédéric Pousin, 46–65. London: Tauris.

Théberge, Paul, Kyle Devine, and Tom Everrett, eds. 2015. *Living Stereo: Histories and Cultures of Multichannel Sound*. New York: Bloomsbury Academic.

Thomas, June Manning, and Marsha Ritzdorf, eds. 1997. *Urban Planning and the African American Community: In the Shadows*. Thousand Oaks, CA: Sage.

Thompson, Emily. 2004. *The Soundscape of Modernity: Architectural Acoustics and the Culture of Listening in America, 1900–1933*. Cambridge, MA: MIT Press.

Thompson, Marie. 2017. *Beyond Unwanted Sound: Noise, Affect, and Aesthetic Moralism*. New York: Bloomsbury Academic.

Thrift, Nigel. 2007. *Non-Representational Theory: Space, Politics, Affect*. London: Routledge.

Timmins, John Francis. 1976. "Noise Pollution and the Law." Master's thesis, Dalhousie University, Halifax, Nova Scotia.

Tompkins, Peter, and Christopher Bird. 1989. *The Secret Life of Plants*. New York: Harper and Row.

Torgerson, Dial. 1969. "Boats Battle Waves to Pick up Jet Remnants but Find No Clues." *Los Angeles Times*, January 20, 1969.

Tousignant, Noémi. 2018. *Edges of Exposure: Toxicology and the Problem of Capacity in Postcolonial Senegal*. Durham, NC: Duke University Press.

Transcript of Record: Supreme Court of the United States, October Term, 1945. No. 630, the United States, Petitioner vs. Thomas Lee Causby and Wife, Tinie Causby, on Writ of Certiorari to the Court of Claims. https://www.google.com/books/edition/_/B-HQs7UCbWMC?hl=en&gbpv=1.

Trower, Shelley. 2012. *Senses of Vibration: A History of the Pleasure and Pain of Sound*. New York: Bloomsbury.

Truax, Barry. 1999. *Handbook for Acoustic Ecology*. Burnaby, BC: Cambridge Street. http://www.sfu.ca/sonic-studio-webdav/handbook/index.html.

Tsing, Anna Lowenhaupt. 2017. *The Mushroom at the End of the World: On the Possibility of Life in Capitalist Ruins*. Princeton, NJ: Princeton University Press.

Tsunoda, Toshiya. 2002. *Pieces of Air*. Lucky Kitchen—LK 016. CD.

Tunney, John V. 1975. *The Changing Dream*. Garden City, NY: Doubleday.

Turner, Victor W. 1966. *The Ritual Process: Structure and Anti-Structure*. New York: Aldine Transaction.

Turner, Victor W., and Edward M. Bruner, eds. 2001. *The Anthropology of Experience*. Urbana: University of Illinois Press.

UNESCO Courier. 1967. "Noise Pollution" (special issue). 20 (July).

U.S. v. Causby. 328 U.S. 256 (1946). https://supreme.justia.com/cases/federal/us/328/256/.

U.S. EPA. 2017. "Clean Air Act Text." U.S. EPA website. Last updated January 3, 2017. https://www.epa.gov/clean-air-act-overview/clean-air-act-text.

U.S. EPA Office of Noise Abatement and Control. 1971a. *Public Hearings on Noise Abatement and Control*, vol. 1, *Construction Noise*. Washington, DC: U.S. Environmental Protection Agency.

U.S. EPA Office of Noise Abatement and Control. 1971b. *Public Hearings on Noise Abatement and Control*, vol. 2, *Manufacturing and Transportation Noise (Highway and Air)*. Washington, DC: U.S. Environmental Protection Agency.

U.S. EPA Office of Noise Abatement and Control. 1971c. *Public Hearings on Noise Abatement and Control*, vol. 3, *Urban Planning, Architectural Design, and Noise in the Home*. Washington, DC: U.S. Environmental Protection Agency.

U.S. EPA Office of Noise Abatement and Control. 1971d. *Public Hearings on Noise Abatement and Control*, vol. 4, *Standards and Measurement Methods, Legislation and Enforcement Problems*. Washington, DC: U.S. Environmental Protection Agency.

U.S. EPA Office of Noise Abatement and Control. 1971e. *Public Hearings on Noise Abatement and Control*, vol. 5, *Agricultural and Recreational Use Noise*. Washington, DC: U.S. Environmental Protection Agency.

U.S. EPA Office of Noise Abatement and Control. 1971f. *Public Hearings on Noise Abatement and Control*, vol. 6, *Transportation Noise (Rail and Other); Urban Noise Problems and Social Behavior*. Washington, DC: U.S. Environmental Protection Agency.

U.S. EPA Office of Noise Abatement and Control. 1971g. *Public Hearings on Noise Abatement and Control*, vol. 7, *Physiological and Psychological Effects*. Washington, DC: U.S. Environmental Protection Agency.

U.S. EPA Office of Noise Abatement and Control. 1971h. *Public Hearings on Noise Abatement and Control*, vol. 8, *Technology and Economics of Noise Control; National Programs and Their Relations with State and Local Programs*. Washington, DC: U.S. Environmental Protection Agency.

U.S. Fish and Wildlife Service. 1998. *Recovery Plan for the El Segundo Blue Butterfly (Euphilotes Battoides Allyni)*. Portland, OR: U.S. Fish and Wildlife Service.

U.S. House. 1960. *Noise: Its Effect on Man and Machine: Hearings before the Special Investigating Subcommittee of the Committee on Science and Astronautics*. Washington, DC: U.S. Government Printing Office.

U.S. House. 1963. *Aircraft Noise Problems: Hearings Before Subcommittees of the Committee on Interstate and Foreign Commerce*. 86th and 87th Cong. Washington, DC: U.S. Government Printing Office.

U.S. House. 1979. *Aviation Safety and Noise Abatement: Hearings before the Sub-committee on Aviation of the Committee on Public Works and Transportation*. 96th Cong. Washington, DC: U.S. Government Printing Office.

U.S. Senate. 1972. *Noise Pollution: Hearings before the Subcommittee on Air and Water Pollution of the Committee on Public Works*. 92nd Cong. Washington: U.S. Government Printing Office.

U.S. Senate. 1974a. *A Legislative History of the Clean Air Act Amendments of 1970*. Washington, DC: U.S. Government Printing Office.

U.S. Senate. 1974b. *A Legislative History of the Noise Control Act of 1972*. Washington, DC: U.S. Government Printing Office.

Vannini, Phillip, ed. 2015. *Non-Representational Methodologies: Re-Envisioning Research*. New York: Routledge.

Vannini, Phillip, and Jonathan Taggart. 2015. *Off the Grid: Re-Assembling Domestic Life*. New York: Routledge.

Veneklasen, Paul S., and Associates. 1968. *Noise Exposure and Control in the City of Inglewood, California*. Santa Monica, CA: Veneklasen and Associates.

Viveiros de Castro, Eduardo. 2013. "Cannibal Metaphysics: Amerindian Perspectivism." Translated by Peter Skafish. *Radical Philosophy* 182:17–28.

Volcler, Juliette. 2013. *Extremely Loud: Sound as a Weapon*. Translated by Carol Volk. New York: New Press.

Von Recklinghausen, Daniel, and Martin L. Borish. 1960. "Space Diversity Techniques Improve FM Reception." *Audio*, November.

Waldie, D. J. 2005. *Holy Land: A Suburban Memoir*. New York: Norton.

Watson, Traci. 2016. "Rare Butterflies Flying High at Los Angeles Airport." *National Geographic News*, April 21, 2016. https://news.nationalgeographic.com/2016/04/160421-butterflies-endangered-species-animals/.

Weinberger, Pearl, and U. Graefe. 1973. "The Effect of Variable-Frequency Sounds on Plant Growth." *Canadian Journal of Botany* 51 (10): 1851–56. https://doi.org/10.1139/b73-237.

Weiner, Isaac. 2013. *Religion Out Loud: Religious Sound, Public Space, and American Pluralism*. New York: NYU Press.

Weiss, Marc A. 1987. *The Rise of the Community Builders: The American Real Estate Industry and Urban Land Planning*. New York: Columbia University Press.

Weschler, Lawrence. 1998. "L.A. Glows: Why Southern California Doesn't Look Like Any Place Else." *New Yorker*, February 23, 1998.

West, Dick. 1965. "Methods Mentioned to Ease Noise Pollution." *Tyrone (PA) Daily Herald*, June 3, 1965.

Westwick, Peter J., ed. 2012. *Blue Sky Metropolis: The Aerospace Century in Southern California*. Berkeley: Huntington Library and University of California Press.

Whitehead, Mark. 2009. *State, Science and the Skies: Governmentalities of the British Atmosphere*. Oxford: Wiley-Blackwell.

Wilson, Brian, and Ben Greenman. 2016. *I Am Brian Wilson: A Memoir*. Boston: Da Capo.

Wolfe, Cary. 2003. *Zoontologies: The Question of the Animal*. Minneapolis: University of Minnesota Press.

Wyle Laboratories. 1970a. *Guide to the Soundproofing of Existing Homes against Exterior Noise*. Report WCR 70-2. El Segundo, CA: Wyle Laboratories.

Wyle Laboratories. 1970b. *Home Soundproofing Pilot Project for the Los Angeles Department of Airports*. Report WCR 70-1. El Segundo, CA: Wyle Laboratories.

Yusoff, Kathryn. 2013. "Insensible Worlds: Postrelational Ethics, Indeterminacy and the (K)nots of Relating." *Environment and Planning D: Society and Space* 31:208–26. doi:10.1068/d17411.

Zigler, M. J. 1926. Review of *Der Aufbau der tastwelt Zeits. f. Psychol. a. Physiol. d. sinnesorgane*. *Psychological Bulletin* 23 (6): 326–36.

Zuthern, Hester van. 2013–14. "Design for Community Well-Being." Delft Institute of Positive Design, November 2013–May 2014. http://studiolab.ide.tudelft.nl/diopd/projects/design-for-community-well-being/.

Page numbers in italics indicate figures.

improvisation, 12

indefinite urbanism, 6, 17, 155–84

indeterminacy, 5–7, 12, 125, 157; annoyance and, 46, 75; measurement and, 192n11; noise and, 48, 79–95

infrasound, 122

infrastructure: airports and, 19–21; indefinite urbanism and, 156–57; Kovary on, 37; land recycling and, 156

Inglewood, 27, 29; class-action lawsuit by, 48; climate zone of, 149; desegregation in, 166; noise ordinance by, 49–50, 191n6; recordings in, 41

Inglewood Citizens' Health and Welfare Council, 29

Inglewood Residents Protective Association, 48

Ingold, Tim, 127, 201n5

inscription: of airport noise, 16, 38–44; and measurement, 52–53, 59–64; and noise pollution, 86; and perception, 68–70; visceral, 70–75

insects, 177–79

interior, 20, 114, 134, 144, 147

Irigaray, Luce, 9, 89–90

Jackson, John, 13

jet flight, 19, 40–41

Johnson, Lyndon, 195n6, 195n10

Jones, Fred, 29, 32–33

jurisdiction issues, 20, 32–33; EPA versus FAA, 79, 195n7; hearings and, 24–25, 27–33, 36; representatives and, 22–24

Kahn, Douglas, 57, 111, 185n6

Kalas, Rayna, 134

Kapchan, Deborah, 9, 127

Kaplan, Caren, 160

Karban, Richard, 205n19

Kennedy, John F., 195n10

kinesthesia, 120

kites, 127

Klein, Norman M., 2

Knudsen, Vern O., 58, 101, 108, 120, 197n23

Kovary, Yvette, 35–37, 158–60, 160, 169–71, 176

Kowsky, Kim, 170, 175

Krause, Bernie, 199n36

Kryter, Karl, 53–60, 65–67, 89, 189n16, 192n12, 193n16

Kupferman, Theodore R., 81, 85

Lacan, Jacques, 79

Laich, Norm, 163–64, *163*

Lakewood, 130

Lally, Sean, 134

land recycling, 135, 156

language, 30–31

Laplantine, François, 21

Larson Doors, 135

Latham, Alan, 134–35

Latour, Bruno, 58, 86

law. *See* legal issues; legislation; regulation

Law, John, 15

LAWA (Los Angeles World Airports), 67–69, 80, 138–39, 186n2

LAX. *See* Los Angeles International Airport

leakage, acoustical, 142–43

Lefebvre, Henri, 73, 120, 185n5

legal issues: eminent domain and, 94; noise and, 22, 64, 65; verbal testimony and, 27

legislation, 24, 92, 95; environmental, 8, 16, 48–49, 175; noise pollution and, 79–80, 84–88; nuisance law, 22, 24, 47–52; property law, 22, 48, 102, 188–89n12, 204n14. *See also* regulation

legislators. *See* hearings on noise, congressional; representatives, elected

Libby-Owens-Ford Glass Company, 137

light, 6, 152

Lispector, Clarice, 33

listening, 5, 41, 144; atmospheric, 147; average listener and, 65–67; easy, 141, 143; electricity and, 118; music and, 143; nature of, 9–10; public hearings and, 33–34, 93–94; sociability and, 82; tests, 55–60; volumetric, 137–41

Longcore, Travis, 179

Los Angeles: characteristics of, 6, 152; climate of, 130; neighborhoods of, 155–84, 203n6, 204n10

Los Angeles International Airport (LAX), 19–44, 186n2; Noise Abatement Commission, 95; Noise Abatement Zone, 1–17, 2–5; noise complaint systems, 47, 70; soundproofing and, 129–53

Los Angeles World Airports (LAWA), 67–69, 80, 138–39, 186n2

Love, Heather, 13

Lowe, Celia, 46

Loyola Village School, 167

luminance, 73

Lutz, Catherine A., 46, 66

Mabaan, 82–83

Makowski, R., 51

Malabou, Catherine, 174, 176

Manning, Erin, 10, 14, 16, 132, 190n17

maps: aerial images and, 160; community noise survey and, 201n6; flight tracker, 47, 70; heat maps of noise levels, 47, 70–75; Lefebvre on, 73; noise contour maps, 68, 137–38

marking study, 182

Martin, Craig, 186n9

matter/materiality, 1, 12, 15, 17, 151; air and, 100, 108, 164; atmosphere and, 8–11; glass and, 134–35; home building and, 201n4; noise pollution and, 95–103; soundproofing and, 200n3

Mattoni, Rudi, 175–76, 179, 182, 205n16

Mawani, Renisa, 176, 179

Maxwell, Ione, 122

McCormack, Derek, 9, 134–35, 160, 185–86n9, 196n12

McCormack, Patricia, 81–82

McGrath, Don, 42

McLean, Stuart J., 15

measurement: of air versus noise pollution, 97; annoyance and, 50–51, 60–64; hearings and, 52–53, 58, 95–96; indeterminacy and, 192n11; issues with, 52–54; mobilization and, 192n15; of noise, 16, 52–70, 83, 87, 102. See also decibel

medium, 57, 90, 201n5

Merleau-Ponty, Maurice, 27

metaphor: butterflies and, 172, 175, 178–79; noise and, 8

methodology, 7–16, 186n16

metrics/metricization. See measurement

microphones, 38–44, 68, 109–12, 153, 153; and high-fidelity recording, 142; mechanism of, 57; wind and, 102, 126, 179, 181

mingling, 10

misophonia, 193n22

mobilization: gender and, 162, 196n14; measurement and, 192n15; noise and, 64, 65, 92–95

Moser, Louis C., 28, 34

Moulder, Morgan, 33–34, 37

mufflers, 161

Murata, Junichi, 57

murmurs, 16, 105–27

music, 141–48

Muskie, Edmund S., 79, 87

Muzak, 143, 146

Myers, Natasha, 178–79, 183, 205n19

Nadar, 202–3n4

Nancy, Jean-Luc, 144

Nash, Linda, 99, 199n34

National Environmental Policy Act (NEPA), 87

National Noise Abatement Council, 93

National Oceanic and Atmospheric Administration, 197n23

National Opinion Research Council (NORC), 67, 194n4

Ngai, Sianne, 74–75

Nicolaides, Becky M., 165

Nightingale, Carl H., 165–66

Nixon, Richard, 87–88, 195–96n10, 197n23

N.O.I.S.E., 68–69, 93

noise: air conditioning and, 148; as annoyance, 45–75; as atmospheric, 4–5, 86–89, 91, 99–103; definitions of, 23, 58; as environmental, 92–95; experience of, 27–33; measurement of, 52–70, 83, 87; nature of, 7–8; as relational, 34, 41; as weapon, 186n13. See also airport noise

Noise Abatement Office, 79, 87, 195n6

Noise Abatement Zone (LAX), 1–17, 2–5

"Noise Annoys" (Buzzcocks), 46, 190n2

noise contour maps, 68, 137–38

Noise Control Act, 87–89, 92, 197n21

Noise Control Advisory Council, 87

noise ordinances, 49–50, 191n6

noise pollution, 49, 77–103; air pollution versus, 79, 96–98; as atmospheric, 86–89; definition of, 78, 194n4; emergence of term, 80–86, 195n10; matter of, 95–103

Noise Pollution Clearinghouse (NPC), 53, 191n9

noisiness, 55, 57, 59

NORC (National Opinion Research Council), 67, 194n4

nuisance: definition of, 48; law on, 22, 24, 47–52; noise/annoyance and, 47–52; pollution versus, 78

Office of Noise Abatement and Control (ONAC), 87–89, 91–93, 100, 122, 197n21

oobleck, 105

Paterson, Mark, 120

Payne, M., 133, 137

Pearsons, Karl, 60

perceived noise decibel (PNdB), 54–55, 57–60, 143

perceived noise level (PNL), 191–92n10

perception: environmental noise and, 98; inscription and, 68–70; literature on, 186n11; PNdB and, 54–55; term, 190n18

pesticides, 99–100, 199n34

photography: aerial, 158–60, 160, 164, 202–3n4; LAX NAZ, 1–5, 2–5; Nadar and, 86; noise as object and, 86

pilots, 25–26, 34–35

pink noise, 110

pitch, 50

plants, 11, 177–79, 205n19

plasticity, 176, 179

Playa del Rey, 130, 156, 160; desegregation and, 167–68; home removals and, 155, 157, 159, 161; resistance in, 162, 168–71

PNdB (perceived noise decibel), 54–55, 57–60, 143

PNL (perceived noise level), 191–92n10

pollution. See noise pollution

pressure, 115, 120, 132

Prokosch, Walter, 21

property law, 22, 48, 102, 188–89n12, 204n14

property rights, 23, 33, 188–89n12

property values, 158–59, 161–71

proprioception, 10, 120

psychoacoustics, 54–55

public ear, 65–67

Puckett, Lomie, 161–62

Purifoy, Noah, 164

quiet, 82–83, 108, 148. See also silence

race: neighborhoods and, 161–71, 203n6, 204n10; removed homes and, 158; urban noise and, 66–67, 191n7

radio, 26, 146

rainbow color maps (heat maps), 16, 47, 70–75

Reagan, Ronald, 91, 197n21, 197n24

recordings, 109, 141–48

redlining, 162

regulation, 8, 22, 48–50, 58, 80, 95–96. See also legislation

representatives, elected, 21–26, 31–33, 87. See also hearings on noise, congressional

resonance, 11, 17, 73, 120, 132–35, 142–44

restrictive covenants, 162, 164–65, 166, 204n9

riots, 163–65

Rosen, Samuel, 82–83

Rosendahl, Charles E., 25

Russell, Sharman, 205n17

Ryan, William Fitts, 87, 196n15

sand, 135, 157–61, 169–70, 176

Schaeffer, Pierre, 145

Schafer, R. Murray, 78–79, 82–83, 102, 120, 147, 192n15

Scheppele, Kim Lane, 27

schools, 40–41, 148, 166–71, 168

Schultz, Theodore J., 60, 61–62

Schultz, Thomas, 53

Schultz curve, 60, 61–62, 61–63

Schwartz, Hillel, 48, 200n1

Segal, Joseph, 57

segregation, 162, 164–66, 169, 203n6

Seigworth, Gregory J., 73

Senate Subcommittee on Environmental
Pollution, 87
sense (term), 190n18
sensing/sensation: annoyance and, 51; atmospheric, 8–11; butterflies and, 182;
heat maps and, 73; measurement of, 55;
nature of, 111; noise pollution and, 79;
rights and, 31–33; skin and, 29–30; vibration and, 121
Serres, Michel, 7, 10, 30
signal: noise and, 29; television and, 118, *119*
signification, 45, 79
silence, 1, 145–46; noisy, 183–84. *See also*
quiet
skin, 10, 190n17; experience and, 29–30; of
house, 131–33; pollution and, 99–100
Sloterdijk, Peter, 131, 198n33
Smithson, Robert, 170–71
smog, 89, 129
Smog/Riot, 163–64, *163*
smoke, 90, 164
Solà-Morales, Ignasi de, 156
sonic boom, 194n4
sonic weaponry, 186n13
Sopher, Lee L., 26
sound, 5; air and, 90, 109; atmospheric conditions and, 106–7; chickens and, 123–24;
definition of, 114; glass and, 134; heat
maps of noise levels and, 71; high-fidelity,
141–48; larvae and, 177; noise and, 68,
79; plants and, 205n19; Schafer and, 120;
skin and, 30; as touch, 125
Sound Abatement Coordinating Committee, 25, 36
sound analyzer, 113, *113*
soundproofing, 17, 49, 114, 129–53; air conditioning and, 148–53; DIY, 142–43; materials used in, 200n3; process of, 129–30,
200n1
soundscape, 102, 141, 147–48, 192n15
sound transmission class (STC), 136
South Coast Air Quality Management
Agency, 98
space, 22
Spano, Bartholomew, 132–33, 200n2
Spieth, Walter, 193n16
Spigel, Lynn, 118
SST (supersonic transport), 194n4

standards. *See* measurement
Stanford Research Institute, 89
Starosielski, Nicole, 74
Stauffer, Jill, 31
STC (sound transmission class), 136
stereophonic (term), 202n9
stereo recording, 141–48
Sterne, Jonathan, 51, 111
Stevens, Stanley Smith, 55, 143–44
Stevenson, Gordon McKay, Jr., 79
Stewart, Kathleen, 8
Still, Henry, 198n29
Sturken, Marita, 74
supersonic transport (SST), 194n4
Supreme Court, 23
Swensen, Cole, 14, 46
systematization. *See* measurement

Taggart, Jonathan, 72
technology. *See* equipment; microphones
telephone, 58, 140
television, 26, 118, 143
terrain vague, 17, 156, 168
theory, 14, 186n16
thermoception, 10, 16–17, 47, 71–72, 120.
See also heat
Thrift, Nigel, 184
Timberlake, L. E., 24
Timmins, John Francis, 51–52, 60, 64
Tobin, Austin, 59
touch, 10, 29–30, 120, 125
traffic noise, 84, 146–47
tranquility, 31–32
transduction, 57–58, 72, 140, 156, 158, 183;
equipment and, 40, 43, 111–12; land
recycling and, 202n2
transperception, 57
Truax, Barry, 192n15
Tsunoda, Toshiya, 109
Tunney, John, 95, 101, 195n5, 195n7,
198n31
tympanic (term), 111

uncertainty, 5, 9, 54, 62, 95, 102, 157, 164,
174
United Civil Rights Committee, 164
United States Gypsum, 93